CHILDREN ADAPT

ADAPT

Elnora M. Gilfoyle, OTR, FAOTA

Ann P. Grady, OTR, FAOTA

Josephine C. Moore, PhD, OTR, FAOTA

This book is dedicated —
  To those with whom we share our lives —
    Our families, friends, collegues —
      And to all the children
        Who taught us to adapt.

Preface

Children Adapt was conceived in 1973 at a developmental workshop sponsored by the Colorado Occupational Therapy Association. The faculty, Mary Fiorentino, Pat Komich, and the authors of this book shared ideas regarding a developmental approach to pediatric rehabilitation. Recognizing their common interest, plus the need to identify a framework for evaluation and treatment of children, the authors set out to write this text.

The content has undergone its own growth, development, and maturation over the past six years. Many "writings," hours of searching, and days of sharing have been integrated into the present manuscript. Children have been our prime teachers, for their actions provided the stimulus to seek answers, modify concepts, and adapt our beliefs.

Concepts presented in this book provide a perspective regarding the development of movement. We have attempted to answer the question of how children learn to function. We present our theory of development, as well as present a philosophical base for pediatric occupational therapy and a model for designing individual therapeutic programs for children. The core of the concepts, theory, and philosophy is in the adaptation process.

This book, like all children, developed with a great deal of understanding and love. To those who provided the book with "parenting" we want to say a very special thank-you. *Children Adapt* would not have become a reality without the understanding, help, support, patience, encouragement, and sacrifices given to us by Lou Shannon, and Gene and Sean Gilfoyle.

Although we have taken the step to organize and write the material, many persons have contributed to the evolution of the principals and concepts. We appreciate the therapists and staff with whom we have worked, especially the occupational and physical therapists at the Denver Children's Hospital. These friends and collegues have been a major source for knowledge sharing and encouragement. The participants of our workshops and our occupational therapy students from Colorado State University have listened, questioned, and provided feedback which have contributed to our growth and adaptation of beliefs. To these friends and collegues we are grateful. Special appreciation is given to Maggie Johnson for her creative art work, to Mary Fiorentino and Pat Komich for their stimulating idea exchange and assistance with the creation of concepts, and to Wilma West and Jean Ayres who have been prime contributors to the development of pediatric occupational therapy and provided us with stimulus and opportunities for integration of ideas.

But most of all we want to thank the children — our teachers — particularly the children pictured in this book:

Aron	Jennifer
Brad	Joyce
Cindy	Kris
David	Kristin
Emily	Kris and Grant
Eric	Laura
Grant	Meg
Heather	Michael
Jeff	Mike and Tim

and, of course, Sean

Table of Contents

Preface . . . .

Chapter One
Introduction **1**
  Introduction to Movement 1
  Related Research and Developmental Theories 3

Chapter Two
Highlights of Nervous System Development **7**
  Prenatal Development-Highlights 14
  Postnatal Development-Highlights 28
  Appendix 38

Chapter Three
The Spiraling Continuum of Spatiotemporal Adaptation **47**
  Introduction 47
  Spatiotemporal Adaptation 48
  Spiraling Continuum 48
  Spatiotemporal Stress 52
  Summary 54

Chapter Four
The Development of Posture and Movement Strategies **57**
  Posture and Movement Strategies 57
  Development of Strategies 63

Chapter Five
The Development of Purposeful Behaviors **79**
  Creeping 79
  Sitting 90
  Rolling 99
  Standing/Walking 109
  Summary 124

Chapter Six
Developmental Sequences to Standing **127**
  Pull-up Sequence 127
  Complete Rotation Sequence 128
  Partial-Complete Rotation Sequence 130
  Partial Rotation Sequence 131

Symmetrical-Partial Rotation Sequence 132
Symmetrical Sequence 132

Chapter Seven
The Development of Purposeful Activities and Skill **135**
   Introduction 135
   Primitive Phase 138
   Transitional Phase 142
   Mature Phase 146
   Summary 152

Chapter Eight
The Development of Personality **155**
   Related Theorists 155
   Theoretical Framework 161
   Summary 169

Chapter Nine
Spatiotemporal Stress, Distress, and Dysfunction **173**
   Spatiotemporal Stress 173
   Stress Factors 174
   Spatiotemporal Distress 176
   SMS Factors 178
   Distress to Dysfunction 182
   Primitive Signs of Dysfunction 183
   Primitive Pathology 184
   Transitional Pathology 188
   Abnormal Patterns 193
   Summary 194
   Vignettes 195

Chapter Ten
A Model for Therapy **207**
   Introduction 207
   Theoretical Premises 208
   Philosophy of Pediatric Occupational Therapy 209
   Supporting Literature 210
   Principles 211
   Therapeutic Framework 211
   Mode of Action 211
   Summary 215

Epilogue
"We Hold These Truths to be Self-Evident" **219**

Appendix A
The Philosophical Base of Occupational Therapy **223**

Appendix B
Suggested Readings **225**

Chapter One
Introduction

Introduction to Movement

For persons devoted to the health care of children, there is always recognition of the importance of movement and ability of a person to adapt to his surroundings by means of movement. We frequently give credence to the effect of movement and adaptation on the development of a child, his education, and his life.

Movement puts the child in relationship with his surroundings so that through this relationship the child can have an effect upon his environment as well as be affected by his environment. Through this relationship of movement and environment the child adapts. Movement and adaptation are systems of relationships, meaning that movement puts the child in touch with his world, both living and nonliving, and the world provides the challenge to interact.[1] Without movement the child has no contact with his surroundings or his fellow beings. Without movement there is no adaptation and without adaptation there is no life.

Through the adaptation of movement life survives and protects, experiences, develops, and expresses. Movement provides the child with the ability to seek and acquire nutrition, satisfy hunger, seek comfort, and rest. Movement provides a means to protect oneself or to flee from danger.

Movement provides experiences for interaction and perception of the environment including the self, objects, object relationships, movement of objects in space and of the effect of self-movement upon objects. Movement provides new dimensions as the child develops means to explore the environment — first with a safer more secure supporting surface, then with less support as the child is able to maintain his balance. As the child begins to carry objects as he walks, he has a linkage between what he wishes to carry with his hands and his legs to support and get him there. The child makes great strides in adapting his abilities to his desires, motivations, and relationships with his environment. Montessori said

> Man's legs, which are his natural means of transport, carry him to the places where he can work, but this work he does with his hands. He may walk for great distances, and men have come in fact to occupy the whole of the earth's surface, and while this conquest of the land was going on man lived and died. But what they left behind them, as a sign of their passing, was the work of their hands.[1]

Movement not only promotes adaptation with life, but movement provides a heritage.

Movement promotes mental and social development through the expression of thoughts and ideas. Not only are thought and action two parts of the same occurrence but it is through movement that the child can express himself. Movement contributes to expression such as verbalizing language, writing thoughts in words, and communicating ideas and emotions by means of facial expressions, gestures, and body language.[2] Movement and adaptation are viewed in terms of a single whole that is set to work as a system of relationship which promotes purposeful experiences. Within the system, movement provides the power for the child to experience, and adaptation provides the process.

Human adaptation is a dynamic organized process of expanding a child's repertoire of behaviors. Adaptation evolves from the transactional process between a person and the environment. Adaptation has its beginnings in early prenatal life. Behavior develops as an ever expanding pattern resulting from the organization of the nervous system and the environmental surrounding. As a baby develops, he becomes more complex, more highly integrated, and he begins to function as a whole person with a unique self-system.

Although the uniqueness of self is continually evolving from specific transactions between a person and his environment, there are certain commonalities in the transactional process that characterize human development. One is the framework of the adaptation process. Adaptation is described as an organized process of modification in which a child assimilates everything that is happening, accommodates to these experiences, and associates, differentiates, and integrates the new experiences with those previously acquired.[3] What continually emerges is a newly organized modification of previous behaviors. By constantly adapting the experiences of environment with self, a unique individual is continually developing. The creation of a child is not solely a product of cultural experiences nor solely a product of genetic inheritance, but an organized process of environmental adaptation. Each child becomes unique by creating an entirely individualistic and complex "self-system"* derived from all the factors that contribute to development.

Throughout development, a child seeks to expand his environment and pursue his quest for autonomy and competence. A child's autonomy and competence depend upon his ability to move about the environment as he engages in goal-directed, purposeful experiences. Movement and adaptation are such an innate part of functioning that frequently we do not give conscious thought to the existence or value of movement until we are struck with the lack of movement or faced with trying to help a child with a handicap experience movement and develop independence.[4]

Therapists observing children with movement handicaps frequently describe the effect of lack of movement upon the developmental process and the child's total functioning. The child with impaired movement experiences dysfunction in performance and develops purposeless behaviors and activities. Dysfunctional performance has an effect upon the total developmental process, ultimately resulting in developmental deviations and/or disabilities.

The child's developmental process is affected by heredity, the environment, and his state of health or presence of disease: congenital, acute, progressive, or chronic. Any of the factors may interrupt or delay the sequence and rate of growth, maturation, and development. The interruption or delay in the process results in an inability to effectively interact with and adapt behaviors and activities. Immature, primitive, or pathological behaviors accompany dysfunctional performance and they in turn further affect the adaptation process.

A child with dysfunctional performance can benefit from a (re)habilitation† process designed to develop within the individual a more effective way of functioning. (Re)habilitation principles presented in this text are based upon the process of adapting purposeful behavior and activities to performance skills. Knowledge of the adaptation process provides the basis

---

*The term "self-system" was introduced by Gordon[5] and reflects the person's uniqueness which evolves from the developmental process.

†"(Re)habilitation" will be used to describe both habilitation and rehabilitation.

from which one evaluates the presence and degree of dysfunction and selects specific methodology and media to facilitate the adaptation of purposeful behaviors and activities, thus modifying performance.

Pediatric (re)habilitation concerns itself with the treatment and/or remediation of developmental deviations and disabilities. The goal of pediatric (re)habilitation is to facilitate a developmental process by which the child can hopefully achieve his potential for functioning. Since movement is basic to function, facilitation and use of movement is a common element in pediatric (re)habilitation. There are a variety of health care professions within the field of pediatric (re)habilitation which share the goal of facilitating development through movement. Although the professions share a common goal and an overlap in health care services frequently occurs, each profession contributes a unique aspect to the child's developmental program.

The concepts and theories presented in this book relate primarily to the role of occupational therapy as a health care profession within the field of pediatric (re)habilitation. Because the concepts and theories are based upon the process of normal growth, maturation, and development, the information presented in this text can be used and applied by a variety of health care professions concerned with children.

The unique contribution of occupational therapy is facilitation of purposeful activities to be adapted by the person for acquisition of performance skills: self-care, work, play, recreational, and leisure activities.[6] Pediatric occupational therapy bases its principals and concepts on the premise that a child's active participation with purposeful activity is meaningful to the nervous system to facilitate maturation and development. Purposeful activity is the media used with occupational therapy programs. The occupational therapy methodology is the mode by which purposeful activity facilitates skill.

The theory of adaptation presented in this book has been developed as a result of clinical observations, related research, and various developmental theories. Factors from the literature have been synthesized and integrated into an adaptation theory and a theoretical framework on which to base facilitation of functioning and modification of a child's performance.

The theory is termed spatiotemporal adaptation to emphasize the process of adjusting basic posture and movement sequences to the gravitational demands of space and to temporal demands of timing movements. The framework of the process is presented as a spiraling continuum of spatiotemporal adaptation. Spiraling describes a process by which lower level primitive postures and movements are adapted to higher level, more mature postures and movements. Through the spiraling spatiotemporal adaptation process, purposeful behaviors and activities are adapted by the self-system and skilled performance evolves.

Related Research and Developmental Theories

A brief review of the information gleaned from literature is summarized to orient the reader to the basis of the theory. The literature which had most influence upon theory development is summarized according to intrauterine, maturational, and environmental factors. The summary is presented here in list form.

Intrauterine Developmental Factors

1. Movement begins during early fetal development with the reflex activity of the fetus being the foundation for sensorimotor behaviors.[3]

2. Sensorimotor behaviors develop as an expanding total pattern, generalized to localized, cephalocaudal, proximal to distal.[7,8,9]

3. Generalized reactions involving the head and trunk develop prior to the localized reactions of the body.[9,10]

4. Generalized reactions of withdrawal develop and remain prepotent over pursuit reactions.[9,10,11]

5. The newborn is dominated by exteroceptive and proprioceptive reflexes and withdrawal reactions with the exception of the pursuit reactions of the mouth.[9,10,11]

6. The specific localized reactions are components of earlier more primitive total response patterns.[8,9,10]

7. The newborn has a crude form of visual perception indicated by preference to patterns.[12]

Maturational Factors

1. The central nervous system has a hierarchical functional organization which is responsible for voluntary sensorimotor activity.[10]

2. Different levels of the central nervous system do not function in isolation, as all parts of the nervous system are influenced by and influence the activities of the other parts.[13]

3. Maturation proceeds in a cephalocaudal, generalized to localized and proximal to distal direction.[14]

4. Most of the cortex is not functioning as a control for behavior at birth.[14]

5. The behavior patterns of early infancy are believed to be primarily under subcortical control.[14,15,16]

6. The maturation of the nervous system is not uniform, therefore, several maturational levels occur simultaneously in relation to different body segments until the whole is established.[14]

7. Higher cortical development of skill continues to be centered in the superior spinal segments throughout the maturational process.[14]

8. Coordinated movements are a result of various feedback mechanisms of the nervous system.[13,17,18,19,20,21]

9. Nervous system activity is adaptive and does not seem to depend on any specific group of circuits; therefore, "It is unwise to attribute specific patterns of neuronal activity to particular functions of the nervous system."[13]

10. The brain becomes aware of movements through sensorimotor links.[4]

11. The brain builds up patterns of movements and is able to anticipate the purpose for which a movement will be used.[22]

4

Environmental Factors

1. Development is dependent upon organized integration, environmental experiences, and adaptation.[7,23,24,25]

2. Life begins with certain neurological and anatomical structures; however, these structures do not account for functioning itself.[3]

3. Higher functioning results from one's adaptation to the postnatal environment. The feedback from new experiences is associated with the already acquired pre- and postnatal adaptations.[3]

4. The reflexes/reactions of the infant undergo modifications as a result of environmental contact and thus become acquired behaviors. Higher level behaviors are modifications of older more primitive patterns.[3]

5. The behavior the infant possesses is the beginning of the adaptation process which continues to occur throughout life.[3]

6. Movement provides the means by which the child can interact with the environment.[4]

7. During environmental interactions, purposeful movements are made by the child to increase his awareness of space, to manipulate the environment, and to communicate with persons and/or objects within the environment.[4]

8. Sensorimotor activity is important as an integrating mechanism for linking together the developmental progress of physical, intellectual, emotional, and social components.[4]

9. Through the existence of a sensory feedback mechanism, the movement of a child influences his ongoing development, as the level of developmental maturity reached by the child allows progressively more complex sensorimotor behaviors to be exhibited.[4]

The intrauterine, maturational, and environmental factors stated above stress the effects of sensorimotor behaviors (movement) upon the total developmental process. The above identified factors from the literature have influenced the discussion of the concepts and theory of spatiotemporal adaptation as presented in this book.

The following chapters discuss the concepts of neurobehavioral development of the fetus and young child, the theory of spatiotemporal adaptation, the spiraling process, and the developmental progressions of purposeful behaviors and activities. Later chapters relate the theory to dysfunction.

References

1. Montessori M: The Absorbent Mind, ed 9. New York, Dell Pub Co Inc, 1974, p 153.
2. Hebb DO: The Organization of Behavior: A Neurophysiological Theory. New York, John Wiley, 1949.
3. Flavel J: The Developmental Psychology of Jean Piaget. Princeton, Van Nostrand, 1963.
4. Holt K: Movement and child development, in Clinics in Developmental Medicine, no. 55. Philadelphia, Lippincott, 1975.
5. Gordon IJ: Human Development from Birth through Adolescence. New York, Harper & Row, 1969.
6. Hopkins H, Smith H (eds): Willard and Spackman's Occupational Therapy, ed 5. Philadelphia, JB Lippincott Co, 1977.

7. Hunt JMcV: Intelligence and Experience. New York, Ronald Press, 1961.
8. Jacobs MJ: Development of normal motor behavior. Am J Phys Med 46: 41-50, 1967.
9. Twitchell TE: Normal motor development. The Child with Central Nervous System Deficit. Children's Bureau Pub, no 432, US Dept of Health, Education, & Welfare, Washington DC, US Government Printing Office, 1965, pp 85-89.
10. Twitchell TE: Attitudinal reflexes. The Child with Central Nervous System Deficit. Children's Bureau Pub, no. 432, US Dept of Health, Education, & Welfare, Washington DC, US Government Printing Office, 1965, pp 77-84.
11. Szumski AJ: Mechanisms underlying normal motor behavior. Am J Phys Med 46: 52-68, 1967.
12. Fantz RL: Visual perception from birth as shown by pattern selectivity, in Whipple HE (ed): New issues in infant development. Ann NY Acad Sci 118:793-814, 1965.
13. Taylor E (ed): Selected Writings of John Hughlings Jackson. London, Hodder and Stoughton, 1932, p 64.
14. McGraw MB: The Neuromuscular Maturation of the Human Infant. New York, Hafner, 1966.
15. Andre-Thomas: The neurological examination of the infant. Clinics in Developmental Medicine, no 1. Philadelphia, JB Lippincott Co, 1964.
16. Beintema JD: A neurological study of newborn infants. Clinics in Developmental Medicine, no 28. Philadelphia, JB Lippincott Co, 1968.
17. Buchwald JS: Exteroceptive reflexes and movement. Am J Phys Med 46:121-128, 1967.
18. Buchwald JS: General features of nervous system organization. Am J Phys Med 46:88-113, 1967.
19. Buchwald JW: Proprioceptive reflexes and posture. Am J Phys Med 46:104-113, 1967.
20. Eldred E: Peripheral receptors: Their excitation and relation to reflex patterns. Am J Phys Med 46:69-87, 1967.
21. Fischer E: Factors affecting motor learning. Am J Phys Med 46:511-516, 1967.
22. Jones B: The importance of memory traces of motor efferent discharges for learning skilled movements. Dev Med Child Neurol 16:620, 1974.
23. Birch HG, Lefford A: Intersensory development in children. Monogr Soc Res Child Dev 5:28, 1963, Serial no 89.
24. Bruner JS: Course of cognitive growth. Am Psychol 19:1-15, 1964.
25. Munn WE: The evolution and growth of human behavior, ed 2. Boston, Houghton Mifflin, 1965.

Chapter Two
Highlights of Nervous System Development

Prior to a discussion of the developmental aspects of the human organism, a brief introduction to the nervous system is presented. The reader can refamiliarize himself with the seven basic levels, the hierarchy of development, pertinent terminology, important parts of this highly integrated system, and functional relationships (Fig 2-1, 2-2).* Level one represents the spinal cord or the least complex area of the central nervous system (CNS). Level seven,

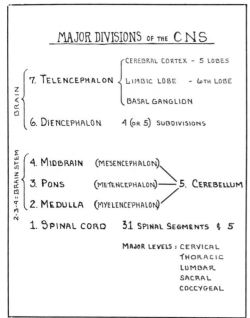

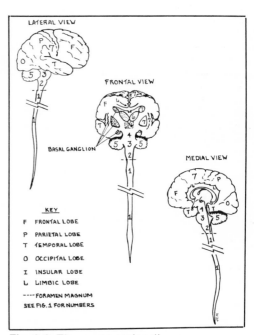

Fig 2-1 The seven major divisions of the central nervous system.

Fig. 2-2 The seven major divisions of the central nervous system.

the telecephalon (distant + brain), is the most highly developed part and the last to reach full maturity.[1–5] This same numbering sequence can be equated with phylogenetic and ontogenetic development, as well as postnatal growth and development of the nervous system. In other words, the lower levels tend to develop and mature much earlier than the higher ones. It is theorized that it may take from 18 (female) to 21 years (male) for the nervous system to reach full maturity.[1–5]

Figures 2-3 and 2-4 show the peripheral nerves which develop outwardly from these seven major levels, These nerves enable the CNS to communicate with the organisms' external and

*Illustrations in Chapter Two by Josephine C. Moore, PhD, OTR, FAOTA

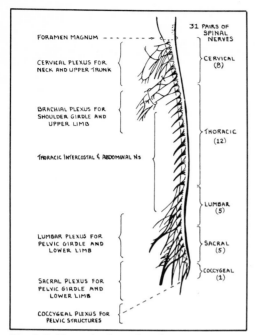

Fig. 2-3 The spinal cord and peripheral nerves.

Labels in figure 2-3:
FORAMEN MAGNUM
31 PAIRS OF SPINAL NERVES
CERVICAL PLEXUS FOR NECK AND UPPER TRUNK
CERVICAL (8)
BRACHIAL PLEXUS FOR SHOULDER GIRDLE AND UPPER LIMB
THORACIC (12)
THORACIC INTERCOSTAL & ABDOMINAL Ns
LUMBAR (5)
LUMBAR PLEXUS FOR PELVIC GIRDLE AND LOWER LIMB
SACRAL (5)
COCCYGEAL (1)
SACRAL PLEXUS FOR PELVIC GIRDLE AND LOWER LIMB
COCCYGEAL PLEXUS FOR PELVIC STRUCTURES

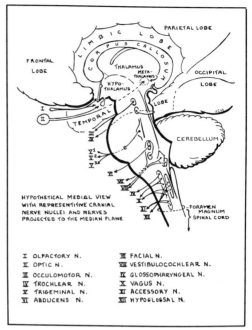

Fig. 2-4 The 12 cranial nerves of the brain and brain stem.

Labels in figure 2-4:
PARIETAL LOBE
FRONTAL LOBE
LIMBIC LOBE
CORPUS CALLOSUM
THALAMUS
META-THALAMUS
HYPO-THALAMUS
OCCIPITAL LOBE
TEMPORAL LOBE
CEREBELLUM
FORAMEN MAGNUM
SPINAL CORD
HYPOTHETICAL MEDIAL VIEW WITH REPRESENTATIVE CRANIAL NERVE NUCLEI AND NERVES PROJECTED TO THE MEDIAN PLANE

I	OLFACTORY N.	VII	FACIAL N.
II	OPTIC N.	VIII	VESTIBULOCOCHLEAR N.
III	OCCULOMOTOR N.	IX	GLOSSOPHARYNGEAL N.
IV	TROCHLEAR N.	X	VAGUS N.
V	TRIGEMINAL N.	XI	ACCESSORY N.
VI	ABDUCENS N.	XII	HYPOGLOSSAL N.

internal environment. Although all of these nerves are sensorimotor in composition (see Table I of Appendix),[1] they are spoken of somewhat differently. Those connected with the spinal cord are called spinal nerves. The 31 pairs of spinal nerves reflect the 31 functional embryonic segments of the spinal cord, ie, 8 cervical, 12 thoracic, 5 lumbar, 5 sacral, and 1 coccygeal. Nerves connected with the brain and brain stem are referred to as cranial nerves. There are 12 pairs of cranial nerves, numbered in sequence from "fore to aft," or as they appear on the base of the brain beginning anteriorly and counting posterio-inferiorially. The first cranial nerve (Cr.n.) is associated with the limbic lobe (level seven); the second Cr.n. with the diencephalon (level six); the third and fourth Cr.ns. with the midbrain (level four); the fifth, sixth, seventh, and part of the eighth with the pons (level three); and the rest of the eighth, and the ninth, tenth, eleventh, and twelveth with the medulla (level two) or the lowest level of the brain stem. Table I of the Appendix presents more detail about the 12 Cr.ns., ie, their names and major functional (sensorimotor) components.

The brain stem (levels two, three, and four) and the cerebellum (level five) can be divided into three functional parts, which can be roughly equated with the developmental stages of these areas of the CNS (Fig 2-5). The central core area, lying anterior to the ventricular system, consists of the primitive brain stem reticular formation, nuclei of the third through the twelveth Cr.ns., ascending older and newer tracts and older descending pathways. Posterior to this central core area, ie, dorsal to the ventricular system, are the roof structures of the brain stem which are intermediate in age. The roof or dorsal part of the medulla consists primarily of the dorsal column pathways extending upward from the spinal cord to reach their synaptic centers (nucleus gracilis, cuneatus, and accessory cuneate nucleus) at higher medullary levels.

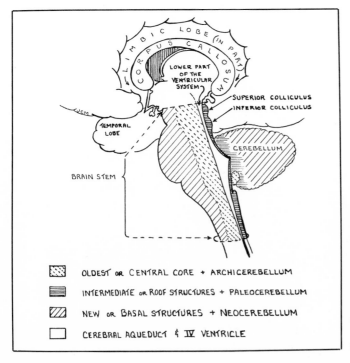

OLDEST or CENTRAL CORE + ARCHICEREBELLUM

INTERMEDIATE or ROOF STRUCTURES + PALEOCEREBELLUM

NEW or BASAL STRUCTURES + NEOCEREBELLUM

CEREBRAL AQUEDUCT & IV VENTRICLE

Fig 2-5 Schematic representation of the developmental ages of the brain stem and cerebellum.

The roof on the pons consists of the different parts of the cerebellum (level five). The roof or tectum of the midbrain is made up of four small elevated bumps, called the superior and inferior colliculi (or corpora quadrigemnia). These midbrain centers are for visual and auditory reflexes, respectively. The newest part of the brain stem is located ventrally, ie, anterior to the old central core structures. This area consists of the phylogenetically recent descending pathways of the CNS, or the corticobulbar, corticopontocerebellar, and corticospinal tracts. These pathways are primarily responsible for voluntary control of skilled functions, informing subcortical centers (such as the thalamus, basal ganglia, and cerebellum) of cortical functions, and modifying incoming sensory stimuli, especially in relation to the newer ascending dorsal column pathways and the dorsal sensory gray areas of the spinal cord.

Level five is the cerebellum or the diminutive brain. It is represented in Fig 2-2 as lying behind the medulla (marrow), pons (bridge), and midbrain (middle brain) or the brain stem, where it is located in the posterior fossa of the cranial vault. Note that there are three lines connecting this structure with the brain stem in Fig 2-1. These lines represent the three pairs of cerebellar peduncles (little feet) or extensions which connect the cerebellum with the brain stem. Generally speaking, the lower two bilateral cerebellar peduncles carry coded messages from almost all centers of the CNS into the cerebellum where they are integrated and recoded. The resultant integrated messages are sent back into the midbrain and adjacent structures of the CNS via the superior cerebellar peduncle for regulation of muscle tone, balance and spatial orientation, coordination, timing, and smoothing out of movement.

The cerebellum (Fig 2-5, 2-6), like other parts of the CNS, develops in uteral in three different stages. The archicerebellum (flocculonodular lobes and uvula) is the oldest and first part of the cerebellum to develop and mature along with the vestibular system. This part is

9

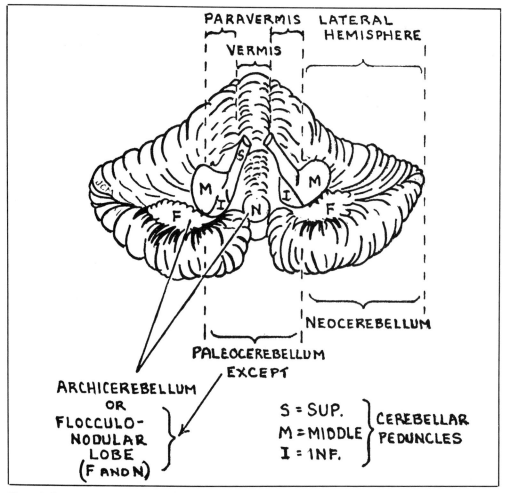

Fig 2-6 Developmental ages of the cerebellum.

sometimes referred to as the vestibulocerebellum. The intermediate part or paleocerebellum matures along with the spinal cord and medulla and is sometimes called the spinocerebellum. Last to develop is the neocerebellum, which matures along with higher brain stem, diencephalic (through + brain), and especially telecephalic (distant + brain) structures. This neo part of the cerebellum comprises most of the lateral hemispheres and can be referred to as the corticopontocerebellum.[1,6]

In summary, the archicerebellum is principally concerned with equilibrium. The paleocerebellum with coordination of trunk and proximal limb bud functions, involving gross coordination, muscle tone, and balance reactions. The neocerebellum is more involved with distal limb and head and neck functions primarily involved in coordination, muscle tone, and spatial orientation of skilled movement and/or the more voluntary and cortically involved kinds of behavior. This same pattern of archi, paleo, neo development of the cerebellum can be seen in the development of infant behavioral patterns during the first 9 to 12 months of postnatal life.[7–11]

Progressing upward to the more complex levels of the nervous system, ie, level six or the diencephalon, (through + brain) more and more parts are added (Fig 2-2, 2-7, and 2-8. Also see Table II of Appendix). The diencephalon, commonly called the thalamus (meaning bridal chamber), is located in the depths, or the most central region, of the brain. This part of the CNS is well named (through + brain), as it acts as the semifinal synaptic, and/or integration, center for all kinds of sensory information (except olfaction) going to higher levels or descending from these centers to lower levels. Note that the thalamus is not just an integration center for sensory functions. Parts of it are concerned with visceral motor functions, others with somatic-motor aspects of movement, emotional tone, vision, hearing, etc (Table II of Appendix). [1,3,12]

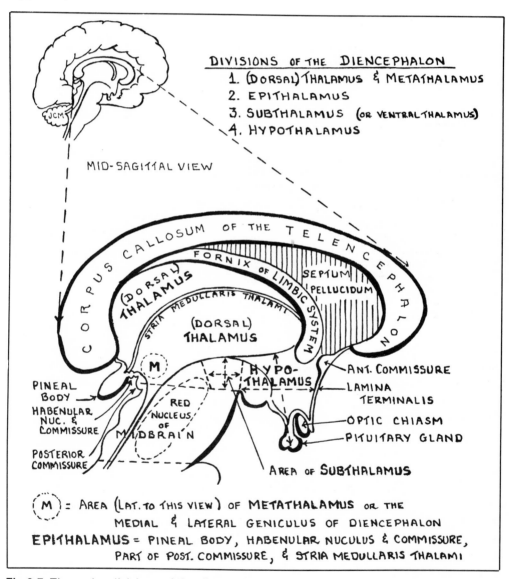

Fig 2-7 The major divisions of the diencephalon.

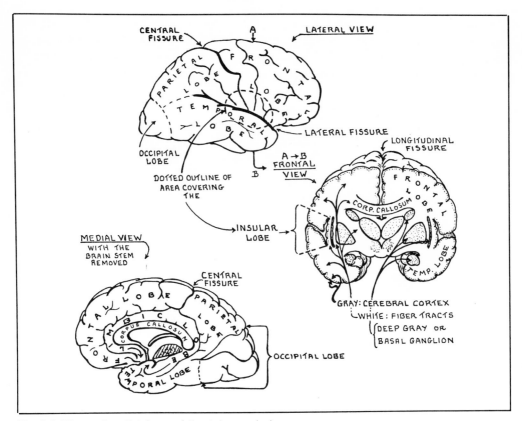

Fig 2-8 The major divisions of the telencephalon.

Level seven is the telencephalon or distant (tel) brain (encephalon) (Fig 2-2, 2-8). One can discuss this area in many ways, both structurally and functionally. Perhaps the least complicated is to subdivide the telencephalon into three major, though highly integrated and interconnected, areas. The older, more centrally located, deep gray cell bodies or nuclear areas are the structures making up the basal ganglia (see Tables IIIa and IIIb of Appendix). These centers partially surround the diencephalon and are believed to be primarily concerned with emotional tone, motor functions, and stereotyped reflexes.[3,12,13] These gray cell centers are found principally at the base of the brain in the embryonic CNS. During development, these cells migrate into their adult positions as shown in the frontal view in Fig 2-8 and Table IIIa. Thus, the deep gray cellular areas are destined to become the caudate nucleus (tail nucleus), the lentiform or lens-shaped nucleus (with the putamen laterally and the globus pallidus medially), the claustrum or gate lying lateral to the lentiform nucleus, and the amygdaloid nucleus found in the medial part of the anterior temporal lobe (see Table IIIb of Appendix).

Surrounding the basal ganglia and the diencephalon is the corpus callosum or the large fiber tract (commissure) which interconnects the two lateral cerebral hemispheres (Fig 2-2, 2-7, 2-8). Surrounding this structure in turn is the oldest lobe of the six lobes of the cerebral cortex or the limbic lobe (Fig 2-5, 2-6, 2-8 and Table IV of Appendix). This lobe, plus many adjacent structures such as the hypothalamus, thalamus, epithalamus, amygdaloid nucleus, basal ganglia, parts of the midbrain, reticular system, and parts of the cerebral cortex, are referred to as the limbic system. This functional region, including the associated components noted, is believed to be primarily responsible for emotional tone or affective behavior, motivation, and the three basic drives, ie, feeding, fighting, and reproduction.[1,12,14]

The last area of the cerebral cortex to develop is believed to be the remaining five lobes, or the insula, parietal, temporal, occipital, and frontal lobes (Fig 2-8 and Table IV of Appendix). However, even these lobes develop in different stages, some areas being older and more concerned with visceral functions such as the insular lobe, others with primary receptive and expressive functions, and still others with higher cognitive and associative functions.[1,2,12,14,15]

Integrating the entire CNS into a functional whole are (1) numerous commissural fibers or interneurons which interconnect both sides of the CNS (Fig 2-9). These kinds of fibers are

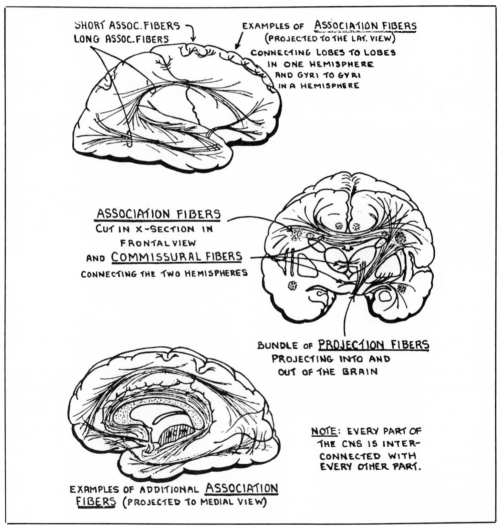

Fig 2-9 Interneuronal fiber systems which connect the entire nervous system into one functional unit.

found at all levels of the CNS: (2) short and long association fibers or interneurons which interconnect one side of the cerebral hemisphere with other parts on the same side, ie, one gyrus to another and/or one lobe to another; and (3) projection fibers or interneurons which project into and out of higher and lower cerebral centers. Thus, in the mature brain one sees a highly integrated system intimately interconnected with all other parts and acting together as a total functional system. How did it get this way? What is important to know in order to understand children who must adapt, especially those who have CNS pathology?

Prenatal Development — Highlights

At about the third week or very early in the fourth week after conception and implantation, the first component of the developing organism to become functional is the circulatory system.[8,16] The primitive heart and vessels begin pumping blood into developing vascular channels. This heart, quite unlike the heart of a child or adult, resembles a muscular expansion of a thin-walled tube. This muscular mass, along with the great vessels extending from it, contracts and expands and over many weeks begins to develop into a heart as we know it. During these critical stages of development, this system is highly vulnerable to trauma. Cardiovascular insult may result in malformation and/or malfunctioning of a part or parts, depending upon what particular area is developing when damage occurs or at what stage development is arrested. Multiple factors, such as genetic defects, toxins, drugs, viri and bacterium, malnutrition, trauma, etc, can cause cardiovascular abnormalities.

Thus the vascular system is believed to be the first viable part of the organism to begin functioning. But by the end of the third week or in the early part of the fourth week of gestation, the CNS begins to form and manifest primitive functions. One should keep in mind, however, that in spite of its early beginning, it is probably the last system in the human organism to fully mature.

Like other systems, the development of the nervous system is genetically predetermined, ie, it is preprogrammed for us from the day of conception. Generally, it can be stated that if everything progresses normally, the nervous system is going to develop in a prescribed sequence, stage by stage, pathway by pathway, and synaptic centers with other synaptic centers, unless it is interrupted.[2,3,5,8,16,17] Like the vascular system or any other system of the organism, trauma or disruption of progress at any critical stage of development (pre- or postnatally) may result in CNS damage, especially to those areas which are undergoing the greatest developmental growth at the moment of insult.

What critical sequence of events takes place during the first 22 to 28 days of life? It is at this time that the neural tube develops.[8,16,17,18] This tube evolves from a flat plate-like structure located on the dorsal area of the embryo (Fig 2-10). Neural crest cells form in a specific area and multiply and migrate dorsomedially, eventually to meet one another and fuse, forming a hollow tube. Fusion begins in the cervical region, then progresses cephalically or above this cervical area and finally caudally. Here may be the first reflection of a cephlocaudal developmental pattern within the nervous system.[8,16,17,18] Various degrees of fusion failure during these different stages of neural tube closure can result in developmental abnormalities of the CNS. However, if development proceeds normally a primitive CNS is developed by the end

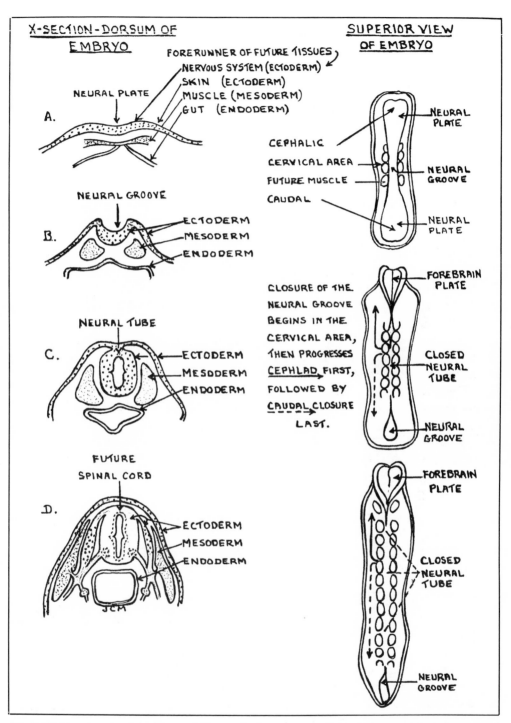

Fig 2-10 Developmental stages of the central nervous system and associated structures.*

*Modified from Hamilton WJ, Boyd JD, Mossman HW: Human Embryology. Baltimore, Williams and Wilkins, 1962.

of the fourth week in utero. This embryonic tube continues to form, expand, and change and can finally be recognized or equated to the seven major divisions of the mature nervous system (Fig 2-11).

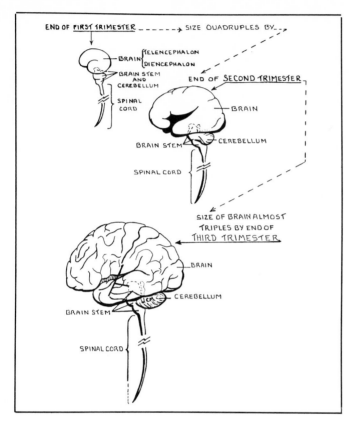

Fig 2-11 The developing central nervous system: First nine months in utero.

During the fifth week tiny limb buds appear in the embryo (Fig 2-12). The upper limb buds precede the development of the lower ones, which appear near the end of the fifth week, once again following the pattern of the cephlocaudal law of development.[8,16,17] One can understand why trauma to the organism at these stages of development can affect either the upper or lower limbs.

As the limb buds grow, three basic structures develop within them: 1) somites, or the beginnings of our muscular, ligamentous, and tendonous tissues; 2) sensorimotor neurons which migrate out from related segments of the spinal cord; and 3) cartilagenous tissue which is the forerunner of our skeletal system (Fig 2-12, 2-13). All three entities (including, or course, vascular, fascial, and lymphatic components) develop and function together. The muscles must have bones upon which to attach in order to create movement and/or stability. They must be innervated in order to contract and relax and also relay messages of this action back to the CNS. In this way, the CNS will be able to tell if everything is properly programmed or, if not, to send through new messages to correct the error. In either event, the nervous system "learns by doing."[3,12,13,20–24] Should a group of neurons destined for a particular muscle mass fail to develop and migrate, or should the neurons develop but the muscle mass fail to

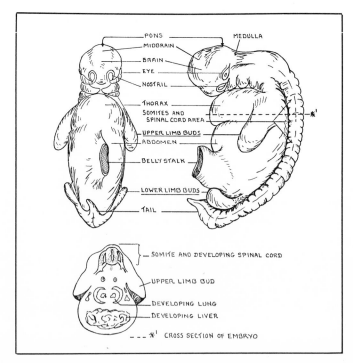

Fig 2-12 Front and side view of the developing embryo showing major structures present at the 10 mm state. Note limb bud development.†

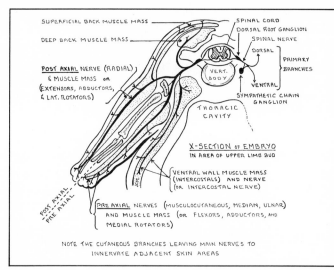

Fig 2-13 Functional organization of neuromuscular components of the upper limb and thorax in the developing embryo. The same type of organization is found in the lower limb-abdominio-pelvic cavity relationship.**

materialize, abnormal development results. Neurons cannot survive without their companion muscles (or glands), just as the muscles (or glands) cannot survive without innervation. This neuromuscular affinity can be likened to the axion: wither the muscle goeth there shall follow the nerves. Loss of one results in degeneration and death of the other.[1,3,12,13,15,25,26]

†Modified from Hamilton WJ, Boyd JD, Mossman HW: Human Embryology. Baltimore, Williams and Wilkins, 1962.
**Modified from Patten BM: Human Embryology, ed 2. New York, The Blakiston Co, 1953.

By the seventh week the embryo is recognizable as a subminiature neuromusculoskeletal organism except the skeleton is still cartilagenous, and the somites or muscle masses still have to mature into their separate entities before they are recognizable as the biceps, triceps, deltoid, soleus, etc. At this time, however, the embryo resembles a creature somewhat like a turtle or rag doll. The limbs or appendages are extended laterally at about a 45° angle from the axial body or head, neck and trunk (Fig 2-12, 2-13). It is at this stage of development that one can best appreciate the simple organization of our major functional muscle groups, ie, the extensors, abductors, and external (lateral) rotators, and the flexors, adductors, and internal (medial) rotators.[2,6] In each limb the extensor groups and its associated muscles develop cephalically or postaxially, ie, above the cartilagenous skeleton forming the central core of the limb (Fig 2-13). Below, caudal or preaxially to the cartilagenous skeleton, the flexor group and its associated synergists develop. It is not until many months later, in utero, that rotation of the limbs begins, first in the upper and later in the lower limbs. Postnatally, it will take a few years before they assume their adult configuration. This rotation factor places the functional muscle groups into the well-known anatomical positions in which we use them once we begin moving about and standing upright. This is best expressed in the lower limbs. Rotation moves the extensor group from a cephalic or superior position into an anterior one. This places many muscles which were relatively straight from origin to insertion into a spiral-like arrangement. It is little wonder that we move about in flowing spiral or diagonal patterns of motion.

Once the nerves migrate into the limbs they begin myelinating. This process takes place some time around the end of the eighth week. When myelination occurs, coded messages from the primitive nervous system are transmitted to the muscles so that they can begin contracting and relaxing and eventually moving the body and limbs. At the same time, myelin formation begins within the CNS. (Two different cell types are involved in the myelination process of the nervous system.[1,6,8,16] In the peripheral nervous system Schwann cells form the myelin or insulating sheath around the peripheral cell processes or the axons of the neurons. In the CNS the oligodendrocytes form the insulation for the nerve processes. See Fig 2-14.) The smallest sized neuronal processes are believed to be the first to myelinate, followed by the intermediate sized ones and then by the largest processes (Fig 2-15). The cell bodies, axon hillock (or the very beginning of the axon), and the dendrites do not myelinate (Fig 2-16). Though these areas remain unmyelinated they are not "bare." They are destined to become the sites of thousands of synapses or junctional areas upon which processes of other cells of the nervous system will eventually synapse (Fig 2-16). Myelination of the nervous system continues after birth for many years. Neurons comprising parts of the cerebral cortex and the pyramidal system, and parts of the proprioceptive, tactile, and vibratory systems are some of the last neurons to become fully functional.[2,5,8] While the axonal processes are myelinating, the dendrites are lengthening and sprouting additional branches (Fig 2-16). Over a long period of time (perhaps for life, and especially following a CNS lesion) more and more dendritic branches appear and eventually little spines or synaptic knobs appear in some areas. Terminals from other nerves will synapse on these spines as well as on the dendritic branches, cell body (or soma), and the axon hillock. Between 1000 and 100,000 (with an average of 10,000) synapses can be found on a single nerve cell body and its processes.[1] This process of dendritic growth and the formation of additional synapses is known to continue for many years and is now believed to be one of the major factors responsible for the plasticity or changeability of the nervous system.[3,12,13,15,22,25,26]

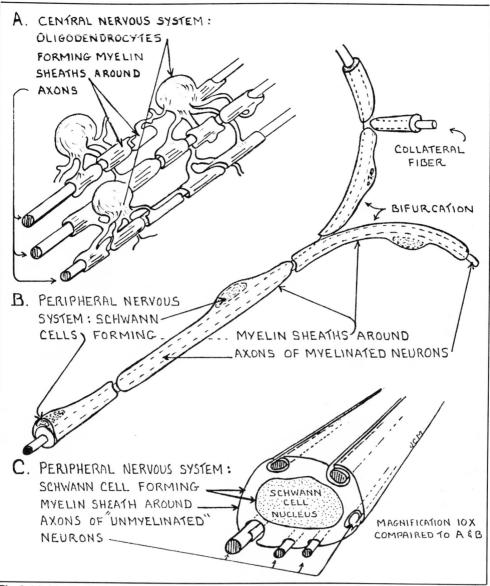

A. CENTRAL NERVOUS SYSTEM: OLIGODENDROCYTES FORMING MYELIN SHEATHS AROUND AXONS

COLLATERAL FIBER

BIFURCATION

B. PERIPHERAL NERVOUS SYSTEM: SCHWANN CELLS FORMING MYELIN SHEATHS AROUND AXONS OF MYELINATED NEURONS

C. PERIPHERAL NERVOUS SYSTEM: SCHWANN CELL FORMING MYELIN SHEATH AROUND AXONS OF "UNMYELINATED" NEURONS

SCHWANN CELL NUCLEUS

MAGNIFICATION 10X COMPARED TO A & B

Fig 2-14 Myelin formation in the central and peripheral nervous system.

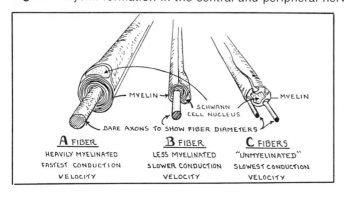

MYELIN
MYELIN
SCHWANN CELL NUCLEUS
BARE AXONS TO SHOW FIBER DIAMETERS

A FIBER
HEAVILY MYELINATED
FASTEST CONDUCTION
VELOCITY

B FIBER
LESS MYELINATED
SLOWER CONDUCTION
VELOCITY

C FIBERS
"UNMYELINATED"
SLOWEST CONDUCTION
VELOCITY

Fig 2-15 Schematic representation of the three kinds of peripheral nerves.

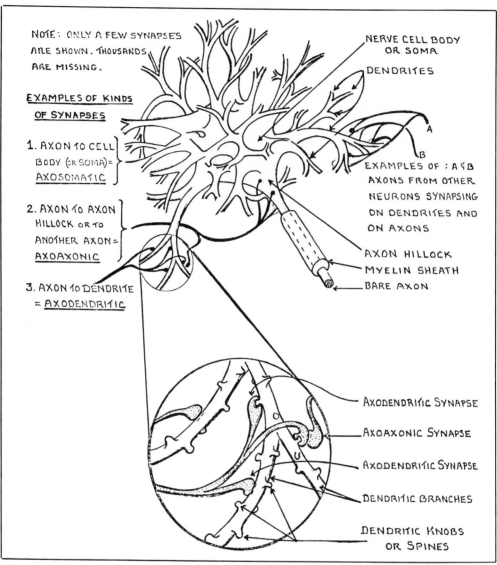

Fig 2-16 A nerve cell body and its processes with different kinds of synapses impinging upon it.

In Fig 2-17, a cross section of the spinal cord shows that the earliest areas to myelinate and become functional are centrally located. Later the more ventral-lateral pathways are myelinated, followed eventually by the most recent tracts, the dorsal columns, and finally the "pyramidal" tracts. Generally speaking, this developmental pattern of the spinal cord reflects the growth of the newborn and the developing child. The first behavioral patterns observed postnatally are those principally concerned with autonomic nervous system reflexes, intra and interspinal segmental reflexes and basic brain stem reticular system functions. Next are the brain stem reflexes coupled with primitive and somewhat fractionated body movements, ie, individual parts are beginning to fractionate or move separately. At this stage the vestibular

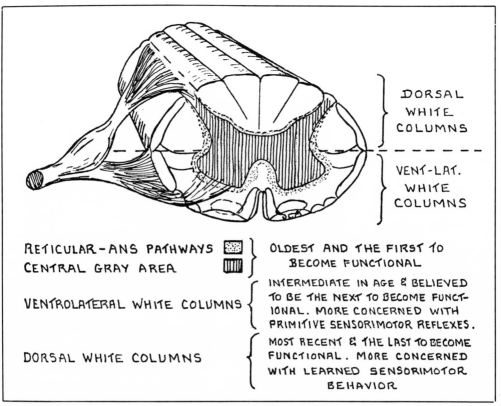

Fig 2-17 Phylogenetic concept of the developmental ages of the spinal cord.

system and the archicerebellum are developing (Fig 2-4, 2-5, 2-6), enabling the infant to achieve balance, muscle tone, and spatial localization of movement patterns. Still later, one observes the beginnings of bilateral and then unilateral exploratory actions. Finally domination by higher CNS centers enables the child to move freely in space, actively explore the environment (dorsal and corticospinal column pathways), control bladder and bowel functions, and communicate this knowledge to others in a meaningful way.

While this developmental sequence is progressing in the spinal cord, what developmental pattern is paralleling it in the brain stem and in the higher levels of the CNS? In the brain stem, cranial nerves 5, 7, 9, 10, and 12 are believed to be the first to myelinate and become functional (Fig 2-4 and Appendix I).[5,8,16,19] The fifth Cr.n. or trigeminal (tri, meaning three, and gemina, meaning twin) has several important functions that are necessary to know in order to understand primitive survival reflexes and normal postnatal development. One component of the fifth Cr.n. is responsible for supplying the entire face and part of the tongue with sensory reception (Fig 2-18). The three divisions of the nerve — ophthalmic, maxillary, and mandibular — enable the developing embryo, fetus, and later the newborn to receive different sensations such as gross touch, pain, temperature changes, pressure, and tactile information. Another part of the fifth Cr.n. is responsible for innervation of the muscles of mastication. These muscles are initially used in the rooting and sucking reflexes, later for chewing and helping to initiate swallowing, and still later for communication. Another function

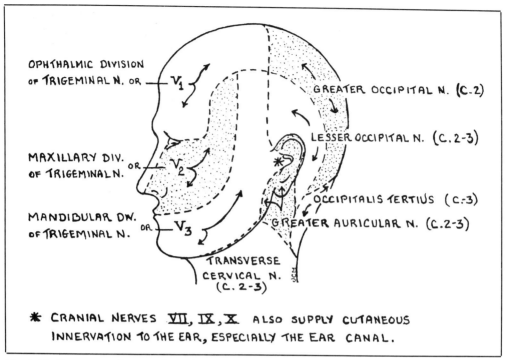

Fig 2-18 Cutaneous innervation of the head.

of the fifth Cr.n. is concerned with hearing or control of the tensor muscle of the tympanic membrane (tensor tympani), a very tiny muscle which is partly responsible for regulation of sound into the middle and inner ear. Thus the fifth Cr.n. is responsible initially for feeling objects that touch the face and obtaining that object so that it can be sucked.

The seventh Cr.n. or facial nerve develops and functions right along with the fifth Cr.n. (Fig 2-4 and Table I of Appendix). Like the fifth, it has several major functions that are involved in the development of the primitive reflexes and later on in such important functions as speaking or verbal and nonverbal communication. One part of the seventh Cr.n. innervates the muscles of facial expression. This enables the organism to open and close its eyes, purse the lips or grasp an object with them, smile, cry, etc. Another part is responsible for regulating two of the three pairs of salivatory glands (the submandibular and the sublingual) which are necessary adjuncts in chewing and in the digestive process. A small component is concerned with taste reception on the anterior two thirds of the tongue and another with a small muscle of the middle ear, the stapedius, which is also concerned with hearing.

Cranial nerves nine and ten (glossopharyngeal and vagus respectively) are also vitally necessary in order to develop the primitive rooting and sucking reflexes (Fig 2-4 and Table I of Appendix). Both nerves are involved in regulation of glandular secretions, the ninth controlling the parotid or the third pair of salivary glands, while the tenth regulates other glands of the digestive system as well as many vital organs such as the heart, lungs, etc. Both nerves innervate swallowing muscles of the pharynx and larynx, structures which will also be used later in life for breathing and phonation. Finally, both nerves innervate taste buds on the posterior aspect of the tongue and walls of the posterior oral cavity.

The twelfth Cr.n. or hypoglossal nerve innervates the tongue musculature which is necessary initially for performing the sucking and swallowing reflexes, later for chewing and swallowing, and eventually for language functions (Fig 2-4 and Table I of Appendix). These five brain stem nerves develop, myelinate, and function together very early in embryonic life. This is brought about, in part, due to the early development of a pathway called the medial longitudinal fasciculus or MLF. This tract begins to myelinate and function along with the development of the cranial nerves of the brain stem. It is located in the old central core of the brain stem and extends into the cervical levels of the spinal cord (Fig 2-19). This fiber bundle

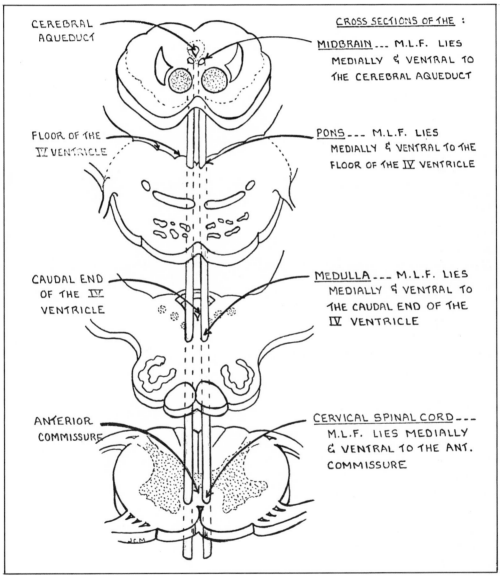

Fig 2-19 The medial longitudinal fasciculus (MLF) of the brain stem and spinal cord. (Size of MLF is enlarged to show the relationships to surrounding structures.)

essentially consists of ascending and descending neuronal processes which are bilaterally represented. It is also one of the principal pathways of the vestibular complex (thus enabling this system to exert a powerful influence upon these cranial nerve nuclei), the reticular formation, and cervical levels of the spinal cord. Later in development additional components will be added to this tract. These are interneurons from cortical and subcortical centers. This is one of many pathways over which these higher areas can exert their influences upon brain stem cranial nerve nuclei and upper levels of the spinal cord.

By the end of the first trimester the organism is capable of using the primitive rooting and sucking reflexes, and indeed it begins to do this in utero. However, just prior to this time, some primitive avoidance reflexes are manifested. These reflexes will eventually be dampened or controlled by higher centers before the rooting and sucking reflexes can dominate. These avoidance reflexes first appear during the last few weeks or at the end of the first trimester.[5,8,16,19] Touching or stroking the oral area causes the embryo's head to turn away from the stimulus. By the end of the twelfth week, it not only turns its head away, but the eyelids, which are closed and relaxed, squeeze tightly shut as an additional response to the oral stimulus. A little later the reflex spreads caudally and movement occurs in the upper limbs and trunk, followed later by movement in the lower limbs. The reflex spreads cephlo-caudally reflecting the growth that is occurring within the nervous system. The next avoidance reflex appears slightly later. This is the eye avoidance reflex. Shining a light into the eyes (even though they are closed) results in the same sequence of tight eyelid closure, head and neck turning, followed by a total body avoidance reflex. Thus avoidance reflexes (and there are many others which could be mentioned) are normal during certain stages of development. It is believed that the residuals of some of these primitive reflexes, seen later in the newborn and developing child, may be manifestations of CNS trauma, either due to arrested development or malfunctioning of higher centers which are damaged and fail to override or control these lower brain-stem-spinal-cord reflexes.

During the beginning of the second trimester or at the end of the twelfth week and progressing into the next few weeks, the oral avoidance reflexes disappear. At this time the fetus is capable of moving his upper limbs toward his mouth. The digital protrusions, destined to become fingers, are grasped by the lips and are sucked. It is well known that babies can be born with calluses on their hands due to continual sucking in utero.[5,17,19] Also, this movement, coupled with touching of one part of the body by another part, represents an additional set of stimuli or input into the developing fetus. In this way, the nervous system sets up its own patterns of repetitive stimuli, ie, rooting, sucking, and swallowing. One could say that the nervous system is programming itself over the intervening five or six months to be highly proficient in performing these basic survival reflexes of rooting, sucking, swallowing, digestion, and elimination. In so doing, it is theorized that this additional sensory input helps to stimulate dendritic growth, further myelination of neuronal processes and pathways, and the formation of new synapses.

To explain this concept further, once the developing organism begins self-stimulation, such as in utero movements, sucking, swallowing, etc. a new set of developmental reflexes are believed to be established. Prior to this time, sensory input and motor output is very generalized and occurs more or less at random or as separate functional entities. As the sensory and motor neurons develop, myelinate, and establish synaptic connections with each other, with adjacent spinal cord segments, and supraspinal centers, primitive sensorimotor reflexes are established. At this time a stimulus can evoke a very generalized but nonpurposeful total body response. With further growth of neuronal processes, peripheral receptors, additional synaptic connections, and finally one body part interacting with another (ie, hands with the face), feedback stimuli or additional sensory impulses resulting from movement and contact make for new synapses, thus changing the total reflexive movement patterns within the organism. Initially the hand and mouth probably come together in a trial and error fashion or as a result of nonpurposeful or coincidental behavior. With repeated contact new sensations are generated along with new feedback information from the successful movement pattern. This information is sent into the CNS and establishes additional sets of complex reflex patterns. Therefore, the nervous system no longer functions just on a simple sensory to motor reflex level. Rather it begins to function on a *sensory-motor-sensory* (feedback) system. It is at this stage that the nervous system begins to monitor nonpurposeful reflex actions which are the result of stimuli from the internal and external environment. And it is at this time that it begins to build up important relay pathways and interneurons which interconnect all sensorimotosensory reflex arcs. Therefore the embryo begins to make purposeful, though noncortical, adjustments in relation to movement because of the feedback information it continually receives. In this way, normal, though stereotyped, predictable patterns of reflexive behavior are gradually laid down or impressed upon the developing pathways and synaptic centers of the CNS.

During the second trimester, or the fourth, fifth and sixth month of development, many more changes take place. By four months the mother can begin to feel "quickening" or movement of the fetus. At this stage, total body reflexes are occurring. The fetus moves about with kicking, turning, and rolling motions.[17,19] By five months it is capable of reacting to loud sounds, such as music. These vibrations can create excessive movements in the fetus which in turn may cause the mother to turn off the sound. However, the auditory input which seems to be of major importance to the fetus is the continual beat of the mother's heart. Research has shown that hospitalized newborns are more contented in a nursery equipped with the recording of a heart beat. The infants appear to develop faster, have less colic, and adjust to their new environment much more quickly than do babies in a nursery lacking this sound.[5,19] Undoubtedly this same principle applies when one places a clock or metronome beside a newly acquired puppy. It sleeps much better and does not disturb the household with its lonesome cries throughout the night.

During the second trimester the eye avoidance reflex to light becomes stronger, as do many total body reflexes. At about the same time, a distal limb grasp reflex appears in the upper and lower limbs. For some reason this reflex is much more powerful than the one which is seen after birth.[11,17] This primitive grasp reflex when properly stimulated causes a tight fisting of the hands and curling of the toes and feet. It can be powerful enough to support the total weight of the fetus. In fact, if this reflex persists for a short time after birth, the infant can be suspended from any object placed within its grasp, such as a sash cord, fingers of the examiner, etc.[11] However, this reflex usually disappears at or just before birth and is replaced by a more normal and less firm grasp reflex. The earlier one may simulate the grasp reflex seen in other animals, such as the infant monkey clinging safely to its mother's fur as she moves swiftly in the forest.

There are many additional reflexes and stages of development which could be noted.

However, it is not the purpose here to delve deeply into this area of prenatal development. There are many excellent texts covering this subject. Only the highlights of various stages of development are noted in order to illustrate two fundamental concepts: 1) that the nervous system develops in an organized preprogrammed cephlocaudal sequence; and 2) that this is reflected outwardly as a central to peripheral and proximal to distal developmental pattern in regards to the development of the head, neck, body, and the extremities.

The next examination includes the surface of the brain and its development (Fig 2-20). At about the end of the fifth or in the sixth month in utero, the fetus has a rather large but smooth

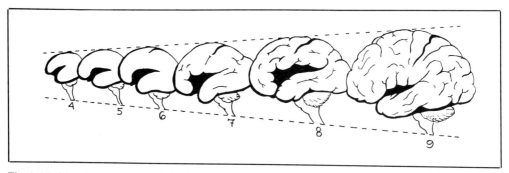

Fig 2-20 Monthly stages of fetal brain development. Also see Fig 2-11 and 2-21.‡

brain. Only the lateral, central, and longitudinal fissures are present. Notice that the lateral fissure is open and that the insular lobe deep to it is visible. This is especially noticeable on the dominate hemisphere, and it is at this time that cerebral dominance can be determined.[2,4,16] During the next month the major lobes of the brain are subdivided by secondary and tertiary fissures, as gyri and sulci, or convolutions, appear reflecting extensive vascularization and growth of neuronal processes, neuroglia, myelination, synaptic formation, and further development of interneuronal circuits. In other words, the surface of the brain is expanding along with the pathways and connections that are projecting into and out from it. Late in the seventh month or during the eighth, many of the major convolutions are well developed, and the lateral fissure is beginning to close over the insula, especially on the left side of the brain. Several different areas of the brain, including the ventricles, develop more extensively in the left hemisphere (in the majority of the population), than they do in the right hemisphere. Even the developing vascular pattern of the brain reflects this difference.[4,27,28,29] Thus, at or before the seventh month in utero, our preprogrammed nervous system has already established which hemisphere shall be dominant for communication and handedness and which will be more involved with abstractions, emotions, and possibly such things as artistic talents.[2,4,27,28,29] By the end of the eighth month the brain almost resembles a small-sized adult brain (Fig 2-20, 2-21). However, it will be many years before full growth is reached, especially in those areas responsible for mature cognitive and higher perceptual functions.

---

‡Modified from Patten BM: Human Embryology, ed 2. New York, The Blakistan Co, 1953. From Hamilton WJ, Boyd JD, Mossman HW: Human Embryology. Baltimore, Williams & Wilkins, 1962.

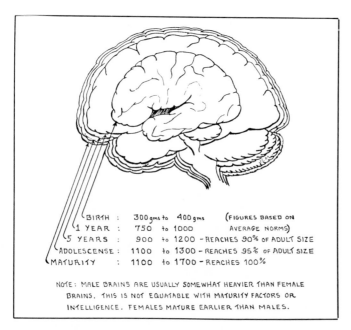

BIRTH   :   300 gms to 400 gms   (FIGURES BASED ON
1 YEAR   :   750 to 1000   AVERAGE NORMS)
5 YEARS   :   900 to 1200 – REACHES 90% OF ADULT SIZE
ADOLESCENSE : 1100 to 1300 – REACHES 95% OF ADULT SIZE
MATURITY   :   1100 to 1700 – REACHES 100%

NOTE: MALE BRAINS ARE USUALLY SOMEWHAT HEAVIER THAN FEMALE
BRAINS. THIS IS NOT EQUATABLE WITH MATURITY FACTORS OR
INTELLIGENCE. FEMALES MATURE EARLIER THAN MALES.

Fig 2-21 Postnatal development of the brain.

While the cortex of the brain has been evolving, other parts of the nervous system are reaching fetal maturity. The eyes, along with their pathways and synaptic centers, are developing so that they can react not only to light, but have the ability to make scanning movements, tract objects, move in a conjugate manner, and focus on near and far objects. Likewise, the auditory centers are beginning to perceive more critically so that the CNS can begin to differentiate sounds that are soothing to the organism or are threatening or strange. Also during the last trimester the fetus may begin hiccupping. It has been theorized that this function might be responsible, in part, for strengthening the diaphragm and the muscles of respiration in preparation for breathing.[2]

As normal growth and development proceeds, additional primitive reflexes appear, such as the symmetrical and asymmetrical tonic neck, optokinetic, babinski reflex, and many more. These will not be enumerated here. They are covered in excellent detail in other texts.[7,9,10,11,14,26] What is important to remember is that as each new level of the CNS develops, additional pathways are myelinated, and new connections or synapses are formed between the lower and higher centers of the system. This in turn enables higher reflexes to develop along with more complex behavioral patterns and override or dampen the more primitive reflexes. Each new sequence of events results in an increased amount of self-stimulation or feedback into the nervous system. This in turn is believed to help in the myelination process, the formation of new synapses and additional circuitry in higher centers which eventually results in more purposeful reflexive and coordinated patterns of movement. This preprogrammed growth and developmental sequence can be equated to a target with ever-widening spiral-like circles surrounding a central area (Fig 2-22). The peri-oral region of the face is found at the center of the target and represents the parts of the fifth, seventh, ninth, tenth, and twelfth cranial nerves which first become functional. As growth and development continues, the next spiraling circle develops. More cranial nerves become functional, and the

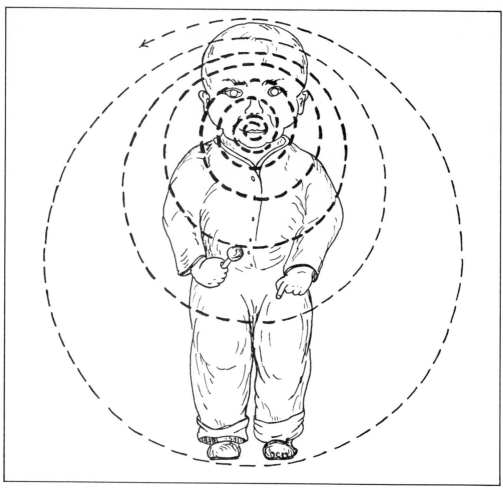

Fig 2-22 Concept of pre and postnatal development. (Adapted to the "Spiraling Continuum" theory) showing the cephalocaudal law of development, beginning peri-orally and expanding ever outward to eventually encompass the highest levels of cognitive behavior.

primitive avoidance reflexes develop. Ever-widening spirals represent the development of upper, and later, lower limb functions, along with growth or primary cortical centers (Fig 2-22) and their subcortical connections, including growth of the ever enlarging cerebellar centers. Finally when the last spiral matures, the organism is ready for birth. This same sequence of events parallels the postnatal developmental patterns of behavior.

Postnatal Development — Highlights

After birth the infant lies relatively quietly, either on its back or stomach, with its upper and lower limbs relaxed, somewhat laterally extended (though semiflexed at the elbow and knee joints) and externally rotated. Complete rotation of the limbs into the adult configuration, as mentioned previously, is still a forthcoming event. Passive movement of the limbs into this adult position will create resistive movements, demonstrating that the baby is unwilling and as yet unable to assume this position. Actually the limbs are not ready to tolerate this rotational pattern.[2,11] It is no wonder that many infants and very young children appear extremely bowlegged and crawl and creep with their limbs in an externally rotated and widely abducted position. In some youngsters it can take up to two or three years before their limbs can achieve the full rotational pattern of the older child.

Another interesting point to consider when examining the newborn, especially one which is suspected of having a CNS lesion, is to be sure that it is awake. One may find many of the reflexes of the newborn to be suppressed when testing the infant in the supine position. The natural tendency of the infant's nervous system is to go to sleep when placed in the fully reclining supine or prone position. Placing the baby in a semi-reclining or slightly elevated position, or supporting its head and upper trunk somewhat above the surface of the crib, tends to awaken the nervous system. This elevated position enables the eyes to open involuntarily, thus adding additional stimuli to the baby's nervous system. Lying the infant supine (unless it is crying and upset) automatically initiates a reflex which moves the eyeballs upward and at the same time closes the eyelids. Thus it is wise, before making a decision in regards to normal or pathological reflexes of the newborn, to be sure that the infant is awake and is functioning at its optimum.[2]

The following examination includes the growth and development of the vertebral column and spinal cord of the baby (Fig 2-23). At birth the newborn has an extremely flexible vertebral column. If one were to dissect the total column out of an infant cadaver, one would find it is very pliable and can be hyperflexed, hyperextended, and laterally rotated with extreme ease. *In vivo,* however, it is C-shaped, ie, if the baby is propped up into a sitting position the total body assumes a totally flexed pattern (Fig 2-23,A). It is not until head raising

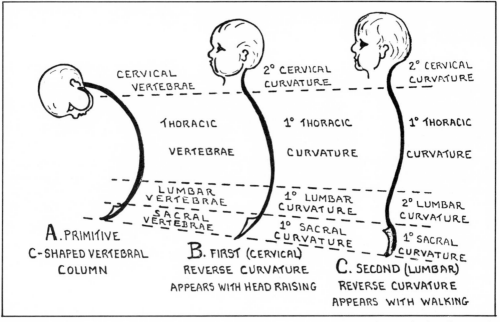

Fig 2-23 Changes in the curvature of the vertebral column accompanying early development.

begins that this C-shaped pattern changes. As head raising improves and strength is acquired, the upper vertebral bodies or cervical vertebrae begin to assume a reverse curvature (Fig 2-23,B). However, the remainder of the column stays flexed or C-shaped for many more months. Once the child begins standing, then cruising, and finally unsteady walking, the second reverse curve, or lumbar curve, begins to form (Fig 2-23,C). The thoracic and sacral segments retain the original or primitive concave or C-shaped pattern, while the cervical and later the lumbar areas obtain their secondary and permanent convex curvatures. The lumbar curve becomes fixed during the time that the child is walking freely and only after many months of this activity.[2,6] Due to anatomical differences, the female usually has a greater lumbar curvature than does the male, which is reflected in later life by the greater protrusion posteriorly of pelvic girdle structures in the female as opposed to the male. The vertebral column finally loses its highly flexible abilities once these curves are fully developed, a process which takes many years and lasts into the teens.

Concurrent with these changes are structural changes occurring in each individual vertebrae (Fig 2-24). Each part of a vertebrae has its own separate growth centers.[6] It is from these areas that bone grows outwardly in all directions to eventually fuse with adjacent parts of a given vertebrae. For most of the vertebrae, it takes from three to six years for this process to reach its final stage of development, ie, complete fusion of all of the separate growth centers into a recognizable vertebrae.[2,18,30] It is not too uncommon for fusion failure to occur between a lamina and a spinous process or to have a growth center missing in a spinous process, especially in the lumbar region of the vertebral column. This usually goes unnoticed and does not interfere with function if only one or possibly two spinous processes or laminae are missing. The massive amount of ligamentous structures and deep back muscles, coupled with the superior and inferior facets and joint capsules of each vertebrae, all help to hold the

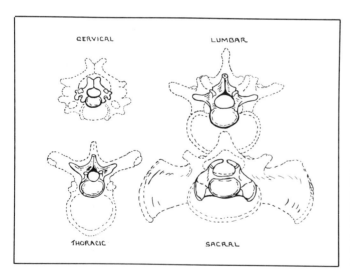

CERVICAL   LUMBAR

THORACIC   SACRAL

Fig 2-24 Typical vertebrae illustrating the difference in relative size between immature and mature vertebrae. At birth only the primary growth centers of each vertebrae consist of bone, the rest is cartilaginous.*

---

*Modified from Patten BM: Human Embryology, ed 2. New York, The Blakistan Co, 1953. From Anson BJ (ed): Morris' Human Anatomy, ed 12. New York, McGraw-Hill Book Co, 1966. From Goss CM (ed): Gray's Anatomy of the Human Body, ed 28. Philadelphia, Lea & Febiger, 1966.

vertebral column together, yet enables it to bend relatively freely in its limited planes of motion. The last bone of the vertebral column to fuse is the atlas or the first cervical vertebrae adjacent to the skull. This particular vertebrae takes from five to nine years to reach full maturity.[2,18,30] It is no wonder that youngsters are so supple in comparison to adults.

At the same time that the different parts of a vertebrae are fusing together, lengthening of the vertebral column is also occurring due to growth of the vertebral bodies and adjacent parts. During fetal development, the spinal cord, lying within the vertebral foramen, is the same length as the vertebral column (Fig 2-25). As growth and development progresses, the spinal cord grows more slowly or lengthens disproportionally to the total length of the faster growing vertebral column. The spinal cord of the baby ends at about the level of the second or third lumbar vertebrae.[1,6] In the adult it can end at thoracic level 12 in very tall individuals, the lower level of the first lumbar vertebrae in most people, or at the lower level of the second lumbar vertebrae in very short people.[1,6] This growth differential between the spinal cord and the vertebrae accounts for the downward slant of the nerve roots as they leave the spinal cord and descend to their respective intervertebral foramena, from whence they emerge as spinal nerves before bifurcating into peripheral nerves. This downward slant of the nerve roots is especially noticeable in the lower thoracic and lumbosacral levels of the spinal cord. More important perhaps is the realization that the segments of the spinal cord from which these nerve roots emerge do not match up with their corresponding vertebral levels once this differential growth is completed, or when full stature is reached in the middle to late teens. Therefore cord injuries in the very young child will affect higher levels of the spinal cord in relation to the vertebrae involved than would be true in the older child or the mature adult (Fig 2-25). This is especially true for the lower thoracic and lumbosacral levels of the spinal cord.

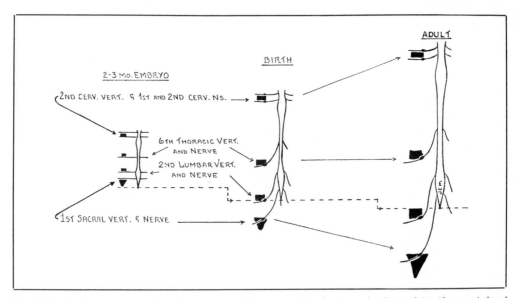

Fig 2-25 Schematic drawing to show relative length of the spinal cord to the vertebral column. With differential growth of the vertebral column in relation to the spinal cord, the nerve roots are displaced caudalward from their point of origin in the cord to their point of exit at the intervertebral foramen. See text for additional differences.

At birth the newborn has a rather large calvaria or skull cap in comparison to the facial structures and the rest of the body. Though the calvaria does not grow as much in relation to the rest of the musculo-skeletal system, it will increase in volume four to five times from birth to maturity.[2] At the same time the facial structures increase 12 times in volume and are the last areas of the musculoskeletal system to reach the adult configuration, especially in the male. Reflecting the expansion of the calvaria is the change taking place within it, ie, the growth of the brain (Fig 2-21). At birth the volume of the brain is about 400cc. At about two years of age it has a volume of about 950cc, more than doubling in size during these 24 months. By the time full maturity is reached the volume of the brain is between 1300 and 1500cc.[2] (Note that in Fig 2-21 this is expressed in gram weight instead of volume.) Female brains are usually slightly smaller than the male though this in no way reflects a lesser degree of intelligence. Variability in volume, give or take a few 100cc, cannot be equated with intellectual ability assuming that normal growth and development has taken place.

These figures should give one a rough idea of the tremendous amount of change taking place within the CNS in relation to dendritic, axonal, and collateral growth of neurons, myelination, synaptic formation, and vascularization, as well as the potential for change which can occur during the development of the immature nervous system. It is little wonder that therapists prefer to treat the newborn or young child instead of being forced to wait until the child reaches school age. It is at this early age that the brain more than doubles in volume and is probably the most plastic and the easiest to modify and to demonstrate significant changes due to therapeutic intervention.

These potential changes in relation to the plasticity of the nervous system can be expressed in another way. Studies on lower animals, ie, the rat, have demonstrated that the growth of the immature brain can be accelerated or slowed down in relation to normal growth rates of litter mate controls.[13] Conditions of sensory deprivation, such as malnutrition, lack of care and handling, disease, crowded quarters, etc, can result in a decrease in the growth of the developing brain. At the same time an enriched environment, expressed by introducing just the opposite set of conditions noted above, can result in an increase in brain growth. This is not to say that the rat brain can mature in half or a quarter of the time it normally takes. Rather, under experimental conditions the brains of rats in an enriched environment are advanced at each stage of development while those under the deprived conditions are retarded. To express this in different terms, the gram weight of the control brain is X at each stage of development, while those of the enriched brain is X-plus and the deprived brain X-minus. These differences are reflected outwardly in the behavioral development of the animal and microscopically in the amount of dendritic growth, synaptic knobs, the degree of myelination taking place within the CNS of each group, and many additional biochemical factors.[13,31] Even though rats are not humans there is reason to believe that these same set of conditions, ie, an enriched environment, a "normal" environment, and one that is sensorally deprived, will have similar effects upon the early growth and development of the human nervous system to some unknown degree. This might help explain some of the great variation seen in the growth and developmental patterns of infants and young children and even young adults who are considered "normal." It is still debatable however, if early sensory deprivation, short of actual CNS trauma, causes long lasting effects on the developing human nervous system.[12,13,20–24,31] Certainly in an environment that is sensorally deprived for many years or for the entire lifetime of the individual, one questions if the nervous system ever "catches up" in development or is indeed a normal nervous system in comparison to individuals reared in a normal environment or an enriched one. However, research tends to show that a "normal" nervous system can "catch up" if removed from its poor environment and placed in one that is normal or especially in one that is enriched. Changes may take several years to express themselves, but the nervous system is highly plastic and eventually compensation or adaptation can result. [12,13,20–24,31] In the brain-injured infant or child, all of these factors are, of course, compounded. One might speculate that in the prenatal or postnatal infant with CNS trauma, an internal state of sensory deprivation is manifested. This condition is expressed externally by sensorimotor abnormalities. Feedback from these overtly expressed actions into the pathological nervous system is going to further compound the growth and developmental lag in this system. Extrapolating further, one could theorize that if the infant is then raised in a deprived environment, CNS development is further jeopardized, or chances for normal growth and development are more than doubly compounded. If a normal environment is impressed upon this centrally deprived nervous system, perhaps some progress can be made depending upon the severity of the damage. But I would contend that it takes an enriched environment, such as sensorimotor integrative therapy, to begin to make an impression upon the growth and development of this damaged CNS, or before meaningful results reflect some degree of organization taking place within the brain-damaged organism.

What areas of the brain appear to grow more during postnatal development in comparison to other areas? What areas are believed to be the last to develop or reach full maturity? It was noted that by the end of the fifth month or early in the sixth month in utero, cerebral dominance could be determined by gross examination of the brain (Figs 2-13, 2-22, 2-23). Prior to and after birth both cerebral hemispheres continue to grow in all areas, but the parts which overlie the lateral fissure, especially in the left hemisphere, appear to grow faster and/or develop larger convolutions than in the right hemisphere. This figure varies from 85% to 98% of any given population according to reports of various authors. [2–4, 27,28] The three specific areas in the left hemisphere are called the frontal, parietal, and temporal operculum (lid or cover) and are destined to become the language center of the brain (Fig 2-8, 2-26). In the left frontal and parietal operculum are found Broca's convolution or the motor speech area and that part of the sensorimotor strip primarily responsible for reception and expression of head and neck structures involved in feeding, swallowing, and later in communication (Fig 2-26, 2-27). In the left temporal operculum, convolutions found in the lateral fissure are concerned with reception of sound. This area is known as the transverse temporal gyrus or Heschl's convolution. Other areas of the parietal operculum, posterior to the sensorimotor strip, may be concerned with reception of coded messages from the vestibular system (Fig 2-26). Further posteriorly is an area which may have more to do with written language. Interconnecting all of these areas is the arcuate fasciculus, a white subcortical fiber tract tying all of these centers together, as well as adjacent centers which are concerned with vision, the limbic system, thalamic functions, memory, other functional parts of the body, etc (Fig 2-26). Commissural fibers also interconnect these areas and others with the right hemisphere (Fig 2-8, 2-9). As the language area develops, other primary receptive and expressive centers are developing such as the primary visual center in the occipital lobe, the remainder of the sensorimotor strip in the frontoparietal lobes and area 8 in the frontal lobe, which is concerned with conjugate

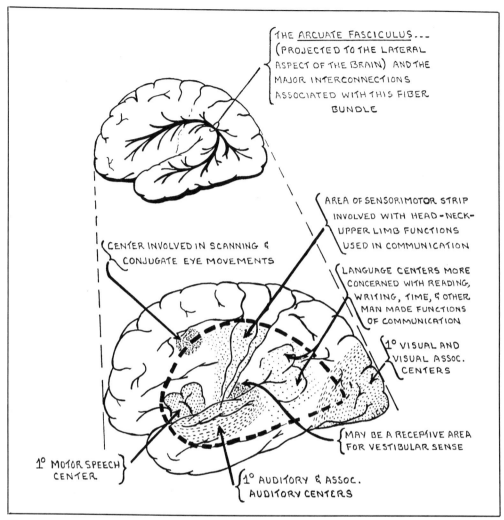

THE <u>ARCUATE FASCICULUS</u>...
(PROJECTED TO THE LATERAL
ASPECT OF THE BRAIN) AND THE
MAJOR INTERCONNECTIONS
ASSOCIATED WITH THIS FIBER
BUNDLE

CENTER INVOLVED IN SCANNING &
CONJUGATE EYE MOVEMENTS

AREA OF SENSORIMOTOR STRIP
INVOLVED WITH HEAD-NECK-
UPPER LIMB FUNCTIONS
USED IN COMMUNICATION

LANGUAGE CENTERS MORE
CONCERNED WITH READING,
WRITING, TIME, & OTHER
MAN MADE FUNCTIONS
OF COMMUNICATION

1° VISUAL AND
VISUAL ASSOC.
CENTERS

MAY BE A RECEPTIVE AREA
FOR VESTIBULAR SENSE

1° MOTOR SPEECH
CENTER

1° AUDITORY & ASSOC.
AUDITORY CENTERS

Fig 2-26 The arcuate fasciculus in relation to the cortical areas of the brain primarily concerned with communication indicate outline of communication center of the brain.

eye movements and scanning motions that are necessary for the development of normal vision (Fig 2-27). As these primary centers develop, adjacent association centers begin to function (Fig 2-27). Current ideas concerning function of the nervous system indicates that the primary centers of the cerebral cortex process information at a level that is not entirely conscious. That is, the system is aware that something is seen or heard or felt, but this information is of little value to the system except perhaps for causing basic protective or expressive reflexes. The stimuli becomes meaningful when it is recoded and transmitted from the primary receptive areas into the adjacent association areas. These association areas enable the system to know or be consciously aware of what it is hearing (seeing or feeling) and to associate this information with past experiences. In this way the nervous system learns by

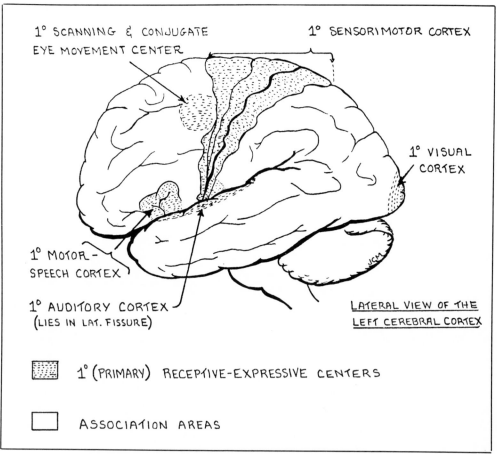

1° SCANNING & CONJUGATE EYE MOVEMENT CENTER

1° SENSORIMOTOR CORTEX

1° VISUAL CORTEX

1° MOTOR-SPEECH CORTEX

1° AUDITORY CORTEX (LIES IN LAT. FISSURE)

LATERAL VIEW OF THE LEFT CEREBRAL CORTEX

1° (PRIMARY) RECEPTIVE-EXPRESSIVE CENTERS

ASSOCIATION AREAS

Fig 2-27 Association areas constitute the major part of man's cerebral cortex in comparison to the primary receptive-expressive centers.

doing or knows how to respond to a given set of stimuli. As development progresses, additional short and long association, commissural and projection fibers (Fig 2-9, 2-27) interconnect different primary and association centers so that eventually a visual stimulus can and will set off receptors in other association areas, causing associative sensations to occur, such as smell, sound, feeling, etc, along with the visual stimulus. Always coupled with any given sensation are emotional overtones or affective behavioral reactions. This is due to the numerous relay pathways which interconnect the limbic system with practically all other parts of the brain, brain stem, and spinal cord. Thus, in the newborn one sees an organism with an immature but very active brain operating more on the level of the primary centers of the brain and principally with the more primitive ventrolateral projection pathways functioning into and out of the developing brain. As development progresses the commissural and short and long association pathways myelinate and function. As new events or input occurs each day, these modify yesterday's experiences, which in turn changes the developing nervous system. Over a period of time the infant begins to make meaningful associations from experimental exploration and manipulation of the environment, and develops his or her own individual personality. As the association centers and interconnecting pathways mature, memory is laid down. This in turn modifies future behavior, dampens or inhibits primitive reflexes, and begins to establish more purposeful sensorimotor patterns of behavior.

One cannot state that the dominate left hemisphere matures faster than the nondominate one, as they both develop together. Yet for some unknown, genetically predetermined reason, the left hemisphere is destined to mature into the communication center in the great majority of people, controlling both the language functions and body movements as well as being more analytical or concrete in nature (Fig 2-26). The right hemisphere is destined to be more abstract and more concerned with spatial concepts and artistic abilities, and it is perhaps more intricately associated with the emotional background tone of our daily lives.[4,12,13,28,29] Eccles[29] goes so far as to speculate that the left hemisphere may be our conscious or verbal brain, while the right one may be the unconscious or nonverbal brain.

In spite of the fact that our nervous system is preprogrammed to develop a dominate and a subdominate cerebral hemisphere, research shows that following CNS trauma to the cerebral cortex in one hemisphere (at least for certain centers such as language and gross sensorimotor behavior), the opposite hemisphere appears capable, to some unknown extent, in taking over the function that has been lost in the opposite side.[3,11–13,24,31] However, the earlier the trauma occurs the better the prospect that the opposite hemisphere will assume the lost function. As growth and development proceed and CNS maturity is reached, it remains questionable if the opposite hemisphere can, or is able to, assume some major functions lost on the other side. However, during the first 20 years of life, at a time when a great deal of memory storage is laid down and more and more interconnecting pathways mature (first projection fibers, then commissural, and finally association fibers [Fig 2-9]), it is theorized that areas adjacent to the injured areas or secondary centers may assume some of the lost function. Whichever is the case, the CNS remains plastic throughout life, even though plasticity decreases with advancing age. It is known that following CNS trauma, new dendritic processes develop and grow around the injured area and establish new synapses with neurons which have survived the initial trauma, provided it is not too extensive.[3,12,15,24,25] Like the developing nervous system which constantly needs meaningful and purposeful stimuli in order to develop and survive, the traumatized nervous system must also have purposeful stimuli to force it to establish new connections and learn to adapt, so that the system can attempt to function in a more purposeful manner.[13] Granted, once neurons die they cannot be rejuvenated or replaced. But it is believed that quality therapeutic intervention can stimulate other neurons and subliminal circuits which can take over and attempt to function and help compensate for that which was lost.[13]

In summary, the nervous system develops in certain preprogrammed sequences and in a cephlocaudal proximal to distal direction. This is expressed in the development of the neural tube, later in the initial behavioral patterns expressed by the developing embryo and fetus, and later during postnatal development. In spite of this genetic predetermination, plasticity remains. Each nervous system develops its own individualistic personality, acting and reacting to the internal environment and later the external environment, in an infinite variety of ways. And even though developmental behavior can be determined or matched to an "average" scale of norms, especially in the first several years of maturation, such is not the case if CNS trauma occurs. This obviously upsets the norms, usually produces developmental lags, and leaves the individual in an unpredictable state in regard to future potentials. Fortunately, many children adapt and learn to handle their disabilities within the limitations of their capabilities, especially if an enriched environment such as sensorimotor integrative therapy is introduced as a major factor during the postnatal growth and developmental stages of their lives.

References

1. Barr ML: The Human Nervous System, ed 2. New York, Harper & Row Pubs Inc, 1974.
2. Crelin ES: Functional Anatomy of the Newborn. New Haven, Yale Univ Press, 1973.
3. Eccles JC: The Understanding of the Brain. New York, McGraw-Hill Book Co, 1973.
4. Levy J: Lateral specialization of the human brain: Behavioral manifestations and possible evolutionary basis, in Kiger JA Jr (ed): Biology of Behavior. Corvallis, Oregon State Univ Press, 1972.
5. Moore JC: The developing nervous system in relation to techniques in treating physical dysfunction, in Zamir LJ (ed): Expanding Dimensions in Rehabilitation. Springfield, Illinois, C C Thomas Pubs, 1969.
6. Grant JC, Basmajian JV: Grant's Method of Anatomy, ed 7. Baltimore, William & Wilkins Co., 1965.
7. Bronisch FW: The Clinically Important Reflexes. New York, Grune & Stratton, 1952.
8. Falkner F (ed): Human Development. Philadelphia, W B Saunders Co, 1966.
9. Fiorentino MR: Normal and Abnormal Development. The Influence of Primitive Reflexes on Motor Development. Springfield, Illinois, C C Thomas Pubs, 1972.
10. Fiorentino MR: Reflex Testing Methods for Evaluating CNS Development. Springfield, Illinois, C C Thomas Pubs, 1963.
11. Peiper A: Cerebral Function in Infancy and Childhood. New York, Consultants Bureau, 1963.
12. Smythies JR: Brain Mechanisms and Behavior. New York, Academic Press, 1970.
13. Bach-y-Rita P: Brain Mechanisms in Sensory Substitution. New York, Academic Press, 1972.
14. Ruch TC, Patton HD, Woodbury JW, et al: Neurophysiology, ed 2. Philadelphia, W B Saunders Co, 1965.
15. Eccles JC: The Physiology of Synapses. New York, Academic Press, 1964.
16. Hamilton WJ, Boyd JD, Mossman HW: Human Embryology. Baltimore, William & Wilkins Co, 1962.
17. Nilsson L, Ingelman-Sundberg A, Wirsen C: A Child is Born, The Drama of Life Before Birth. New York, Dell Pub Co Inc, 1965.
18. Anson BJ (ed): Morris' Human Anatomy, ed 12. New York, McGraw-Hill Book Co, 1966.
19. Tanner JM, Taylor GR: Growth. New York, Life Science Library, Time, 1965.
20. Hinde RA: Biological Basis of Human Social Behavior. New York, McGraw-Hill Book Co, 1974.
21. Lorenz K: Evolution and Modifications of Behavior. Chicago, Univ Chicago Press, 1965.
22. Melzack R: Effects of early experience on behavior: Experimental and conceptual considerations. Psychopathology of Perception. New York, Grune & Stratton, 1965.
23. Tinbergen N: Ethology and stress diseases. Science 185:41-45, 1974.
24. Wallace P: Complex environments: Effects on brain development. Science 185:1035-1037, 1974.
25. Marx JL: Nerve growth factor: Regulatory role examined. Science 185:930, 1974.
26. Roberts E, Kuriyama K: Strategies for study of synaptic organization. Science 185:964, 1974.
27. Geschwind N: Cerebral dominance and anatomic asymmetry. N Engl J Med 287:194-195, 1972.
28. Kimura D: The asymmetry of the human brain. Sci Am 228:70-78, 1973.
29. LeMay M, Culebras A: The human brain — Morphologic differences in the hemispheres demonstrable by carotid arteriography. N Engl J Med 287:168-170, 1972.
30. Patten BM: Human Embryology, ed 2. New York, The Blakiston Co, 1953.
31. Held R: Plasticity in sensory motor systems. Sci Am 213:84, 1965.

Appendix

Table 1a

Sensory Components of the 12 Cranial Nerves

Name	*Code*	(E) = Exteroceptive components (P) = Proprioceptive components (I) = Interoceptive components
I. OLFACTORY N. (olfacto - to smell, to detect an odor)	(I)	Receptive hair cells in upper nasal mucosa → olfactory bulb and tract → limbic system.
II. OPTIC N. (optikos = meaning the eye or vision)	(E)	Rods and cones of retina → optic n., chiasm, tract → lat. geniculate nuclei of diencephalon and midbrain nuclei and to visual cortex of telencephalon.
III. OCULOMOTOR N. (oculus = eye motor = motion)	(P)	5 eye muscles → midbrain nuclei of V → Retic. system and to diencephalic/telencephalic centers.
IV. TROCHLEAR N. (troché = wheel or pulley)	(P)	From superior oblique eye muscle → midbrain nuclei of V → Retic. system and diencephalic/telencephalic centers.
V. TRIGEMINAL N. (tri = three geminus = twin) V^1 = ophthalmic ÷ V^2 = maxillary ÷ V^3 = mandibular ÷	(E)	Skin of face, mucous membrane of nose and mouth anterior tongue → V Cr. n. nuclei in pons → to Retic. system and to dienceph/telenceph. centers.
	(P)	From muscles supplied by V, temp-mandib. joint, tensor tympani mus. of middle ear, tooth sockets → V cr. n. nuclei in pons → Retic. system and dienceph/telencephalic centers.
VI. ABDUCENS N. (abduco = to abduct)	(P)	From lat. rectus eye musc. → midbrain nuclei of V → Retic. system and dienceph/telenceph. centers.
VII. FACIAL N. (facies = the face)	(P)	Stapedius mus. of middle ear → brain stem nuclei → Retic. system and dienceph/telenceph. centers.
	(I)	Deep tissues of the face and ant. two thirds tongue for taste → pontine nuclei concerned with taste and interoception → Retic. system and dienceph/telenceph. centers.
VIII. VESTIBULO - (vestibulum = an entrance)	(P)	Semicircular canals and vestibule of inner ear (utricle and sacculus) → vestib. nuclei and archicerebellum → brain stem nuclei, Retic. system, spinal cord and dienceph/telenceph centers.

Table 1a (cont.)
Sensory Components of the 12 Cranial Nerves

Name	Code	(E) = Exteroceptive components (P) = Proprioceptive components (I) = Interoceptive components

VIII. COCHLEAR N.
(cochlea = a snail
or anything in
spiral form)

(E) Organ of Corti (inner ear) → cochlear nuclei of brain stem → inferior colliculi of midbrain and medial geniculate nuclei of dienceph. → auditory cortex of telencephalon.

IX. GLOSSOPHARYNGEAL N.
(glossa = tongue +
pharynx = throat)

(E) Small area of ear and ear canal → brain stem nuclei of V, and general sensations of post one half of tongue → Retic. system and higher dienceph/telencephalic centers.

(P) Stylopharyngeous muscle of pharynx → brain stem nuclei → Retic. system and higher dienceph/telencephalic centers.

(I) Taste receptors post. one third)
    of tongue   )
Carotid sinus baroreceptors   )→ brain stem
Carotid body chemoreceptors)
Receptors of pharynx   )
nuclei → Retic. system and dienceph/telenceph centers.

X. VAGUS N.
(vago = to wander)

(E) Small area of ear canal and general sensations of base of tongue and palatal areas → brain stem nuclei → Retic. system and dienceph/telenceph centers.

(P) Muscles of palate, tonsilar arch, pharynx, larynx and esophagus → brain stem nuclei and Retic. system and dienceph/telenceph centers.

(I) Taste receptors of base tongue and palate, sensations from pharynx, larynx, esophagus, heart, lungs, abdominal viscera, aortic body and sinus, etc. → brain stem nuclei → Retic. system, etc.

XI. ACCESSORY N.
(spinal and bulbar
parts)

(Accessory to X and cervical cord levels C 1-6). Really not a cranial nerve. See under Cr.N. X for bulbar part of Accessory N. Spinal part concerned with sensations from Sternomastoid and Trapezius muscles → cervical cord levels C 1-6.

XII. HYPOGLOSSAL N.
(hypo = under +
glossa = tongue)

(E) general sensations via Cr. N.'s V, IX, X.

(P) Tongue musculature → brain stem nuclei → Retic. system and dienceph/telenceph centers.

Table 1b
Motor Components of the 12 Cranial Nerves

I. OLFACTORY N.
(olfacto - to smell,
detect an odor)

Efferent nerves to olfactory bulbs from telencephalon, possibly for enhancing, dampening or adapting to odors.

II. OPTIC N.
(optikos = eye
or vision)

Efferent nerves from superior colliculi of midbrain to retina. Possibly for enhancing visual acuity, ie, modifying peripheral vision.

III. OCULOMOTOR N.
(oculus = eye
motor = motion)

Efferent fibers from midbrain nuclei to five eye muscles (sup., inf. and med. recti and inf. oblique, and levator palpebrae superioris mus. of upper eyelid) for eye movements, convergence-divergence, scanning and tracking reflexes.

Efferent (ANS) fibers from Edinger-Westphal nuclei of midbrain to eye (ciliary musc. and constrictor papillae mus.) for light and accommodation reflexes.

IV. TROCHLEAR N.
(troché = wheel
or pulley)

Efferent fibers from midbrain nuclei to superior oblique eye mus. for eye movements, convergence-divergence, scanning and tracking reflexes.

V. TRIGEMINAL N.
(tri = three +
geminus = twin)

Efferent fibers from pontine nuclei to muscles of mastication, including the ant. digastrics, tensor veli palatine of soft palate, and the mylohyoids, for sucking, chewing, swallowing and later phonation.

Efferent fibers from the same pontine nuclei to tensor tympani muscle of middle ear for regulation (in part) of sound.

VI. ABDUCENS N.
(abducto - to
abduct)

Efferent fibers from pontine nuclei to lateral rectus eye muscles for lateral eye movements and convergence-divergence, scanning and tracking reflexes.

VII. FACIAL N.
(facies = the face)

Efferent fibers from pontine nuclei to muscles of facial expression, including the posterior digastrics, and stylohyoid muscles for rooting, sucking, chewing, swallowing, and later for verbal/nonverbal communication.

Efferent (ANS) fibers from pontine nuclei to lacrimal gland for lubrication of eyes (tears): to sublingual and submandibular glands for secretions (salivation) necessary for normal sucking and chewing and digestion; to nasal and sinus glands for moisturizing nasal-sinus passages.

Table 1b (cont.)
Motor Components of the 12 Cranial Nerves

VIII. VESTIBULAR DIVISION (vestibulum = entrance)	Efferent fibers from vestibular nuclei of brain stem to receptors of the vestibule and semicircular canals of the inner ear . . . function debatable. Numerous efferent components to the vestibular nuclei of the brain stem from adjoining structures within the CNS, may act to enhance or depress vestibular stimulus arriving from the receptor organs of the inner ear.
VIII. COCHLEAR DIVISION (cochlea = a snail or anything in spiral form)	Efferent fibers from medullary nuclei to organ of Corti of inner ear . . . may function, in part, as a dampener to certain sounds or vibrations in this receptor organ.
IX. GLOSSOPHARYNGEAL N. (glossa = tongue + pharynx = throat)	Efferent fibers from medullary nuclei to stylopharyngeus muscles for swallowing and phonation reflexes, also functions, in part, in the gag reflex. Efferent (ANS) fibers from medullary nuclei to the parotid gland for secretions (salivation) necessary for normal sucking, chewing and digestive functions.
X. VAGUS N. (vago = to wander)	Efferent fibers from medullary nuclei to muscles of the palate, uvula and palatal arch (in part), pharynx, larynx (vocal cords) and esophagus, for swallowing, digestion, and vocalization. Efferent fibers from medullary nuclei (ANS) to glands of the digestive system. Efferent fibers from medullary nuclei (ANS) to smooth and cardiac musculature of internal organs of thoracic and abdomino-pelvic cavities.
XI. ACCESSORY N. (accessory to X and cervical cord levels C 1-6. Really not a cranial nerve)	1. Bulbar division: See under X Cranial N. 2. Spinal division: Efferent fibers from spinal cord levels C 1-5 or 6, ventral horn nuclei to sternomastoid and trapezius muscles.
XII. HYPOGLOSSAL N. (hypo = under + glossa = tongue)	Efferent fibers from medullary nuclei to the intrinsic musculature of the tongue and to genioglossus, hypoglossus and styloglossus (or extrinsic muscles of the tongue) for sucking, chewing, swallowing, and phonation.

Table 2
General Functions of the Diencephalon

Major Structure	Major Subdivisions	Functional Components
EPITHALAMUS	1. Habenular nucleus and associated components	Part of circuity of the olfactory system and limbic system whereby smell and basic emotional background tone (or affective behavior) can influence the brain stem reticular formation and nuclei of the ANS.
	2. Pineal body or gland	Hormonal secretions (endocrine gland) concerned with growth and development, especially as regards the gonads.
DORSAL THALAMUS	1. Reticular nuclei	A continuation at diencephalic levels of the brain stem reticular formation (especially the reticular activating system) which then relays impulses to the entire cerebral cortex.
	2. Association Reticular Nuclei (or intralaminer and midline nuclei)	An extension of the brain stem reticular formation into the diencephalon. These fibers do not project directly to higher telencephalic centers, rather they relay impulses to adjacent diencephalic nuclei.
	3. Specific (dorsal) thalamic nuclei (or Ventral Thalamic Nuclei)	Integration and relay nuclear centers for a) reception of general sensations (touch, pain, temp., vibrations, pressure, proprioception, etc); b) the special sensation of taste; and c) motor impulses from lower centers which are then relayed to the sensorimotor cortex of the cerebral hemispheres.
	4. Nonspecific (dorsal) Thalamic Nuclei (or the anterior medial, and laterial thalamic nuclei including the pulvinar)	Interneuronal or reciprocal fiber connections between these named diencephalic centers and the association cortex of the cerebral hemispheres.

Table 2 (cont.)
General Functions of the Diencephalon

METHATHALAMUS	1. Medial Geniculate Nucleus of the (Dorsal) Thalamus	A specific integration center for auditory sensations which are then relayed in part to the auditory cortex of the cerebral hemispheres.
	2. Laterial Geniculate Nucleus of the (Dorsal) Thalamus	A specific integration center for visual sensations which are then relayed, in part, to the visual cortex of the cerebral hemispheres.
SUBTHALAMUS (also known as the Ventral Thalamus.)	1. Specific sensory pathways	Rostral extension of the principal ascending sensory pathways (fasciculi) of the body and head through the brain stem on their way to the specific thalamic nuclear centers.
	2. Subcortical motor pathways	Rostral extension of fibers from the cerebellum red nucleus, substantia nigra and globus pallidus enroute to specific thalamic nuclei and to lower brain stem structures.
	3. Reticular fibers	Continuation of the midbrain ascending reticular system enroute to thalamic nuclei.
	4. Subthalamic nucleus	An "extrapyramidal" or interneuronal motoneuron center possibly for regulation of muscle tone and movement especially as regards the axial skeleton.
HYPOTHALAMUS	Many specific subdivisions or nuclear centers are recognized, all of which are too numerous and too complex to note here. Simply stated, the hypothalamus is principally concerned with:	1. Homeostatic mechanisms, ie, master controller of: a) hormonal regulation b) metabolism c) water balance d) temperature regulation e) osmotic pressure f) ANS (both sympathetic and parasympathetic systems) g) et al 2. Regulation, in part, of emotional tone along with the limbic system and cerebral cortex.

Table 3a
Basal Ganglia—Terminology (Correlate with Table 3b)

1a. BASAL GANGLIA: *Anatomically* this part of the telencephalon consists of four deep gray nuclear areas:
   1) Caudate nucleus (tail + cell bodies)
   2) Lenticular nucleus (lens shaped + cell bodies)
   3) Claustrum (gate + cell body area)
   4) Amygdala or Amygdaloid nucleus (almond shaped + cell bodies)

1b. BASAL GANGLIA: *Physiologically* this term can be used to indicate three subcortical motor centers principally concerned with the "extrapyramidal" system:
   1) Corpus striatum (a telencephalic structure of the basal ganglia)
   2) Subthalamus (a diencephalic structure)
   3) Substantia nigra (a mesencephalic or midbrain structure)

2. CORPUS STRIATUM: The caudate nucleus and the lenticular (or lentiform) nucleus considered as one structure.

3. LENTICULAR NUCLEUS: A synonym for LENTIFORM (lens + form or shape) nucleus.

4. LENTIFORM NUCLEUS: The putamen (lateral part) and the globus pallidus (medial part) considered as one structure. (See also LENTICULAR NUCLEUS).

5. NEOSTRIATUM: A phylogenetic term for the newer or lateral part of the lentiform nucleus, ie, the putamen, plus the caudate nucleus.

6. PALEOSTRIATUM: A phylogenetic term for the older or medial part of the lentiform nucleus, ie, the globus pallidus.

7. PALLIDUM: A synonym for the globus pallidus or paleostriatum.

8. STRIATUM: A synonym for neostriatum.

Table 3b
General Functions of the Basal Ganglia (See Table 3a for explanation of terms)

AMYGDALOID NUCLEUS:

A smaller and older part of this nucleus is concerned with olfaction (smell). The newer and larger part is concerned with the limbic system.

BASAL GANGLIA:

A phylogenetically older area of deep gray matter of the telencephalon primarily responsible for stereotyped (motor or "extrapyramidal") reflexes. In man this area is capable of being controlled or overridden at times by higher centers (COEPS), ie, the Cortically Originating ExtraPyramidal System. Lesions of the physiological parts of the basal ganglia (corpus striatum, subthalamus, and substantia nigra) cause dyskinesias, ie, uncontrollable movements which are purposeless and make voluntary movements difficult if not impossible. Degree of involvement depends upon the exact location and the extent or severity of the lesion.

BASAL GANGLIA and (Dorsal) THALAMUS:

Primarily responsible for subcortical sensorimotor integrative mechanisms and/or reflexes involved in human behavior.

NEOSTRIATUM:

The phylogenetically newer component of the basal ganglia which is more concerned with inhibitory functions in relation to stereotyped reflex behavior.

PALEOSTRIATUM:

The phylogenetically older component of the basal ganglia which is more concerned with excitatory functions in relation to stereotyped reflex behavior.

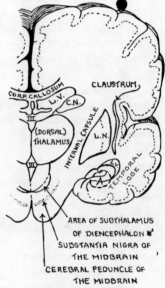

AREA OF SUBTHALAMUS OF DIENCEPHALON *'
SUBSTANTIA NIGRA OF THE MIDBRAIN
CEREBRAL PEDUNCLE OF THE MIDBRAIN

A = AMYGDALOID NUCLEUS *'
LN = LENTICULAR NUCLEUS
LV = LATERAL VENTRICLE
III = THIRD VENTRICLE
*' = STRUCTURE LIES SLIGHTLY ANTERIOR TO THIS FRONTAL VIEW OF THE BRAIN

Table 4

General Functions of the Six Lobes of the Cerebral Cortex of the Telencephalon

FRONTAL LOBES (correlate with Fig 2-8, 2-26, 2-27)

1. PREFRONTAL LOBES or the ASSOCIATION AREAS OF THE FRONTAL LOBES: More concerned with affective behavior, ie, the emotional background tone of all voluntary and involuntary functions which constitute an individuals' total personality. A phylogenetically newer area of the cerebral cortex.

2. POSTERIOR and POSTERIOINFERIOR AREAS of the FRONTAL LOBES or the 1° (primary) centers: More concerned with the reception and expression of semiautomatic or learned reflexes having to do with sensorimotor functions, languages (in the dominant hemisphere), and voluntary eye movements.

INSULAR LOBES or INSULA (Island of Reil):

More concerned with visceral functions, ie, gustatory and autonomic nervous system functions. Believed to be a very old phylogenetic structure.

LIMBIC LOBES:

In lower animals this is the Rhinencephalon or smell-brain. In primates (especially in man) only a small part is for olfaction. The majority of this area is concerned with basic drives, emotional tone including visceral reactions, and (in part) the ability to have both short term and long term memory.

OCCIPITAL LOBES:

Primarily responsible for the reception of visual input at the cortical level, and (in part) responsible for the ability to associate these kinds of stimuli with past memories.

PARIETAL LOBES:

1. 1° CENTERS or POST-CENTRAL GYRI of the parietal lobes: More concerned with the reception and expression of semiautomatic or learned reflexes having to do with sensorimotor functions and language.

2. ASSOCIATION CENTERS: More concerned in the dominant hemisphere with language functions, ie, association of all senses (vision, hearing, writing, speaking, feeling, etc) involved in verbal and nonverbal communication. In the nondominant hemisphere probably more concerned with spatial-temporal relationships and the emotional overtones of verbal and nonverbal communication.

TEMPORAL LOBES:

1. 1° CENTERS or TRANSVERSE TEMPORAL GYRUS (of Heschl): More concerned with cortical reception of sound

2. ASSOCIATION CENTERS: More concerned with language functions especially in regards to association of memory such as visual, auditory, tactile, smell, speech, etc, that is involved in verbal and nonverbal communication.

Chapter Three
The Spiraling Continuum of Spatiotemporal Adaptation

Introduction

Children adapt throughout their developmental life span. The adaptation process which results from transactions between the individual and his environment of space and time is termed spatiotemporal adaptation. The development of spatiotemporal adaptation is a spiraling process for the unfolding of complex performance skills from primitive patterns of posture and movement. During the spiraling process of development, primitive postures and movements of the newborn are modified and integrated into complex posture and movement strategies. Spontaneous actions and primitive posture and movement strategies are adapted to purposeful behaviors observed during early stages of development. Purposeful behaviors are the foundations for the development of complex strategies which are adapted to perform purposeful activities and develop skill.

Transactions between the child and his environment serve a dual purpose according to the adaptation concept of development. The environment provides a source of stimulation for functional change in bodily structures and processes which are the means to influence and be influenced by the environment. The adaptation process matures with alteration of functions and enhances growth, maturation, and development of the underlying systems. There are commonalities in the anatomical and biological structures and systems of man which account for similarities in development among individuals. However, each individual develops a unique system or his own self-system within the common structures. The self-system autonomously integrates experiences from the environment which in turn enhance the individual's unique development. The uniqueness of a person is the product of spatiotemporal adaptation.

Throughout the progressions of development, environmental interaction provides experiences necessary to develop strategies of posture and movement. Basic posture and movement strategies are adapted to purposeful behaviors which include rolling, sitting, creeping, standing/walking. Purposeful behaviors emerge as selected patterns of posture and movement linked together into specific developmental sequences reflecting higher level functioning. Attainment of purposeful behaviors are innate goals for the child during early stages of development. As purposeful behaviors are repeated, the newly developed complex sequences of posture and movement are differentiated from the original innate goal and directed toward events within the environment. For example, a child first walks for the joy of having attained the ability to walk. As he repeats the experience, his walking pattern becomes automatic and he directs it toward the purpose of walking to some specific place or activity. With repetition, automatic patterns develop and performance skills emerge. The automatic patterns of reciprocal sequences used for walking becomes available for differentiation and adaptation to such higher level skills as running and skipping. Throughout development, as purposeful behaviors are adapted to goal-directed events within the environment, purposeful activities evolve and a variety of complex performance skills emerge.

Spatiotemporal Adaptation

Transactions with the environment take place within the dimensions of space and time. Space, or spatial, refers to the area surrounding an individual, including the supporting surface for the body, the gravitational and three dimensional space surrounding the body, and the space occupied by the body or by other persons or objects within the area. Spatial dimensions encompass the environment in which a person exists and functions. Time, or temporal aspects of adaptation, are defined as the duration, regulation, memory, and sequence of a person's actions, body movements, or movements of other persons or objects within the area.[1] Temporal dimensions encompass the sequencing (planning) and timing (processing) of actions in relation to stationary or moving objects. Spatiotemporal adaptation is defined as the continuous, ongoing state or act of adjusting those bodily processes required to function within a given space and at a given time.

In order to utilize the theory of spatiotemporal adaptation and apply the concept to the spiraling process of development, the reader must have an understanding of the four components of the adaptation process. The components are termed *assimilation, accommodation, association,* and *differentiation.*[2]

Assimilation is the sensory process of receiving information external to and within the system. To illustrate, a ball is seen as coming toward one's self and the hands are felt as being inside one's pockets. The information is "taken-in" or assimilated into the system. As the information is received by the self-system, the individual will modify his posture and adjust the position of the hands in preparation for catching the ball. The response or the the motor process of adjusting the body to react to the incoming stimulation is termed *accommodation.* The third component, *association,* is the organized process of relating sensory information with the motor act being experienced as well as calling up previously acquired behavior for relating present and past experiences with each other. For example, the visual stimulation of the moving ball is related with the accommodation of the body, and the present act of catching the ball is related with past experiences of ball catching. *Differentiation* is the process of discriminating those essential elements of a specific behavior which are pertinent to a given situation, distinguishing those that are not thereby modifying or altering the behavior in some manner; for example, an individual discriminates the forearm pattern necessary to catch the ball by distinguishing the amount of elbow flexion and supination necessary and thus modifying the forearm position for more efficient ball catching.

Spiraling Continuum

The process of adapting lower level primitive patterns of posture and movement to higher level complex skills is the framework of the spatiotemporal adaptation theory. The framework

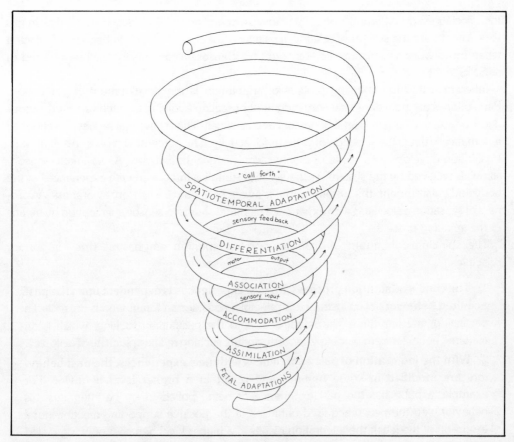

Fig 3-1 Spiraling Continuum of Spatiotemporal Adaptation.

is illustrated by the ever-widening and upward continuum of a spiral (Fig 3-1). The spiraling continuum illustrates the ongoing process of development while the spiral-effect emphasizes the integration of the old with the new. The spiraling process of spatiotemporal adaptation has a developmental sequence and matures as a result of environmental experiences and modification of the maturing nervous system to eventually encompass the highest levels of complex functioning.

The spiraling process includes the integration of sensory input, motor output, and sensory feedback. The assimilation component is the sensory input, accommodation is viewed as the motor output and the association-differentiation components are the vital part of sensory feedback which occurs as a person functions within the environment.

When the environment provides a new experience for a child, he adapts to the experience with an acquired behavior. The nervous system integrates the sensory feedback from the new experience with the actions of the acquired behavior. Through integration the self-system organizes the information from the experience. Integration of new with old is dependent upon and results in the modification of the nervous system. Association and differentiation of the information further facilitates higher level performance. Therefore, maturation results from the spiraling process of sensorimotor-sensory integration. The term sensorimotor-*sensory* emphasizes the relationship of sensory input, motor output, and the importance of feedback for association and differentiation. Thus movement and adaptation must be judged from this view as both are the system of relationships which is a single whole that becomes perfected when set to work as sensorimotor-sensory unit. Sensorimotor-sensory shall be referred to as SMS.

Inherent within the spiraling process of adaptation is the development of perception. Perception is an individual's sensory judgment or feeling evolving through repeated experiences adapted from purposeful behaviors and activities. The perceptual process functions to automatically direct the selection of patterns for activity. The perceptual process results in skill. Perception develops as a result of highly complex SMS integration. As an infant, sensory stimuli is received by the system; as the sensory stimuli is integrated with experiences of the body and environment, the system becomes aware or acquires a sensory awareness. Awareness of sensation associated with experience ultimately leads to sensory perception by means of the spiraling process.

The spiraling continuum of spatiotemporal adaptation emphasizes three important principles:

1. **The child's adaptation process with new experiences is dependent upon the past acquired behaviors.** To illustrate this principle, consider an infant who is presented a pacifier for the first time. The infant adapts to the pacifier by sucking, which is an acquired behavior from past experiences (rooting, sucking reflexes, sucking of a nipple).

2. **With the integration of past experiences with new experiences, the past behaviors are modified in some manner and result in a higher level behavior.** For example, a baby has the past experience of being pulled to sit; he integrates this behavior with the newly acquired behavior of the positive supporting reaction (total extension of the legs); the integration results in a higher level behavior of being pulled to stand.

3. **The integration of higher level behaviors influences and increases the maturity of the lower level behaviors.** To illustrate this principle, consider a child who integrates the higher level behavior of forearm supination with the earlier acquired pronated reaching and grasping patterns. The integration of these two behaviors increases the maturity of reaching and grasping; with integration the child can reach forward and supinate simultaneously to adapt the limb position to the object he is attempting to grasp.

Therefore, in the spiraling continuum of spatiotemporal adaptation, a child does not acquire totally new behaviors, rather new behaviors are higher level modifications of the older lower level reactions.[2] To further illustrate, consider the foot contact reflexes of the neonate that facilitate total flexion and extension movements of the lower extremities. With maturation and environmental experiences, lower level reactions are modified for higher level patterns of reciprocation. The lower level reactions are integrated into the ontogenic sequence to the extent that they may lose their original identity, but their trace effect contribute to higher level spatiotemporal adaptations. In the above example of foot contact reflexes, the original total flexion and extension movements are not present in higher level patterns of reciprocation; however, the trace effects of total flexion and extension are differentiated to form reciprocal patterns for creeping and walking.

In summary, a child's ability to function within his environment is dependent upon his adaptation to and with that environment. The process of spatiotemporal adaptation consists of assimilation, accommodation, association, and differentiation. The adaptation process is illustrated by a spiral and is termed the spiraling continuum of spatiotemporal adaptation. The spiraling framework emphasizes that adaptation of new environmental experiences is dependent upon past behaviors and that with integration of new experiences, higher level adaptations of past behaviors result. The development of spatiotemporal adaptation is dependent upon and results in the maturational changes within the nervous system.

Spatiotemporal Stress

As the child is adapting basic posture and movement strategies to purposeful behaviors and purposeful activities, the challenge of the process and the demands of the environment may exceed his functional capacities. The child may experience spatiotemporal stress. In a stress situation, aspects of lower level posture and movement strategies may influence the adaptation process. The use of lower level strategies is often apparent during the course of normal development when a child meets a new experience. For example, influences of the lower level prone extension posture (pivot prone), can be observed in early sitting and walking postures (Fig 3-2, 3-3, 3-4). The scapular adduction, shoulder retraction, and elbow flexion pattern of the lower level prone extension posture facilitates the necessary trunk extension for early sitting and standing. When the child first assumes sitting and standing, he will utilize a pattern similar to a prone extension posture to facilitate trunk extension necessary for maintaining the vertical postures of sitting and standing. As vertical postures are repeated, lower level reactions are differentiated so that the essential elements are integrated to form higher level adaptations. With the above example, the essential elements of postural extensor tone are differentiated from the prone extension pattern and integrated into the higher level adaptation of trunk stability in vertical postures (Fig 3-5).

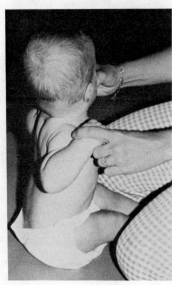

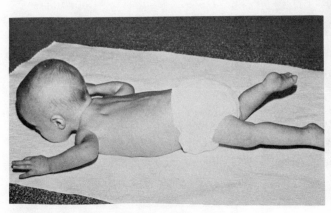

Fig 3-2 Prone Extension Posture.

Fig 3-3 Early Sitting.

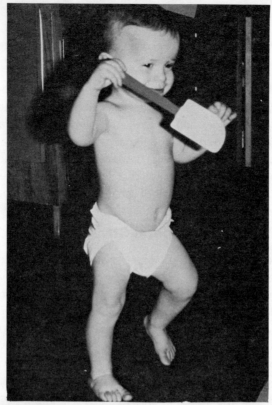

Fig 3-4 Early Standing.

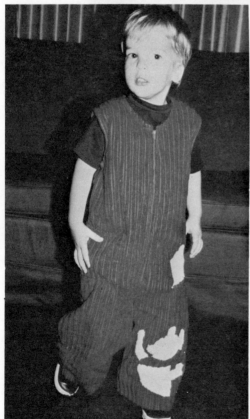

Fig 3-5 Standing/Walking.

Fig 3-6 Vertical Righting.

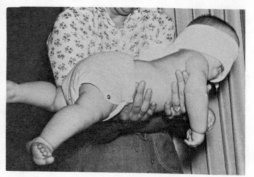

Fig 3-7 Asymmetrical Posture.

Fig 3-8 Walking on Balance Beam — eyes open.

Fig 3-9 Walking on Balance Beam — eyes closed.

The effects of stress upon a child's spatiotemporal adaptation is further illustrated in Figures 3-6 and 3-7. Figure 3-6 illustrates a child adapting with a beginning form of the Landau reaction (note the extension patterns of the body). The boy in Figure 3-7 is blindfolded, which temporarily changes one parameter of his sensory integrative patterns. The temporary alteration of sensory integration interrupts the midline stability of the Laundau reaction. The child adapts to this stress situation with a lower level pattern of asymmetrical stability.

The boy in Figure 3-8 demonstrates the stress phenomenon on a higher level of performance behaviors. While walking on a balance beam with his eyes open, the boy is able to adapt with a mature equilibrium reaction with his upper extremities. Compare the equilibrium reaction illustrated in Figure 3-8 with the reaction in Figure 3-9. The child in Figure 3-9 is walking the balance beam with his eyes closed, which alters his sensory integration. He adapts with a lower level immature equilibrium reaction (note the asymmetrical upper extremity pattern). In both sets of figures (3-8 and 3-9) the changing integration that occurs with vision occluded results in spatiotemporal stress, and the child adapts with a more primitive pattern of posture and movement.

The normal child will frequently utilize lower level responses to adapt to the environmental demands during the transitional phases of developmental progressions. For example, a child may be able to assume and maintain the all-fours creeping position, but will revert to a prone crawling posture to move his body forward. As the child repeats this sequence, he associates the reciprocal movement pattern of prone crawling with the stability and equilibrium reactions utilized to maintain a creeping position. In the normal developmental progression, the child associates, differentiates, and integrates the reciprocal elements of the old prone progression with his new ability to attain the all-fours position. Integration of new with old promotes a higher level reciprocal creeping behavior. Stability and equilibrium in the all-fours position are further developed by moving in that position. The child has successfully adapted mature posture and movement reactions to meet the challenge of the process and the demands of the environment.

Milani-Comparetti and Gidoni state:

> The mature individual makes use of equilibrium reactions and the more primitive mechanisms take over when the challenge exceeds the functional capacities of the more refined response.[3]

During normal developmental progressions a child will adapt with more primitive behaviors in three situations:

1. when adapting to new experiences,
2. when the SMS integrative process is temporarily altered, and
3. during the transitional phases of the developmental progressions.

During normal development the nervous system will associate and differentiate certain elements of lower level reactions, and the child will integrate these aspects of the behavior into higher levels reactions. Association and differentiation occur with repeated environmental experiences and the maturation of the nervous system.

When the nervous system cannot differentiate the essential elements from lower level behaviors and integrate these elements into higher level reactions, a child will repeatedly adapt with more primitive posture and movement strategies. When primitive reactions or lower level behaviors persist and are repeatedly elicited, the persistent primitive behaviors will interfere with normal developmental progressions. As a result a developmental deviation may occur, and the child experiences spatiotemporal distress.

Summary

The theoretical framework of the spatiotemporal adaptation process is the spiraling continuum of development. Spiraling emphasizes that the adaptation of new environmental experiences is dependent upon past behaviors and that with the introduction of new experiences, higher level adaptations of the past behaviors result. The spiraling continuum of adaptation occurs through the process of SMS integration which has four components: assimilation, accommodation, association, and differentiation. The development of spatiotemporal adaptation is dependent upon and results in the maturation of the nervous system. The spiraling of spatiotemporal adaptations is based on the following:

1. The adaptation process of SMS integration is dependent upon the interaction between nervous system maturation and environmental experiences.

2. The adaptation process is hierarchical with increasingly higher level behaviors gradually emerging from the lower level behaviors as a result of continual environmental interaction.

3. Lower level SMS behaviors will emerge during the adaptation process when the

environmental demands exceed the functional capacities of a child.

4. A developmental deviation occurs if lower level behaviors persist and are not modified by the adaptation process.

References

1. Jones B: The importance of memory traces of motor efferent discharges for learning skilled movements. Dev Med Child Neurol 16:620, 1974.
2. Flavell J: The Developmental Psychology of Jean Piaget. Princeton, Van Nostrand Co, 1963.
3. Milani-Comparetti A, Gidoni E: Routine developmental examination in normal and retarded children. Dev Med Child Neurol 9:631-638, 1967.

Chapter Four

The Development of Posture and Movement Strategies

Posture and movement strategies are patterns of movement and control which are adapted to perform purposeful behaviors, activities, and skills. Strategies are responsible for moving or maintaining body segments in coordination with each other and in relation to the spatiotemporal environment. Posture and movement strategies combine functions of nervous, muscular, and skeletal systems (neuromusculo-skeletal functions), thus forming the basic foundation of the adaptation process. Neuromusculo-skeletal functions are the bodily processes used to interact with and adapt to the environment. Sensory assimilations are received by neuromusculo-skeletal receptors, motor accommodations are carried out by neuromusculo-skeletal structures and mechanisms, and sensory feedback is transmitted from and by neuromusculo-skeletal systems. Neuromusculo-skeletal systems transmit tactile (including pressure) and proprioceptive (including vestibular) information from within the body and from the area immediately surrounding the body. Tactile and proprioceptive, or somatosensory perception, plays a significant role in linking neuromusculo-skeletal functions together to form posture and movement strategies. Therefore, somatosensory perception will be emphasized in this chapter.

Visual and auditory systems also play an important role in spatiotemporal adaptation by providing information about the more distant environment. Visual and auditory information facilitates strategies in a variety of ways: initiation or cessation of movement in relation to sight or sound, guidance and knowledge of results of movement by means of vision or audition, and learning through imitation or verbal direction. Adaptation of strategies to interact with more distance environment is accomplished by associating somatosensory, visual, and auditory information and responses. Vision and audition are involved in the development of posture and movement strategies; however, vision and audition are more significant in adaptation of posture and movement strategies to purposeful behaviors, activities and skills, and will be briefly discussed in subsequent chapters.

Posture and Movement Strategies

Posture and movement strategies supply ability to "move" or "not move" in certain predictable patterns determined by the purpose of moving or ceasing movement. Postural strategies control movement and movement strategies give rise to purposeful action.[1] Movement strategies promote and sequence changes in position of body or body parts. Movement strategies combine muscle actions so that one movement flows into another. Action by one group of muscles sequentially enhances or dampens actions by other groups of muscles. Sequence of flow develops from repetition of selected movement strategies adapted to specific purposes. With repetition, neural pathways are established so that a particular sequence of movement is associated with outcomes of performance. Once selected, movement strategies are associated with specific outcomes; a strategy can be automatically elicited as soon as the individual anticipates a desired outcome.

Perceptual sets develop when certain movement strategies are consistantly selected to achieve specific outcomes. Perceptual sets are set into motion and monitored by sensory perceptions of the immediate and distance environment integrated with actions from the strategy. The concept of perceptual sets will be further explored in Chapter Seven.

Movement strategies require control of timing, direction, and strength as well as simultaneous control of body position in space during movement. Postural strategies control both movement and body position during movement by distributing normal postural tone in specific patterns. Normal postural tone is defined as muscle tone sufficient to support posture while simultaneously allowing movement within and from the posture.[2] For example, sitting and rotating to reach for an object, or holding a pencil and writing, or rising from sitting to standing are accomplished by using normal postural tone as background from which movement emanates and ends.

Postural strategies are organized into dynamic postural sets. Postural sets are bodily adjustments made by the individual in preparation for a specific activity. The appropriate postural set for an activity is determined from information about the state of the body, surrounding environment, and specific nature of activity to be performed. When postural tone is automatically distributed in sets, muscle groups around certain body segments are activated to maintain position while other segments move.[3] Or, muscle groups may be activated counter to a movement strategy in order to dampen speed and range of movement. Postural sets will be identified in this chapter and in Chapter 5.

The neuromusculo-skeletal components of posture and movement strategies include reflexes and reactions which mature according to specific functions (Fig 4-1), muscles and muscle groups which develop specific patterns of mobility and stability (Fig 4-2), and bone and joint structures which grow to support neuromuscular actions. Posture and movement strategies are activated by means of automatic reflexes and reactions which facilitate or dampen appropriate muscle actions, promote skeletal alignment and re-alignment, and transmit feedback from the body and the environment.[3,4]

Reflexes and Reactions

Automatic reflexes and reactions are functions of the central nervous system.[4] They are neurological mechanisms which affect predictable patterns of posture and/or movements. Reflexes and reactions distribute muscle tone in specific posture and movement strategies according to whether the strategies are adapted to purposeful behaviors (rolling, creeping, walking, reaching, etc) or adapted to purposeful activities (feeding oneself, cutting a circle from the paper, walking to the store, etc). The terms ''reflex'' and ''reaction'' are used to describe specific responses or series of responses to particular sensory input or combination of sensory stimuli. ''Reactions are distinguished from reflexes by their greater complexity and inconstancy of the response.''[5] According to this distinction, the term *reflex* is preferred to

REFLEXES AND REACTIONS

Reflex/Reaction	Description	Phase	Related Muscle Functions
1. Phasic Reflexes			
Rooting	Touch to corner of mouth elicits head turning towards stimulated side	Primitive	Activation
Moro	Gentle head drop in supported supine posture elicits abduction-extension of arms, followed by arms coming together in arc over body	Primitive	Activation
Flexor Withdrawal	Touch-pressure to sole of foot of extended leg elicits flexion and withdrawal of stimulated leg	Primitive	Activation
Crossed Extension	Touch-pressure to sole of foot of leg held in extension elicits flexion, followed by extension, of opposite leg	Primitive	Activation
Crawling	Sufficient leg flexion-foot dorsiflexion in prone for sole to touch surface elicits extension of leg and flexion of opposite, or crawling movements	Primitive	Activation
Stepping	Held in upright position so feet touch surface elicits alternating flexion-extension stepping movements, especially if trunk is bent forward	Primitive	Activation
Placing-Legs	Held in upright position and dorsum of foot touched by table edge elicits flexion followed by extension of leg so foot is placed on table.	Primitive	Activation, Co-activation
Placing-Arms	Touch to dorsum of hand from table elicits arm flexion followed by placing hand on table	Primitive	Activation
Avoiding	Light touch on the palm or dorsum of the flexed hand elicits finger extension	Primitive	Activation
2. Tonic Reflexes			
Tonic Labyrinthine	Positioning in supine elicits general extension pattern throughout body; positioning in prone elicits general flexion pattern	Primitive	Activation, Co-activation
Asymmetrical Tonic Neck	Head turning elicits extension of face-side arm and leg and flexion of skull-side arm and leg	Primitive	Activation, Co-activation
Symmetrical Tonic Neck	Head dorsiflexion elicits arm extension and leg flexion; head ventroflexion elicits arm flexion and leg extension	Primitive	Activation, Co-activation
Magnet	Touch-pressure to sole of foot with leg flexed elicits extension of leg touched	Primitive	Co-activation

Reflex/Reaction	Description	Phase	Related Muscle Functions
Primary Standing	Held in upright position so feet touch surface elicits extension of legs to "stand"	Primitive	Co-activation
Plantar Grasp	Touch-pressure to ball of foot elicits flexion of toes	Primitive	Activation Co-activation
Traction	Pressure on the palm of hand elicits finger flexion followed flexion of arm	Primitive	Activation Co-activation
Grasp Reflex	Pressure on the palm of hand and stretch to finger flexors elicits finger flexion	Primitive	Activation Co-activation
3. *Vertical Righting Reactions*			
Labyrinthine Acting on Head	Movement in space causes head and trunk to align in or toward vertical orientation in space	Transitional	Activation
Body Righting Acting on Head	Asymmetrical touch-pressure from supporting surface causes head and trunk to align in or toward vertical orientation in space	Transitional	Activation
Optical Righting	Visual awareness causes head and trunk to align in or toward vertical orientation in space	Transitional	Activation
4. *Rotational Righting Reactions*			
Neck Righting	Neck rotation causes the rest of the body to turn in same direction to align head and trunk with each other	Transitional	Activation
Body Righting Acting on Body	Rotation of one body segment causes adjacent body segments to rotate in sequence in the same direction to align head and trunk with each other	Transitional	Activation
5. *Supporting Reactions*	Touch-pressure from supporting surface to body support receptors causes maintained extension of trunk, arms, or legs to hold position	Transitional Mature	Co-activation Combined Mobility and Stability actions
6. *Protective Reactions*	Moving in space and changing touch-pressure from supporting surface causes arms or legs to extend and protect the body as needed	Transitional Mature	Activation

60

		Predominate Phases	Related Postural Sets
7. *Midline Stability Reactions* (All Positions)	Vertical alignment with gravity is maintained by constant adjustment in response to gravity	Transitional Mature	Blended Mobility and Stability Functions
8. *Equilibrium Reactions* (All Positions)	Compensatory movements used to regain midline stability if alignment with gravity is significantly disturbed	Mature	Blended Mobility and Stability Functions

Figure 4-2
MUSCLE FUNCTIONS[8]

Muscle Function	Description	Predominate Phases	Related Postural Sets
1. Activation (mobility)	Complete shortening of agonist and lengthening of antagonist to develop muscles	*Primitive Transitional	Dependent upon external sources of postural control
2. Co-activation (stability)	Simultaneous contraction of agonist and antagonist around joints to hold position	Primitive *Transitional	Fixation-Support Set
3. Combined Mobility (activation) and Stability (co-activation) actions	Movement around midline and proximal joints with extremities fixed distally to support movement	Transitional	Bilateral-Linear Set
4. Blended Mobility and Stability Functions	Free movement in space with control from midline and proximal joints; or controlled movement of objects in space	Transitional *Mature	Weight-Shift Set Movement-Counter-Movement Set

*Indicates most predominate phase

describe some of the fetal and neonatal responses which are simple, more predictable, and probably result from one or two sources of sensory stimulation, such as tactile and vestibular. The term *reaction* applies to more complex responses which result from integration of simultaneous sensory input, such as tactile, proprioceptive, visual, and auditory. Reactions usually develop from infancy and may be retained with maturity, eg, the parachute (protective extension) reaction. This text will generally follow the above distinction in terminology.

Much of the terminology used to describe human reflexes and reactions originated with experiments performed on lower animals. Experimentation on lower animals allowed interruption of selected areas of central nervous system control. As a result, more isolated reactions were observed and attributed to specific sensory systems. Some reflexes and reactions identified by animal experimentation were termed according to specific sensory input which appeared to be responsible for the response, for example, labyrinthine righting acting on the head. Terminology describing experimental animal reflexes and reactions has frequently been applied to human responses in behavioral observations of the developing child.[6]

There are some similarities between the experimental animal and the developing human infant, eg, both are functioning without their highest levels of central nervous system control.[6] There are also differences. The most important difference is that the experimental animal demonstrates function which is controlled by a more specific area in the nervous system within the confines of the experiment. In normal human development, it is not possible to observe isolated areas of central nervous system control, even at the subcortical level. Human reflexes and reactions develop in sequence and interact with each other. Therefore, it is dififcult to attribute any behavior to only one source of sensory input, although one may predominate depending upon various stimuli from the environment. Human reflexes and reactions are being integrated and adapted as they develop.

Muscle Functions

Stability and mobility muscle function is dependent upon maturation of CNS reflexes and reactions and upon physiological development of specific muscles and muscle groups according to their primary function, ie, stability or mobility.[3,7] Mobility actions produce "moveability" or change. Mobility actions function as part of movement strategies to carry out a desired sequence of changes in position of the body and/or body segments. Some muscle groups, especially muscles used for skill activity, function primarily as mobilizers. Mobilizers are characterized by their ability to act with range, speed, and accuracy.[3,7] Mobilizers are usually activated in reciprocal patterns and make use of a wide range of motion.

Stability actions produce "stay-ability," or regulation of change. Stability actions dampen mobility to control movement of the body and/or body segments during changes in position. Some groups, especially more proximal muscles, function more as stabilizers. Stabilizers readily respond to constant stimuli from gravity and from the supporting surface.[3,7] Stabilizers maintain contraction in shortened ranges at the midline and around proximal joints for postural stability and control of movement. Stability actions are blended with mobility actions to control posture and movement. Most of the information in this text concerning muscle development has been synthesized from the literature. In addition, clinical observations of children have provided input for analyzing normal and abnormal development of muscle functions.

Posture and movement strategies do not exist in isolation or account fully for function but provide underlying mechanisms and support for function. Posture and movement strategies are continually being adapted to purposeful behaviors and activities or skills, even as the neuromusculo-skeletal functions comprising strategies are maturing. Adaptation of strategies to behaviors and activities during development modifies the strategies and provides linkages necessary to develop certain predictable, consistantly available patterns of posture and movement beyond the simple reflex level.[8] In addition, maturing posture and movement strategies support development of progressively higher levels of behavior and activity through the adaptation process.

There are occasions when posture and movement strategies may be consciously isolated. In exercise situations, increased range of motion or increased strength is usually the immediate goal. However, even in an exercise situation, the long-range goal is often enhancement or restoration for performance of behaviors, activities, or skill. Preparation for performance through exercise temporarily isolates and directs the patterns of movement and control.

Posture and movement strategies are being extracted from behaviors and activities in this chapter so that the reader can examine the components and development of strategies in preparation for subsequent discussion regarding adaptation of strategies to behaviors and activities.

Development of Strategies

Movement begins in utero.[1] Underlying neurological mechanisms for movement are sufficiently established before birth to transmit stimuli for essentially reflexive movements. Specific movements of the body and body segments are present and some bodily functions which reflect movement, such as swallowing, have been noted.[1] Reflexive fetal movements include flexion or extension of an extremity, moving the body as a whole, and even coordinating movements in patterns required for sucking or swallowing. When the baby is born, fetal reflexes and movement patterns are adapted to extrauterine life. The neonate's movements often appear to serve no particular purpose because early movements do not seem to culminate in a specific purpose or goal, except for survival movements related to feeding, breathing, etc.[9] However, neonatal movements provide the means by which transactions with the environment are enacted and complex purposeful movements develop. A neonate's behavioral repertoire, expanded by stimulation from his new environment, initiates the spiraling continuum of spatiotemporal adaptation.

The baby's extrauterine world adds new dimensions to his fetal experiences. Gravity is a significant force to move against. Gravity adds impetus to strengthen early movements and build muscle function into patterns for stability underlying postural control against gravity.[1] The postnatal spatiotemporal environment adds new somatosensory input and considerable visual and auditory input. Although the neonate cannot act upon all the new stimuli, he begins to organize his primitive movements into sequences to orient to new sources of input. The neonate moves to look at an object or stops moving to listen or pulls away or cuddles to a touch. The infant begins to associate movement with different sensory experiences and modify movement for the most effective ways of interacting with his new environment.[1]

Primitive patterns of the fetus and neonate possess the essential elements for higher level functioning.[8] Rather than developing wholly new patterns of behavior, primitive behaviors are modified and adapted for more complex functioning. There are three general phases of development: *primitive* phase, *transitional* phase, and *mature* phase. The phases characterize development of strategies (Fig 4-3), as well as behaviors and activities controlled by strategies.

During the primitive phase, the infant adapts fetal movement to develop undifferientiated (ie, full range of motion) movement strategies, facilitating mobility by means of primitive reflexes. As the baby moves against gravity, he acquires holding or fixation strategies and prepares for stability functions. Primitive movement and holding strategies are adapted to early functions, such as feeding, protection, spontaneous behaviors, and orientation to the environment. Adaptation of fetal patterns to postnatal functions modifies and expands fetal responses to primitive posture and movement strategies underlying primitive behaviors. By means of the spiraling continuum, primitive strategies are further modified and expanded by transitional strategies.

Undifferentiated movement and holding strategies are adapted to movement synergies and weight-bearing patterns by means of chain reactions.[6] Activation and co-activation of muscle groups is completed as the baby assumes and maintains new postures in space. Fixation-support postural sets develop during primitive and expand into the transitional phase. Coactivation of proximal muscle groups allows the baby to support on extremities before he is able to move from support (Fig 4-4). Once mobility and stability functions are developed, they can be combined as the baby maintains and moves in supported posture. Weight-bearing functions are adapted to provide distal fixation to control movement while movement is superimposed more proximally. A bilateral-linear postural set develops as the baby pushes and pulls in prone, occasionally moves symmetrically in creeping position, and pulls bilaterally to stand (Fig 4-5). The baby is using support reactions to obtain external control from the environment while he develops internal control about the midline and proximal joints.

As the baby adapts transitional strategies to mature strategies, he does so by differentiating mobility and stability functions and by developing automatic balance reactions to distribute mobility and stability muscle tone appropriately. Combined strategies are differentiated by shifting stability functions to one part of the body and freeing other parts for mobility. Weight-shift postural sets (Fig 4-6) develop so that movement in a position or into new positions is characterized by first shifting weight to stabilize a part of the body followed by movement of nonweight portions. Control of movement is preceded by lateral movement to shift weight. Differentiated strategies are adapted to blend mobility and stability under the control of automatic balance reactions.

In the mature phase, internal postural control is available as background for movement. Automatic sequencing of mobility and stability is available for adaptation to any function. Blended strategies form the basis of movement-countermovement postural sets (Fig 4-7). As a result, movement is smoothly executed under the control of appropriate antagonistic movements. With postural sets fully developed, controlled movement strategies continue to be adapted to perceptual sets demanded by higher level functioning.

Primitive Strategies

The primitive phase of development extends from the time of conception until several months after birth. During this time, the baby is supported by and confined within the

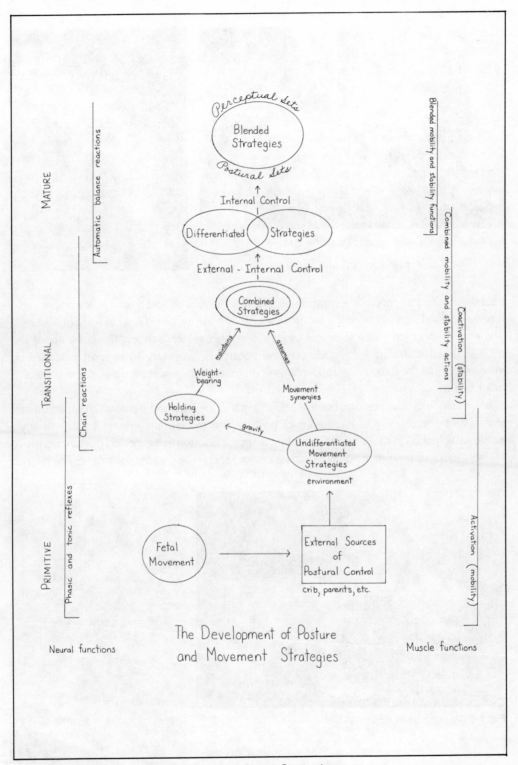

Fig 4-3 Development of Posture and Movement Strategies.

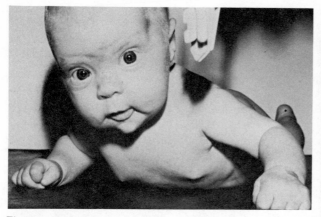

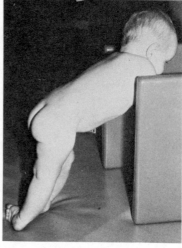

Fig 4-4 Fixation — Support Postural Set.

Fig 4-5 Bilateral-Linear Postural Set.

boundaries of the immediate environment. The fetus, neonate, and young infant respectively receive postural support from the womb, the crib or floor, or being held in someone's arms. The environment provides sources of external control which support the baby about the midline (head and trunk). External postural control is necessary to support posture and movement until the baby can support himself on extremities with internal postural control of head and trunk position.

Sources of external postural control also provide a background from which an infant can move, thus contributing to expansion of posture and movement strategies by the baby's active participation in movement. The infant is secure enough in supported postures to move by using external reference points to initiate (move) and cease (hold) movement. The infant's

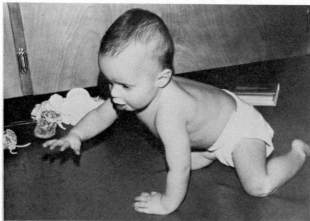

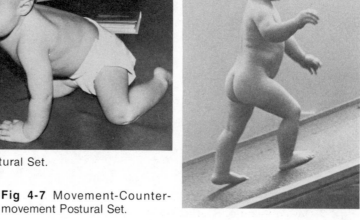

Fig 4-6 Weight Shift Postural Set.

Fig 4-7 Movement-Countermovement Postural Set.

moving and holding patterns are carried out in relation to gravity in the extrauterine environment. Gravity provides a significant force to both stimulate and strengthen movement, ultimately leading to development of strategies supporting internal control of behavior.[1]

The posture and movement strategies active during primitive development tend to cause undifferentiated patterns of movement or holding postures of rest. Primitive strategies generally cause movement or positioning of the neck or limbs rather than affecting the body as a whole. The strategies affect changes in position of body segments in relation to each other, but not significant changes in position of the body in space. The neonate and young infant engage primarily in bilateral or reciprocal flexion and extension movements of the limbs with some rotary movement beginning to develop about the neck region as well. The infant moves from semiflexed to fully extended postures, a prerequisite to develop antigravity postural control. He uses a full range of flexion against gravity, a prerequisite for useful flexion for activity, and begins to develop rotation around the body axis, a prerequisite for combining flexion and extension into coordinated rotation patterns at higher levels of development.[10] Primitive posture and movement strategies are utilized as they develop for such primitive behaviors as head lift, primitive support on arms, and first attempts to roll. Primitive strategies also underlie baby's first activities, for example, feeding and swiping at a toy.[8]

Primitive strategies are developed by means of subcortical neural mechanisms which activate muscles and muscle groups in undifferentiated movement patterns and initiate co-activation of muscle groups in primitive holding patterns.[3]. Subcortical neural mechanisms can be classified as phasic and tonic reflexes.[4] The two classifications may not be mutually exclusive, but the classifications reflect the apparent purposes of each.

Phasic reflexes (Fig 4-8) originate from a variety of exteroceptive, interoceptive, and proprioceptive assimilations. Phasic reflexes usually produce observable movement in response to touch, pressure, movement of the body, or sight or sound received.[8] Some phasic reflexes are part of movement strategies which serve survival functions, such as taking nourishment into the body, for example, rooting, sucking, etc. Others serve protective purposes, causing withdrawal from unknown sources of stimulation, for example, avoiding responses, while some relate to strategies which are forerunners of more complex behaviors. For example, reflexes like crossed-extension[6] cause reciprocal limb activity which prepares for development of higher level reciprocal patterns of movement after postural control has been established.

Phasic reflexes activate muscles and muscle groups through a complete range of motion.[8] Agonist muscles are activated in shortening contractions. Antagonist muscles are dampened and lengthened by reciprocal innervation. Movement through a complete range of motion both by shortening and lengthening is necessary for muscles to develop physiologically through a complete range of motion.[3] Muscle groups with similar function are also aided in developing synergistic action by being activated through complete ranges of motion simultaneously. The outcome of phasic reflexes activating muscle and muscle groups through complete ranges of motion is the development of mobility and strategies reflecting undifferentiated patterns of movement.

Sensory assimilations which initiate primitive mobility also provide feedback from the peripheral to the central nervous system, increasing the baby's awareness of self and envi-

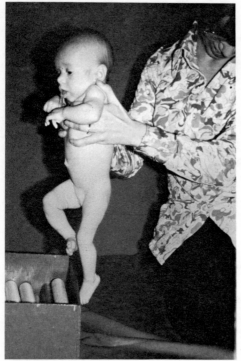

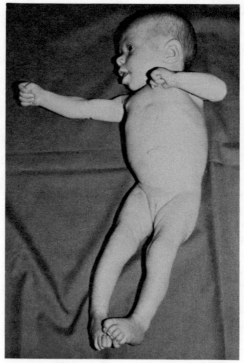

Fig 4-8 Phasic Reflex.   **Fig 4-9** Tonic Reflex.

ronment. Reflexive motor accommodations provide additional exteroceptive, interoceptive, and proprioceptive information about changing positions and motions of body segments. The baby begins to associate certain sensory input with certain predictable responses, such as moving to a touch to obtain the nipple.[9] The baby can repeat familiar movement patterns to obtain desired results. Spontaneous head turning may indicate hunger as the infant associates head turning from the rooting reflex with search for the nipple to satisfy hunger. The infant begins to link together a specific outcome or to adapt primitive movement strategies to primitive behaviors and activities.

Tonic reflexes (Fig 4-9) also originate from a variety of exteroceptive, interoceptive, and proprioceptive assimilations. Tonic reflexes are usually seen as postures assumed in response to the position of head and trunk in space or in relation to each other; for example, the tonic labyrinthine reflex or asymmetrical tonic neck reflex.[4] Muscle tone is distributed in specific postural patterns causing cessation of movement or fixation. Most frequently, the midline of the body and proximal joints are affected by tonic reflexes. These are the segments of the body which will eventually provide stabilization to support posture and control movement. Some tonic reflexes distribute tone in opposite patterns on either side of the midline (asymmetrical tonic neck reflex), or above and below the waistline (symmetrical tonic neck reflex). Such differences in distribution may predict types of stabilization patterns which will develop for postural control at higher levels.

Distribution of muscle tone in primitive postural patterns activates muscles and muscle groups in holding contractions at a particular point within the range of motion, frequently at the end of the range of either flexion or extension. Agonist and antagonists muscle groups are prepared for simultaneous partial activation, or co-activation within the range to provide stability.[1,3] Holding strategies produced by tonic reflexes initiate development of stability muscle functions. Stability development is expanded by holding strategies adapted to behaviors requiring action against gravity, eg, head lift in prone.

As the baby assumes and maintains primitive postures, he receives feedback from muscle tone distributed in specific holding strategies. As the baby moves from one primitive holding pattern to another, he receives additional feedback about changes in distribution of tone. Distribution of tone and the baby's awareness of changes in distribution prepares for primitive postural strategies to be adapted to higher levels of internal postural control.

Transitional Strategies

Primitive behaviors are modified for mature function by means of transitional strategies. The transitional phase of development begins a few months after birth and culminates when the child achieves the internal posture and movement control characteristic of mature performance for each behavior. During the transitional phase, the baby develops and utilizes strategies which allow him to move his body in and around in space. Movement of the body as a unit assists the baby to further activate muscle groups and develop synergies of movement needed to assume new positions in space. In addition to expanded activation of muscle groups into synergies, muscle functions for co-activation develop to support weight-bearing on extremities in new positions. As transition proceeds, the baby combines mobility and stability functions from synergies and weight-bearing into combined strategies in order to gain postural control over movement and to prepare to move from weight-bearing postures.[1] Toward the end of the transitional phase, combined strategies are differentiated according to posture or movement functions in preparation for blending strategies for mature performance.

During transition, the baby moves about in the environment. He rises to and maintains new positions in space by using chain reactions.[6] He progresses from primitive dependence on the environment for total support to supporting himself and moving by means of his own extremities. The infant gains more independence in his spatial environment by adapting primitive reflexes to transitional reactions, hence facilitating higher level strategies and behaviors.

Transitional strategies develop by means of chain reactions, including vertical righting reactions,[8] rotational righting reactions,[8] support reactions,[2] and protective reactions.[4] Chain reactions are neurological mechanisms which occur when an initial movement is followed by certain other predictable movements. The chain reaction mechanism makes it easier for certain other movements to follow an initial movement.[6] As reported by Holt,[1] Peiper described chain reactions as follows:

> The initial chain reflexes . . . and . . . all the ensuing reflexes and the postures dependent upon them follow strict laws; these bring the child through reflexes of which he is not conscious, into the exact position under the given conditions to maintain the equilibrium which would otherwise be lost.[1]

Chain reactions help establish links between movements so that one movement automatically flows or is followed by the next appropriate movement. As a result, movement sequences are activated, developed, and available as underlying patterns for transitional behaviors. The baby uses chain reactions to insure postural integrity during transition. Since he is moving in space before internal postural control is fully established, he must be certain that body segments move in sequence and new postures are maintained.

Chain reactions include righting reactions designed to control the position of head and trunk in space and to facilitate movement from one position to another. Righting reactions cause the head and trunk to align in space and with each other.[2,4] Righting reactions can be grouped according to the type of body alignment and direction of movement most characteristic of the reaction. The groups are termed vertical righting reactions and rotational righting reactions. The two groups of reactions develop parallel with one another, ie, the infant moves his head and trunk in either a vertical or rotational direction, for example, vertical prone head raising or rotational rolling. The essential difference between the two groups of reactions during their parallel development is the direction of movement and the groups of muscles activated. Vertical righting reactions activate muscles to move the midline of the body into alignment with the center of gravity, ie, move toward vertical. Muscle groups activated will be adapted to stability about the midline to maintain a vertical posture. Rotational righting reactions activate muscles to move body segments around the central axis of the body so that segments maintain alignment with each other. Muscle groups activated will be adapted to mobility about the midline for rotating away from and back toward the center of gravity.

Vertical righting reactions (Fig 4-10) include labyrinthine righting acting on the head, body righting acting on the head, and optical righting.[2,4] The reactions are termed according to sensory receptors assumed to be primarily responsible for the reaction. Labyrinthine righting is most likely initiated when the infant moves or is moved in space; the labyrinths are stimulated and the infant rights his head. Body righting on head begins when the infant receives asymmetrical or localized pressure to the body from the supporting surface and rights his head toward vertical. Later development of optical righting comes from visual reception. The baby rights his head in order to orient visually to the world. The different sensory assimilations result in the same accommodation of vertical righting. When the assimilations are received simultaneously, they are integrated so that a single source of input as a stimulus for vertical righting is no longer identifiable.

Vertical righting reactions are not present at birth but develop with central nervous system maturation and environmental contact. The reactions are adapted from primitive behaviors of head lift and head align. Vertical righting begins with the head moving against gravity to right itself vertically in prone, supine, and lateral positions. Neck muscles are activated and develop extension, flexion, and lateral flexion. With further maturation, movement of the head elicits a vertical chain reaction. The stimulus for righting is transferred from neck to trunk muscle groups, and trunk muscles are activated in synergy with neck muscles through a complete range of motion. As the trunk follows the head, the baby assumes a prone extension posture, participates in pull to sit, or raises head and trunk in sidelying. Vertical righting reactions are used during transition to maintain head and trunk alignment as well as to develop higher level stability reactions. Neck and trunk muscle groups develop toward midline, preparing for co-activation around the midline in order to maintain vertical alignment with the center of gravity.

70

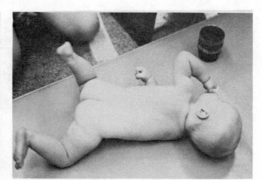

Fig 4-10 Vertical Righting.   **Fig 4-11** Rotational Righting.

Vertical righting reactions also activate extremity musculature by chain reactions in patterns corresponding to activated neck-trunk synergy. As extension develops in neck and trunk, the upper and then lower extremities develop full extension; as head and neck flex, flexion spreads to affect the extremities; when lateral flexion develops, the corresponding upper, then lower extremities extend and abduct. The extremity patterns activated by vertical chain reactions are undifferentiated; however, musculature is activated which will be adapted to protective and balance reactions after extremity support reactions are developed.

Rotational righting reactions (Fig 4-11) include neck righting and body righting on the body.[2,4] Rotational righting reactions are not present at birth but are adapted from primitive turning behaviors. The reactions are termed according to whether rotation is initiated by turning the head or by turning a trunk segment. Rotational righting reactions activate muscles which cause head and trunk to rotate around the central axis of the body. Primary sensory assimilations needed to initiate neck righting are tactile input stimulating head turning and proprioceptive input from neck muscles activated in turning. However, visual and auditory receptions are rapidly integrated as sources of stimuli for rotational righting. The baby may turn his head toward a sound or to look at a toy. If sufficient rotation is placed upon the central axis of the body, other body segments will automatically follow in the same direction to maintain alignment.

Neck righting is initiated by independent head turning. Rotation of the neck stimulates neck proprioceptors, labyrinths, and rotates vertebral segments. The combined stimuli from neck rotation is transmitted to the trunk by chain reaction. The trunk follows to align itself with the head in sidelying. Neck righting moves the trunk and limbs as a unit because differentiation of body segments has developed only between the head and trunk, and not between the upper trunk and pelvis.

However, the trunk elongates as the baby rolls from supine to sidelying. Elongation of the trunk stimulates proprioceptors and activates trunk muscles which the baby uses to move from sidelying to prone. Elongation, increased tactile pressure in sidelying, and assistance from extremities pushing and pulling stimulate trunk muscles and facilitates a body righting on body reaction. Repetition of body righting on body reaction facilitates rotation between upper trunk and pelvis and differentiates body segments. Differentiation of trunk segments is necessary for deliberate rolling from sidelying to prone. Rotation between body segments also means that the infant can initiate rolling by rotating head, upper or lower trunk, significantly

 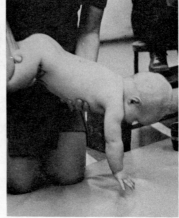

Fig 4-12 Support Reaction.   **Fig 4-13** Protective Reaction.

modifying his rolling pattern. As the child initiates rotational righting by turning an upper or lower trunk segment, he does so by pulling with the appropriate extremity. At first, the extremity moves in line with the body segment; eventually, the extremity will cross the midline of the body during rolling.[10]

Differentiation of body segments by maturation of rotational righting reactions brings about development of counter-rotation. Since body segments can move independent of each other and muscles groups have developed to rotate segments in either direction, the child can rotate one segment in one direction and interrupt the pattern by rotating another segment in an opposite direction.[8] The effect of rotation-counter-rotation is to begin to balance rotation around the midline and modify the complete rotation pattern. When rotation-counter-rotation strategies are affecting the midline, the shoulder and hip on the same side are observed to move in opposite directions. Rotation-counter-rotation patterns of movement achieve significance throughout development as they are adapted to complex functions.[10]

Both vertical and rotational righting reactions activate muscle groups which move the body as a whole in space. Righting reactions control movement in a particular sequence so that transitory equilibrium is not lost during movement.[6] New positions achieved by means of righting reactions are stabilized and maintained by development of support reactions.

Support reactions (Fig 4-12) develop from adaptation of primitive holding strategies. Support reactions are elicited when supporting areas of the body (palm of hand, sole of foot, buttocks) contact the supporting surface.[2] Exteroceptive stimulation from touch to the surface and proprioceptive stimulation from pressure and stretch of distal musculature produce sensory assimilations for support reactions. The motor accommodation is accomplished by co-activation of muscle groups of the appropriate extremity or about the midline. Tactile-pressure input causes an initial movement away from the source. The baby essentially pushes away from the source of stimulation (supporting surface) while maintaining contact with supporting surface. Following the chain of movements away from a contact point, muscle groups are co-activated with antagonists to stabilize around joints and bear weight or support posture in that position. When palms of the hands contact the supporting surface, the baby extends arms to push up to support in an on-hands position. When sensory assimilations are localized on the buttocks, the baby straightens his neck and trunk to sit in a vertical posture. Similarly, as soles of the feet contact the surface, lower extremities and then neck-trunk muscles are co-activated for standing.

Support receptors are a major source of input to alert the system to any changes in posture. As a person moves or is moved in space, pressure from the supporting surface to the body surface is altered. Pressure may be increased, localized, moving, or completely changed to another area of the body. Alterations in tactile-pressure input received cause automatic changes in distribution of supporting responses in order to adjust a position in space. Support functions may be transferred from one extremity to another, from one side of the body to the other, or from upper to lower body segments and reverse.

Support for posture is trunk-centered before the baby develops support reactions. At every level of development, the extremities support new postures before any purposeful movement in the posture develops. Once the limbs are freed from total support, they can protect the body by extending, reversing the chain effect from support reactions to protective reactions.

Protective reactions (Fig 4-13) of the extremities allow a person to seek out or return to a support base to sequence movement flow or to protect the body when environment demands exceed the individual's capacity to adapt.[1,4] Protective reactions are elicited as accommodations to vestibular assimilations from moving in space, tactile-pressure alterations from supporting surfaces, and visual/auditory awareness of impending change. These assimilations are integrated and available to initiate extension of extremities toward the supporting surface whenever protection from falling or use of support for moving is required. Following initial input for a limb extension synergy, the pattern is completed by chain reactions. Development of protective reactions contributes to activation of limb extensors through a complete range of motion.

Once protective reactions are developed, they are always available for use in their original form, ie, given appropriate input, extremities automatically extend in any plane of the body to protect by seeking support. In addition, protective reactions are adapted to alternate with support reactions in performance of such reciprocal behaviors as walking. Protective reactions are also adapted to activities and skills and used to seek out pivot points on the supporting surface in order to turn cartwheels or hop.

The advent of righting reactions and support-protective reactions during transition from primitive to mature functioning organize posture and movement strategies into transition sets. After the baby develops mobility to assume postures and stability to maintain postures, mobility and stability patterns are combined into strategies adapted to new behaviors. Combined strategies[3] are initially adapted in *bilateral-linear sets*. Bilateral-linear sets allow the baby to move forward and back through space. The baby adapts extremity support reactions to continue external control distally while he superimposes mobility upon stability more proximally. By rocking, bouncing, and push-pull patterns, muscle functions are expanded so that ultimately posture can control movement. The baby learns to move with support, thus modifying primitive fixation-support sets which did not allow movement and limit the range of primitive movement.

The progression of development from external to internal control requires that modified mobility and stability functions be differentiated from each other.[3] Differentiated strategies allow *weight-shift sets* to emerge. The baby secures postural control over body position and frees extremities from distal support by shifting weight either symmetrically to upper or lower body segments, or asymmetrically to ipsilateral upper and lower extremities. Once weight has been shifted and postural tone distributed in a new orientation, nonweightbearing extremities are free to let go and move in space. Proximal control over the freely moving extremity is provided by stability adapted from combined mobility-stability functions. During transition, stabilizing and moving is a two-step process. First weight is shifted, then movement follows. The baby stabilizes with upper extremities and moves lower portions into creeping or standing positions. Or, he stabilizes with lower portions of body in sitting and frees hands to reach; or, he shifts weight laterally to reach in prone, or creep or walk. Forward progression of the body is characterized by lateral shift followed by movement forward or a side-to-side, waddling-type progression.

During transition, free movement of the extremities reflect adaptation of control from combined mobility-stability functions. Just as combined function develops in a proximal-distal progression, differentiated postural control over free movement follows. The baby first moves extremities freely from the shoulder or the hip before he isolates more distal movements with proximal segments stabilized. The child adapts transitional movement strategies to activities by shaking a rattle or scribbling with a crayon using shoulder motion, then elbow motion, etc, until mobility and stability are blended for mature function.

Mature Strategies

A child enters into the mature phase of functioning for each behavior as soon as he can independently maintain postures, move within the position and move about the environment in a desired position. The child is able to select and consistently use most appropriate posture and movement strategies for the demands of the environment and the behavior/activity. Mature functioning is controlled by automatic balance reactions blending mobility and stability muscle functions.

Automatic balance reactions adapt posture and movement strategies developed during the transitional phase. With balance reactions available, the child develops internal control with which he maintains and regains balance as he moves in an infinite variety of unique patterns. Automatic reactions include midline stability reactions and equilibrium reactions.[2,4,8]

Midline stability reactions (Fig 4-14) are adapted primarily from *vertical*-rotational righting and support reactions. Midline stability reactions are defined as invisible or barely discernible adjustments in posture around the midline and proximal joints. Stability muscle functions are facilitated by influence from gravity on stretch receptors of postural muscles and from alteration in touch-pressure reception from supporting surface. The child responds with constant, but barely observable, changes in distribution of postural tone which keeps the midline of the body aligned with the center of gravity.[8] The child uses midline stability reactions to maintain vertical postures, even before equilibrium reactions have developed. After equilibrium reactions develop, they are blended with midline stability so that the two types of reactions function on a continuum. Midline reactions control postural adjustments within a confined area related to the center of gravity. As soon as the child moves away from the center significantly, equilibrium reactions are elicited for balance.

Equilibrium reactions (Fig 4-15) are compensatory movements used to regain midline

Fig 4-14 Midline Stability Reaction.   **Fig 4-15** Equilibrium Reaction.

stability when alignment of midline with gravity is significantly disturbed.[8] Equilibrium reactions adapt vertical-*rotational* righting and protective reactions from the transitional phase. Tactile-pressure, vestibular, and visual/auditory assimilations are integrated to produce equilibrium reactions. Equilibrium reactions encompass several observable sequential movements:

1) Movement away from the center of gravity to the extent that balance may be lost elicits rotation of head and upper trunk back toward the center.

2) Lower trunk segments counter-rotate to balance the rotational effect of the upper portions and control the degree of rotation. As upper portions of the body come back to midline, there is a barely observable reverse in the rotation and counter-rotation patterns of the upper and lower segments in order to stop the adjustment at midline.

3) Extremities on one side of the body may extend and abduct to assist the body back toward center-alignment by pulling.

4) Opposite extremities may extend and abduct in preparation to protect and support the body if balance is lost, or if already weight-bearing, opposite extremities experience increase in stability distribution to support the shift in weight-bearing.

A person automatically sequences midline and equilibrium reactions as he establishes and re-establishes his center and freely moves about in space. He can use his automatic balance reactions for control as he moves in relation to a fixed support, such as balancing on a stable object or as he adjusts to a moving source of support, such as standing on a moving subway.[2]

Automatic balance reactions blend mobility and stability muscle functions to achieve mature internal postural control by developing movement-countermovement postural sets.

Movement-countermovement postural sets provide control by stabilizing a movement strategy with a simultaneous antagonistic movement. The affect of countermovement is to balance moving and holding appropriately and automatically so that movement can be readily adapted to behaviors, activities, and skills. Within the central axis, mature postural sets are primarily executed by finely balanced rotation and counter-rotation. Now the child can shift weight to upper body segments, or lower body segments, or laterally and simultaneously move opposite body segments. Forward movement in reaching, crawling, creeping, walking, etc, is characterized by smooth reciprocal patterns with rotation-counter-rotation around the midline, shoulders, and hips on the same side moving in opposite directions, and scapula-humeral and sacral-femoral disassociation which allows limbs to move counter to adjacent trunk segments.[10] In addition, movement within a position is smooth and automatic. If the head and upper trunk rotate away from the center of gravity, for example, reaching from a sitting position, the lower trunk rotates toward the center of gravity to control the upper body and maintain balance. To regain vertical sitting posture, the upper trunk rotates back toward the center and the lower trunk counter-rotates to control the degree of rotation. In addition, if movement away from the center of gravity is rapid, as in loss of balance, the extremities are immediately activated to protect and support.

With internal postural control established centrally, the extremities refine blended mobility-stability functions to engage in behaviors, activities, and skills. Freely-moving extremities are controlled by countermovement of more proximal segments, ie, the shoulder moves back as the hand reaches forward, or the pelvis moves back as the foot swings forward and in reverse, the pelvis moves forward as the leg moves back.[10] In addition, finer control required for manipulation of objects as an extension of the hand calls forth more proximal stability from combined strategies. Movement superimposed on stability is available to direct the hand and object according to perceptual and cognitive monitoring.[3] Movement-countermovement postural sets and adaptation of combined strategies form a basis for organization of movement strategies into perceptual sets. Blended posture and movement strategies organized into postural and perceptual sets are available for mature functioning. The strategies are adapted for performance of an infinite variety of skills, accounting for automatic control of posture and movement while the individual pursues the goals of his actions.

> As a dancer shifts his position he keeps his balance. He does this by taking his center with him, he shifts his center of gravity, re-establishing his equilibrium in the very instant that he has leapt.[11]

References

1. Holt K: Movement and child development. Clinics in Developmental Medicine, no 55. Philadelphia, JB Lippincott Co, 1975, p 2.
2. Bobath B: Abnormal Postural Reflex Activity Caused By Brain Lesion. London, W Heinemann Med Books, 1975.
3. Stockmeyer S: Sensorimotor approach to treatment, in Pearson P, Williams C (eds): Physical Therapy Services in the Developmental Disabilities. Springfield, Ill, Charles C Thomas Pubs 1972, pp 186-222.
4. Fiorentino MR: Reflex testing methods for evaluating D.N.S. development. Springfield, Illinois, Charles C Thomas Pubs, 1965.

5. Andre-Thomas: The neurological examination of the infant. Clinics in Developmental Medicine, no 1. Philadelphia, JB Lippincott Co, 1964, p 11.
6. Peiper A: Cerebral Function in Infancy and Childhood. New York, Consultants Bureau, 1963.
7. Coogler E: Differentiation of human skeletal muscle. A self-instructional package. HEW Grant #5-DOI-AH-50524-02, Georgia State University, 1973.
8. Gilfoyle E, Grady A: Posture and movement, in Hopkins H, Smith H (eds): Willard and Spackman's Occupational Therapy, ed 5. Philadelphia, JB Lippincott Co, 1978, pp 58-80.
9. Touwen B: Neurological development in infancy. Clinics in Developmental Medicine, no 58. Philadelphia, JB Lippincott Co, 1976.
10. Bly L: Lecture Notes, Components of Movement, Neurodevelopmental Treatment Course. Colorado Springs, Colorado, Rocky Mountain Rehabilitation Center, April-May, 1975.
11. Richards MG: Centering. Middletown, Wesleyan Univ Press, 1975, p 38.

Chapter Five
The Development of Purposeful Behaviors

Achievement of the upright posture is an underlying innate goal of a child's developmental quest. To achieve "upright," children adapt posture and movement strategies that are behavior motivated, that is, achievement of the behavior itself is the motivating factor or goal that leads the child to performance. Behavior motivated performances are self-starting and self-perpetuating, thus actions are centered on the bodily processes to achieve the behavior and not on events or objects outside the body.[1] Behaviors are purposeful when their actions are body centered and have meaning for the nervous system.

Behaviors are purposeful when functions associated with actions facilitate a meaningful response for nervous system maturation. Maturation occurs when the child's performance with the behavior produces change and facilitates efforts that are more mature or at a higher level. As purposeful, actions of behaviors are goal-directed, ie, the innate goal to roll, to sit, to creep, and to stand. Once the child has achieved the goal the behavior may be repeated and practiced until it is no longer purposeful. Rather the behavior becomes automatic and available for adaptation to higher level purposeful behaviors, activities and skills.[2]

This chapter will explore progressive development of four basic purposeful behaviors. The four behaviors are discussed according to the primitive, transitional, and mature phases of development. The behaviors include the child's achievement of creeping, sitting, rolling, and standing/walking. Discussion of development of reaching will be incorporated with the discussion of creeping, sitting, and rolling. In addition, reaching and grasping will be further discussed with adaptation of purposeful activities and skill (Chapter Seven).

For clarity, the integrated development of each behavior is presented separately. However, the reader should keep in mind that throughout a child's developmental process, posture and movement strategies of one behavior are also associated and integrated to modify other behaviors.

Integration through the spiraling process of development is discussed in terms of adaptation of posture and movement strategies and emergence of somatosensory perception. Although the somatosensory system receives emphasis in the discussion of purposeful behaviors, the vital role of the visual and auditory systems must not be ignored. External stimuli received by these systems serves as the child's cue to action and may become the primary motivating force for adaptation of purposeful behaviors to activities and higher level skills. Integration of external stimuli with somatosensory stimuli augments perceptual development and spatiotemporal adaptation.[2]

Creeping

Creeping provides a means of locomotion prior to achieving the upright posture. Creeping affords the child opportunities during his early days of development to move about and investigate his environment while assuring a secure position of support by four extremities. Creeping is also a behavior which combines development of postural strategies of the trunk against gravity blended with reciprocal limb movement strategies needed to move the body in space. Posture and movement strategies of creeping are adapted for the essential elements of upright locomotion. During development of creeping, strategies can be integrated and practiced in the more secure all-fours position, thus becoming available as automatic patterns for adaptation to higher level upright positions. Strategies which develop in prone and culminate in creeping are designed to develop extension against gravity. Creeping, as a purposeful behavior, combines extension, flexion, and rotation for postural control about the midline. Creeping also provides the opportunity to develop reciprocal limb movement to move the body into space.

The key behaviors associated with the development of creeping include:

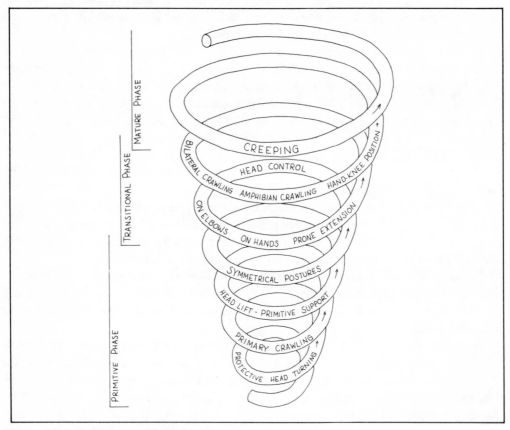

Fig 5-1 Key Behaviors of Creeping.

a) **Primitive phase** — protective head turning, primary crawling, head lift — primitive support and symmetrical postures;

b) **Transitional phase** — head control-on-elbows, on-hands, prone extension, bilateral crawling, amphibian crawling, and hand-knee position;

c) **Mature phase** — creeping.

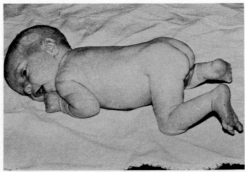

Fig 5-2 Protective Head Turning.

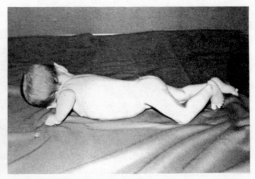

Fig 5-3 Primary Crawling.

Protective Head Turning

The neonate in prone assumes a completely flexed posture. He can dorsiflex his head momentarily and turn his face away from the supporting surface in protective head turning. The flexed posture is influenced by the tonic labyrinthine reflex which distributes flexor tone in a primitive holding pattern. The primitive holding pattern is altered by the adaptation of phasic fetal responses. Protective head turning is an adaptation of an acquired fetal response reported by Twitchell.[3,4] According to Twitchell, the fetus will dorsiflex the head following a tactile stimulation of the midline of the face, turning the head away from stimulation. In addition, Twitchell describes sensory sensibility of the ventral surface that begins as a confined receptive field around the face, especially the area of the mouth, and gradually spreads down the ventral surface of the body. The fetus responds to sensory stimulation of the ventral surface with extension.

The fetal experiences become available for neonatal adaptation of protective head turning and initiation of extension. As the neonate adapts to the prone position with protective head turning, the neck extensors are activated against gravity to modify fetal flexion with head lift. Emergence of extension in prone begins to dampen the flexor influence of the tonic labyrinthine reflex.[5,6,7]

Primary Crawling

In addition to head turning, the flexed posture of the neonate is also altered by primary crawling (Bauer's reflex).[5,6,7] Flexed posture of the lower extremities sometimes increases dorsiflexion of the foot to the extent that the sole of the foot contacts the supporting surface. Tactile pressure on the sole of one foot can cause complete extension of that lower extremity and increased flexion of the opposite extremity. The result of this phasic "crossed extension" strategy is movement of the body forward by primitive reciprocal limb movement. Reflexive kicking patterns of primary crawling and head turning represent activation of muscle groups in undifferentiated movement strategies affecting a segment of the body. Reflexive rhythmical flexion extension movements of primary crawling will be adapted for crawling and creeping when higher level posture and movement strategies control the trunk and limbs.

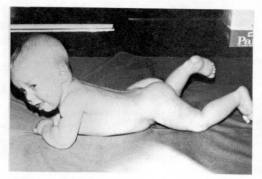

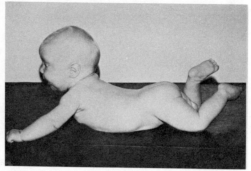

Fig 5-4 Head Lift.

Fig 5-5 Symmetrical Posture.

Head Lift — Primitive Support

Protective head turning is adapted by the infant to deliberately turn head from side to side in prone. Neck extensors are activated against gravity as the head is lifted slightly to turn. Gravity and movement provide stimulus for the baby to initiate head lift from a side turned position toward midline, facilitating neck retraction and primitive upper extremity support. Initial head lift is accompanied by head movement downward toward the shoulders to retract and fix the head on shoulders. Neck retraction is utilized by the infant to stabilize the head on shoulders prior to the time when neck extension facilitates upper trunk extension and upper extremity support as background for neck movement.[8] Neck retraction allows primitive holding so that the upper extremities can begin to move toward alignment with the shoulders. The extremities are not yet available for full weight-bearing. As the infant fixes for primitive support with upper portions of the body, lower portions are adapted in a partially flexed posture with reflexive kicking movements.[9] Primitive support patterns begin to stabilize the upper portion of the body while the reflexive kicking patterns mobilize the lower portion — the foundation for a postural set. Activation and holding patterns further modify tonic labyrinthine and primary crawling reflexes. Head lift and primitive support prepare for development of the symmetrical tonic neck reflex.[2,10,11,12]

Symmetrical Postures

The baby lifts his head in midline and supports himself on symmetrically extended arms with hands fisted and both lower extremities partially flexed. As the neck and spinal extensors lift the upper portion of the body from the supporting surface, primitive support and reflexive kicking patterns are modified. Repetition of head lift initiates vertical head righting reactions to modify neck retraction to neck extension.[8] Assimilations from neck proprioceptors change the distribution of postural tone according to the symmetrical tonic neck reflex.[10,11] The baby raises his head further from the supporting surface activating neck extensors in primitive midline holding. Primitive midline holding provides a postural strategy which allows the infant to maintain head dorsiflexion prior to fully developing righting reactions for neck and trunk extension. The baby can now support himself on extended arms, with arms positioned forward of the shoulders. The change in arm position from primitive support to symmetrical support allows the baby to develop stabilization throughout the range of upper extremity holding. The lower extremities are held in partial flexion which combines symmetrical holding with primitive reflexive kicking patterns. The opposite distribution of extensor tone in upper and flexor-tone in lower segments of the body may be viewed as a primitive form of a postural set.

Primitive stabilization about the midline of the body with holding at different points within the range of upper extremity support provides symmetry and alignment of body segments. Symmetry prepares for further activation of muscle groups through chain reactions and co-activation of muscle groups from support reactions. By the end of the primitive phase, the infant brings his elbows under his shoulders to rest on forearms and support neck and upper trunk extension. His initial attempts to support on elbows are accompanied by abduction of the shoulders to compensate for lack of adequate upper trunk extension. [8]

During the primitive phase, adaptation of the key behaviors of prone (protective head turning, primary crawling, head lift — primitive support and symmetrical postures) have provided the self-system with the basic foundation for the development of creeping. In addition, adapting experiences of behaviors adds new information toward expansion of visual and auditory perceptions. Through actions of behaviors, the baby receives somatosensory stimulation from his body in motion and at rest. Association and integration of somatosensory reception with primitive visual and auditory perceptions facilitates somatosensory awareness of the body in space. [2]

During the transitional phase, primitive responses are modified and adapted to vertical righting and support/protective reactions. These reactions influence development of creeping since extension expands to include the trunk and extremities. Muscles that extend the body are activated against gravity to develop the stability component for postural control. [13,14] Extension of the neck and trunk also brings the body into position to facilitate support, first on upper extremities and then on all-fours. The baby then develops the ability to move his body forward and backward through space supported by four extremities.

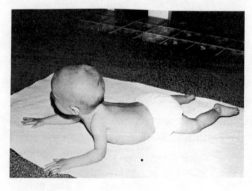

Fig 5-6 On-Elbows.

Head Control — On Elbows

Vertical righting reactions further activate extensors of the neck to develop against gravity, prepare for head and trunk alignment, and provide the stimulus for trunk and extremity extension. As neck extensors and scapular stabilizers are completely activated against gravity, the baby lifts his head and upper portion of the trunk further from the supporting surface. Head raising indicates use of midline extensors to control head and upper trunk position. The baby begins to bear weight on forearms with elbows more adducted and slightly forward of the shoulders.

Now that the baby has achieved symmetrical support behaviors he calls up primitive rotation patterns from protective head turning. Trace effects of the asymmetrical tonic neck reflex can be noted as the head is turned. The asymmetrical tonic neck reflex causes a change in distribution of upper extremity muscle tone. Changes in tone affects the symmetrical posture by initiating asymmetrical stabilization in preparation for lateral weight shift.

As extensors and scapular stabilizers are completely activated against gravity, stimulus for flexor activation is provided through reciprocal innervation.[1] Flexors and extensors interact to enhance synergistic action for co-activation which begins at the neck as the head and trunk align.[14] Co-activation expands to the upper extremities as muscle groups around the shoulders are partially activated at a point within the range to align elbows and shoulders in weight bearing. Having achieved head control and on-elbows security, the baby can grasp objects in forearm supported postures. Visual monitoring of early play stimulates the baby to lower his head from complete extension to align head and trunk further enhancing co-activation. Upper portions of the body maintain a higher level on-elbows support pattern while the baby reinforces activation of lower portions with reciprocal reflexive kicking.[10,11] Combining higher level support of the upper portions with lower level reflexive movements is a forerunner to the development of a postural set.

Postural strategies developed around the neck and shoulders from the on-elbow position provide a stable background to adapt neck rotation from head turning behaviors. With rotation the baby can differentiate head from trunk by turning head on shoulders. Differentiated head turning allows the baby to move head freely without significantly changing the distribution of tone in the upper extremities, thus modifying the affect of the asymmetrical tonic neck reflex. Modification of the primitive asymmetrical stabilization pattern allows the baby to transfer weight to the skull side upper extremity in preparation for weight shift.

On-Hands

Vertical chain reactions expand extension to lower portions of the body. Protective extension reactions are adapted to modify the on-elbows position to on-hands. During early experiences of weight bearing on-hands, primitive postural strategies of upper extremity abduction and fisted hands are called up and adapted to compensate for a lack of internal stability created by the more fully extended posture. Extensors are being activated toward lower portions of the body by means of increased trunk extension created by the on-hands position. Upper extremities are again called upon to support trunk development of activation until co-activation develops in the lower trunk.

Simultaneous with adaptation of protective reactions for upper extremity extension, the Landau reaction[5,6] is adapted to further expand axial extension to pelvis and lower extremities. Combination of upper extremity extension and expansion of extension in the trunk anchors the pelvis to the supporting surface as a stable base for upper body movement. Complete axial extension is adapted to the prone extension posture.[11,14] The infant combines

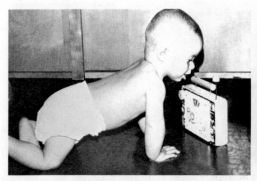

Fig 5-7 On-Hands.

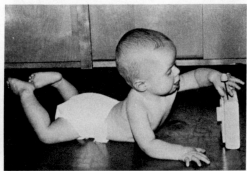

Fig 5-8 On-Elbows Reaching.

shoulder retraction with midline extension to facilitate distal expansion of extension. With full range of extension available in the trunk and extremities, the baby activates full ranges of extension by moving between pivot prone extension posture and support on-hands posture. The extension synergy completes the activation phase in prone and prepares for expansion of co-activation around the midline and proximal joints for postural control.[11,14]

The baby is motivated to move between on-hands and on-elbows positions to repeat the achievement of these purposeful behaviors. Repetition combines upper extremity movement synergies with weight-bearing postures. The hands are fixed to the supporting surface to reinforce more proximal stability. Muscle groups around the shoulders are activated with co-activation as background to control movement. Increasing shoulder control, arm extension developed with on-hands position, and visual surveillance of toys out of immediate range motivates the baby to reach. Sufficient stability on-hands has not been acquired to support weight on one arm and reach. Postural strategies are called up from on-elbows behavior to adapt to the newly developing movement strategy for reaching. The baby assumes the on-elbows position obtaining environmental support and stability to support weight unilaterally. Previously acquired asymmetrical postures and neck rotation are called up to shift weight laterally, thus freeing one extremity to extend into space and reach. The development of a movement strategy for reaching from prone with control represents differentiated mobility and stability development.

Bilateral Crawling

The baby's initial attempts to move around in prone represent adaptation of movement strategies to move in space. Bilateral movements of the upper extremities push and pull the body in a linear fashion and are available for pivoting in a circle. With upper extremities fixed to the supporting surface, the baby pushes his body backward to augment mobility and stability in extension. Pulling forward combines mobility and stability in flexion. Lateral movements of the trunk are enhanced as the baby pulls with one upper extremity, pushes with the other to move in a circle. Occasionally, as the baby is pushing back, he may push into an all-fours position. However, the ability to assume all-fours postures is greatly enhanced by higher level reciprocal crawling.

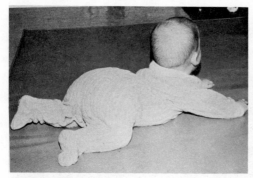

Fig 5-9 Linear Push.

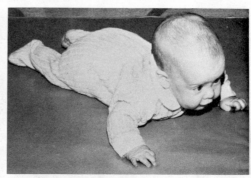

Fig 5-10 Linear Pull.

Fig 5-11 Pivot in Circle.

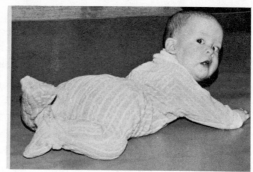

Fig 5-12 Rock Side-to-Side.

Movement strategies developed with initial attempts to move in space are combined with lower level postural strategies and modify on-elbows and on-hands behaviors. Pushing back expands extension distally to open the hands for palmar weight bearing. Support reactions are stimulated and combined with increased extension to facilitate co-activation around the elbows and more adduction of the upper extremities. The adduction-distal extension modification of the on-hands posture provides increased upper extremity stability. Increased stability of the upper extremities combines mobility with stability to rock side to side. Rocking enhances lateral weight shift calling forth the basis for reaching from on-hands. The reaching strategy from on-elbows behavior is adapted to reach from on-hands position. In addition, rocking with hand support and the trunk more fully extended expands rotation within the body axis in a caudal direction. The higher level rotation patterns developed with on-hands rocking modifies the lateral weight shift aspect of on-elbows reaching. Now when the baby is on-elbows and laterally shifts weight to reach out, he may come to the end of the range of lateral weight shift. At the end of the range, he can call forth rotation from rocking on-hands as a means to simultaneously shift weight and rotate toward the midline and reach forward.

Reciprocal Crawling

Movement strategies needed for initial exploration of space are organized into crawling behaviors. Crawling describes trunk-centered reciprocal progression through space. The

Fig 5-13 Crawling.

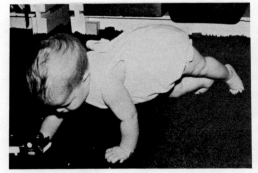

Fig 5-14 Hands-Feet Support.

Fig 5-15 On-Hands Reaching.

environment continues to provide support for the trunk while the extremities adapt strategies from primary crawling, weight shift, and bilateral crawling — pivoting. The baby crawls by using lateral flexion to first shift weight and stabilize on one side of the body, followed by the extremities on the opposite side which reach out and unilaterally pull to move forward.

Chain reactions facilitated by on-hands behavior expand co-activation distally to develop pelvic and hip stability. As internal stability is augmented, the baby adapts reflexive kicking patterns of primary crawling to the higher level prone extended posture. As the baby supports himself on his hands and shifts his weight laterally, the upper trunk rotates back, and the pelvic area is elevated from the supporting surface, thus the amphibian reaction is initiated.[15,16] Amphibian facilitates flexion and abduction of the lower extremity which is adapted to assume all-fours support postures as well as adapted for forward progression. Reciprocal crawling is initiated when one arm is free to reach forward unilaterally and move the body out into space. The lower extremity on the same side can follow in reciprocal amphibian patterns. The previous bilateral linear trunk motion of pushing and pulling the body through space is modified to reciprocal crawling with lateral weight shift.

The baby assumes an all-fours position by adapting the amphibian reaction to previously acquired on-hands support posture. The baby first shifts weight unilaterally, then extends his other arm and flexes his other leg. In the all-fours position, co-activation expands distally to provide internal trunk stability against gravity necessary for higher level purposeful behaviors. As the baby is adapting all-fours, he rocks back and forth and side to side combining mobility and stability. In addition, extension continues to expand distally to complete the development of co-activation in prone, and the baby assumes the hands-feet posture. The youngster moves from all-fours hand-knee support to hands-feet support. Rocking in hand-knee and moving between hand-knee, hands-feet combines movement strategies with weight bearing in higher level positions. Combining mobility and stability prepares for differentiation of functions necessary to modify lower level on-hands behavior and prepare for creeping.[14] Rocking and expanded extension are adapted to modify on-hands reaching behavior from reaching with lateral weight shift to reaching with rotation. When the baby is in an all-fours position and wishes to reach out for an object, he calls forth the on-hands posture in order to anchor his pelvis for support. However, upper extremity weight-shift on-hands is modified by higher level all-fours experience. Rocking with expanded trunk extension also expands the development of trunk rotation distally. The baby differentiates the rotation patterns experienced from on-elbows reaching, adapts experiences from all-fours so that on-hands reaching with lateral weight shift is modified to on-hands reaching with rotation.

During the transitional phase, the self-system selects elements of primitive behaviors to combine stability and mobility actions for interaction with the environment. Somatosensory awareness of the body in relation to itself and in relation to space is augmented from feedback of synergistic actions adapted from key behaviors experienced during transition. Increased somatosensory feedback and sensory input from movement experiences contributes to personal and spatial perceptions of the confined area surrounding the body. Integration of visual perceptions of the environment with somatosensory awareness from transitional actions provides necessary associations for the baby to make a judgment about his capacities to move out into the environment. Somatosensory perceptions evolve from adaptations of transitional behaviors to mature behaviors.

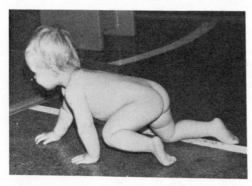

Fig 5-16 Creeping.

Creeping

Creeping describes extremity-supported forward progression dependent upon maturation of balance reactions to sequence posture and movement strategies. Even after the child has assumed the all-fours posture frequently and rocked back and forth in the position with distal support, he continues to call up the more stable, trunk-centered crawling to progress forward. However, the all-fours posture modifies reciprocal crawling and reciprocal strategies are adapted to all-fours posture to develop creeping in the mature phase.

Rocking on all-fours provides opportunity to move the trunk over the extremities, combining mobility with stability about the shoulders and hips simultaneously. Increased stability with mobility at proximal joints allows the child to adapt rotation around the midline as he turns his head and transfers rotation through the trunk distally. Combined muscle actions in all-fours modify reciprocal trunk-centered crawling. Addition of rotation to reciprocal crawling makes it possible for the child to rotate and shift weight, simultaneously moving the body forward by means of rotation around the midline. The child crawls by moving one arm and the opposite leg together. The postural set of upper trunk rotation and lower trunk counter-rotation provides contralateral stabilization for postural background needed for movement.[8] As crawling matures, mobility and stability functions are differentiated: one shoulder moves forward while the pelvis on the same side moves back; the opposite shoulder moves back while the pelvis on that side moves forward, equaling rotation and counter-rotation. Mature crawling also modifies the child's ability to assume all-fours positions. The baby can adapt the midline rotation component from crawling to shift weight unilaterally and simultaneously assume a creeping position.

The child continues to seek out his highest postural level by assuming all-fours, but to move he continues to seek out crawling. As he moves between crawling and creeping, he begins to associate reciprocal movement strategies with higher level all-fours postures. Now, instead of calling forth the more secure posture of crawling to move, he calls up reciprocal movement from crawling and adapts it to all-fours to initiate creeping. Creeping frees the lower extremities to move in space following the same process as the upper extremities, ie, shifting weight and freeing an extremity to move in space. In the process of adapting reciprocation to all-fours posture, movement forward is again accompanied by lateral weight shift. The child shifts weight and secures unilateral weight bearing on hand and knee before moving opposite hand and knee to creep. Creeping with lateral weight shift repeats the side-to-side forward movement which also characterized first attempt to crawl reciprocally.

The side-to-side creeping pattern is modified by adapting rotation components from crawling combined with experiences moving from creep to sit, sit to creep, and pulling to stand. Once again, the extremities are called upon to stabilize while midline and proximal mobility is combined by the child to move from creep to sit and back to creep or pull to stand. The rotary component adapted from both lower and higher level behaviors modifies creeping. Mature creeping with rotation at the midline facilitates weight shift and simultaneous movement forward, allowing opposite upper and lower extremities to move together, and adapting rotation/counter-rotation synergies within the trunk.[8]

Although there are individual variations of creeping patterns[9,14] the spiraling process is constant. The primitive support and reflexive flexion/extension movements are integrated by the self-system as a foundation for higher level development. The primitive behaviors are modified as higher level transitional reactions are adapted for crawling and all-fours support. The integration and adaptation of primitive and transitional experiences expand the baby's repertoire of behaviors which become modified as mature balance reactions influence crawling and creeping. During the developmental quest to move out and interact with the environment, the infant repeats his acquired crawling and creeping behaviors augmenting somatosensory perception of the body in space.

Sitting

Sitting is a vertical antigravity posture which a child develops on his way to standing. Sitting contributes significantly to standing behaviors; in return, the ability to assume sitting is significantly affected by standing/walking as well as other behaviors. Sitting provides the child with a posture which is first purposeful because it combines co-activation of neck and trunk muscles with extremity support to stay upright for the first time all alone. When a child can support himself in sitting securely, he finds it fun to let go of support and see if he can stay upright anyway. When sitting can be maintained, then both hands are free simultaneously for activities. Sitting ability is retained throughout life for the purposes of play, work, rest, socialization, and transportation. Sitting becomes automatic background for new purposes with environmental interactions.

The ability to maintain sitting and eventually assume sitting is primarily dependent on the development of flexion. The baby practices flexion against gravity in supine from both cephalo and caudal directions. He adapts his newly developed flexion to purposes: when he reaches to be picked up or discovers his feet in his mouth, when he is placed in sitting and prevents extension from pulling him over or combines flexion with extension and rotation to speed along the development of creeping and rolling. These behaviors do allow the baby to

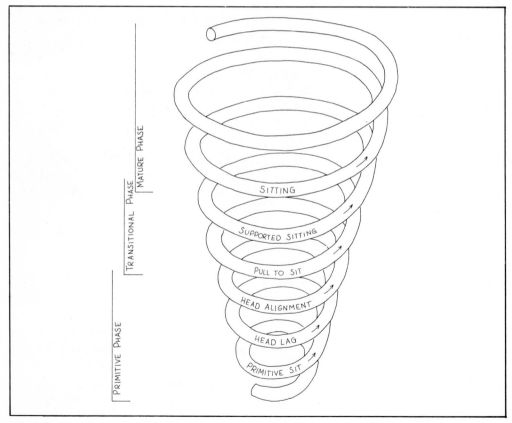

Fig 5-17 Key Behaviors of Sitting.

assume sitting from prone or creeping by assisting with his arms. Adapting the flexion development in supine to behaviors of creeping, rolling, and standing provides the child with the ability to raise his head from supine and come into a sitting position.

The key behaviors associated with the development of sitting include:

a) **Primitive phase** — primitive sit, head lag and head align;
b) **Transitional phase** — pull to sit and supported sitting;
c) **Mature phase** — sitting.

Primitive Sit

When placed and supported in a sitting position the neonate assumes a flexed posture with rounded back. The rounded back posture is adapted from fetal experiences. The literature reports that total body movements of the fetus proceed along the body axis including both flexion and axial extension[15,16] Some newborns will momentarily align head and trunk by adapting fetal axial trunk extension to the supported posture.[1,2] Tactile-proprioceptive reception localized on the buttocks provides input to adapt fetal extension. Primitive sitting provides a preview of support reactions of the transitional phase.

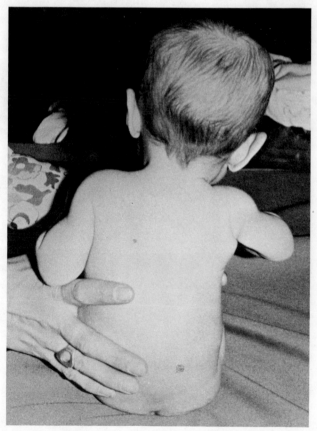

Fig 5-18 Primitive Sit.

Although the infant experiences momentary head and trunk alignment as a primitive form of sitting, development of muscle functions and righting reactions must be experienced and adapted to provide useful head and trunk alignment for vertical postures. The flexion experience of being pulled to sit combined with prone behaviors of extension facilitates head control for sitting upright.

Head Lag

During the neonatal period the infant adapts previously acquired fetal behaviors of flexion and total generalized body movements to the supine posture. Protective reflexes and flexed postures predominate.[5,6,9] Although the lower extremities can be observed to extend in reciprocal kicking patterns, reflexive movements are viewed as a semi-kicking response which occurs within a flexed range.[10,11] During the primitive phase, the neonate adapts phasic and tonic reflexes to alter flexed postures in supine. In addition, behaviors contributing to asymmetrical postures are modified so that the baby develops symmetry in supine. Symmetry in supine posture contributes to the infant's ability to maintain head in midline, engage hands at midline, and move along the midline from supine to sit.

As the neonate in supine is pulled to a sitting position, head lag is observed.[7] Head lag is indicative of influence of the tonic labyrinthine reflex (TLR) as well as lack of controlled neck flexion against gravity. The tonic labyrinthine reflex dampens the primitive flexion response by distributing extensor tone in supine.[6,7]

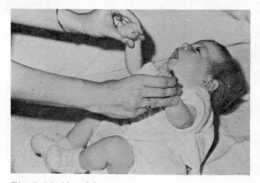

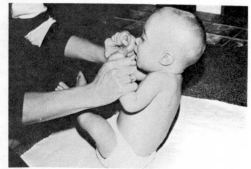

Fig 5-19 Head Lag.   **Fig 5-20** Head Align.

The Moro reflex also plays a role in altering the primitive flexed posture in supine and promoting primitive symmetrical movement strategies. As the infant experiences movement of the body in supine, vestibular reception elicits bilateral extension-abduction movements to the upper extremities followed by adduction and flexion to bring the arms together in an arc over the body.[15]

The Moro reflex[6,7] activates upper extremity muscle groups through ranges of extension-abduction and flexion-adduction. The primitive extensor strategies which alter fetal flexion also provide the stimulus for reciprocal flexion against gravity to develop as the baby is pulled to sit. However, total extension will need to be modified by other primitive strategies in order to combine flexion and extension and move into sitting from supine.

Head Align

After a few weeks the infant aligns the head with the axis of the trunk as he is being pulled to sit.[6,15] The initial neck flexion noted with head alignment can be attributed to past acquired behaviors associated with sucking and pressure on the palms. Somatosensory reception of associated sucking,[6] and pressure on the palms[16] facilitates neck flexion. In addition, proprioceptive stimulation on the palms elicits a total upper extremity flexion synergy associated with the traction response.[3,4] The infant adapts these primitive reactions to align head with trunk while being pulled to sit.

The symmetrical tonic neck reflex also changes distributions of muscle tone to modify the effect of total flexion or extension on supine behaviors. Efforts to flex the neck and align head with trunk stimulate neck proprioceptors and distribute more flexor tone in the upper extremities, reinforcing the effect of sucking and traction. Lower portions of the body are extended, adding to the effect of the tonic labyrinthine and indicative of the law of cephalocaudal development. The symmetrical distribution of tone prepares for differentiation of upper and lower body segments on either side of the waistline. This primitive differentiation of body segments is a forerunner of a postural set which will combine different upper and lower body strategies for getting to the sitting position.

Head and trunk alignment from pull to sit is the beginning of midline holding in supine.[8] By the end of the primitive phase the baby has developed sufficient symmetry to maintain the head in midline. Upper extremity movement strategies develop with the use of shoulder stability as background to begin to move the arms up against gravity from symmetrical postures. Concurrently, movement through space stimulates the labyrinths and increases stimulation to the buttocks.

Adapting experiences of primitive sit, head lag and head align provide primitive posture and movement strategies to augment somatosensory reception of the body in space. Integrating visual/auditory perceptions from external stimuli with sensory receptions of being pulled to sit enhances the baby's primitive perceptual repertoire and somatosensory reception. As a result of the intersensory integration, somatosensory awareness evolves. The combined somatosensory integration facilitates vertical righting reactions and support reactions so that the baby can eventually maintain and assume sitting.

Pull To Sit

In the beginning of the transitional phase, the baby is influenced by vertical righting and support/protective reactions as he is pulled to sit. Vertical righting reactions activate neck flexors and the baby raises his head. By means of chain reactions, initial head raising transmits flexion from neck to trunk and hips expanding flexion activation.[6,7,10,15] As the baby participates more as he is pulled to sit, flexion is activated throughout the range so that he fully flexes his trunk and hips. In addition to flexion developing in supine, the baby adapts extension developed in prone which facilitates the body to arch in supine. Body arching activates extension synergies to combine with flexion synergies developing in supine postures. Flexion synergies are further developed as the baby initiates flexion from a cephaloc caudal direction. The baby in supine mobilizes his lower portions of the body to bring his feet to his mouth.

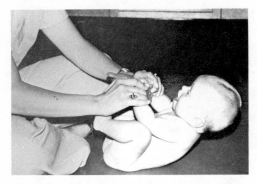 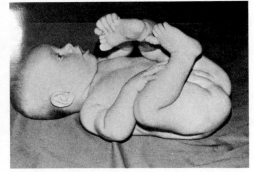

Fig 5-21 Pull-to-Sit.　　　　　　　　　**Fig 5-22** Feet-to-Mouth.

Feet-to-mouth actions mobilize the pelvis to move into posterior tilt, thus differentiating body segments and prepare for rotation at higher levels.[8] Playing with feet represents an awareness of body parts as well as an element of control over posture and movement sequences. The infant's ability to bring his feet to his mouth contributes to tactile exploration of body parts which enhances somatosensory awareness.

Body arching is adapted to bridging. The pelvis is mobilized in an anterior tilt by bridging with knees flexed and soles of the feet contacting the supporting surface.[8] Upper trunk and foot contact support provide stability for the baby to extend the hips against gravity and bridge. Bridging reinforces extension of the hips and differentiates knees from hips. Moving between "foot-to-mouth" and bridging positions differentiates the lower portions of the body from the upper portions in preparation for sitting. In addition, the experiences in supine which fully activate flexors and extensors are combined to develop co-activation around the midline. With differentiation, and co-activation, the baby can maintain upper body extension upon lower body flexion to sit with support

Supported Sitting

Posture and movement strategies of the transitional phase are suggestive of higher level independent sitting. However, the baby will not be able to assume or maintain upright sitting postures until the behaviors associated with rolling and prone progression have developed for adaptation to vertical postures.

Attempts to maintain sitting during transition are with support from extended arms, an adaptation of protective extension.[10,14] Association of protective reactions with sitting positions illustrates somatosensory awareness of the body in space. With awareness, the baby, anticipating the activity, reaches out to be picked up thus initiating being pulled to sit as well as further developing pelvic mobility. At this time, the baby flexes his neck more readily, uses less trunk and leg flexion, and requires only a light hand hold.[14] Repeated experiences with being pulled to sit localizes tactile pressure from the supporting surface to the buttocks. Localization of pressure on the buttocks confines the area of sensory input which increases sensory assimilations for vertical righting in sitting.

Integration of visual and somatosensory assimilations provides information for the baby to make a sensory judgment about his abilities and thus call up the protective extension strategies

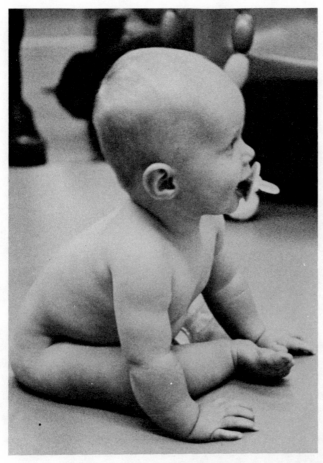

Fig 5-23 Supported Sitting.

from the on-hands behavior to prop forward. Lack of trunk control in sitting calls forth the more primitive pattern of support on arms with fisted hands. However, as the baby props himself with support, the opportunity for neck and co-activation is provided to develop midline stability in sitting position. [12,14]

Co-activation of the upper trunk and use of the lower trunk as a stable base modifies supported sitting. The lower extremities are stabilized in a frog-like posture for wide-base support. Propping forward matures to support on open hands, and the baby now props both forward and laterally. Maturation of support reactions allows the baby to maintain vertical alignment and combine mobility and stability in supported sitting. As he turns his head in supported sitting, his trunk rotates by chain reactions. Rotation is combined with co-activation so he can hold on in sitting and rotate around the midline. Rotation superimposed upon the supported vertical postures alerts the baby to changes in alignment with gravity by altering buttocks pressure. Rotation with support from the hands and buttocks will develop a postural set which allows him to stabilize lower portions of the body and rotate upper portions away from the midline.

The acquired ability to maintain supported sitting and move the head and upper trunk upon lower portions enhances interactions with the environment from the sitting position. New

dimensions are added to the baby's visual perceptual repertoire and somatosensory awareness is augmented to initiate a somatosensory perception of the vertical position of the body
in space.

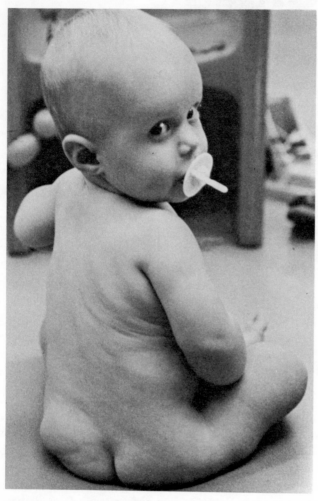

Fig 5-24 Unsupported Sitting.

Sitting

Independent sitting develops from adaptation and integration of behaviors experienced
during the spiraling process from supine posture to sit, prone postures to creep, and rolling.
The youngster acquires the ability to assume and maintain the vertical posture in sitting. As
co-activation develops the baby can lift his hands and sit unsupported.[14] At times the baby will
adapt lower level prone extension posture to reinforce trunk stability. Influence of lower level
postures adapted to sitting is an example of the spiraling process. Shoulder retraction
experienced with prone extension posture is called up to facilitate trunk extension in unsupported sitting. As the baby experiences sitting with retraction, he facilitates vertical alignment
with gravity and develops internal trunk stability. He can differentiate the necessary extension

96

adapted from the prone posture to sit without utilizing the more primitive retraction pattern to maintain the posture.

The supporting reaction of the buttocks alerts the baby to any changes in the center of

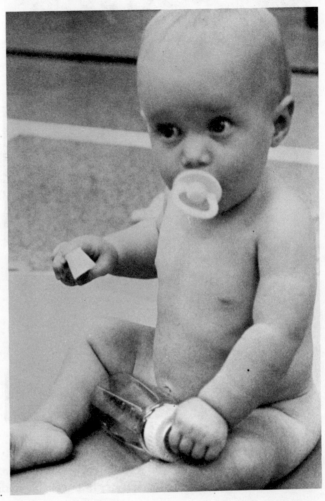

Fig 5-25 Ready for Activity.

gravity and he will readjust his posture to align the body segments in relation to gravity. Midline stability is further developed.

During early experiences with unsupported sitting, the baby may call up extremity support patterns as background to move away from and back to the midline in sitting. He adapts rotation patterns to vertical alignment with support from extremities. In addition, protective reactions develop to prop backwards. The baby is prepared to develop mature automatic balance reactions.

Midline stability and equilibrium reactions in sitting provide background for the baby to reach out without support to be picked up or to reach for a toy. Reaching up recalls earlier experiences of being pulled to sit so that pelvic mobility can be adapted to the vertical position.

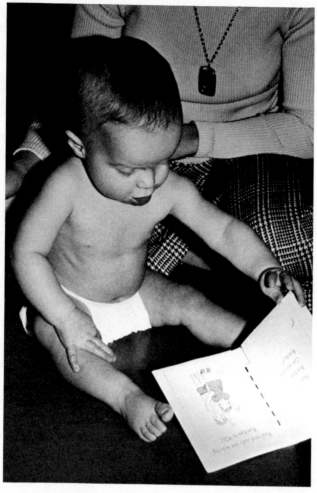

Fig 5-26 Long Sit.

Reaching out without support blends mobility and stability in sitting. The postural set allows the baby to stabilize the lower portion of the body and rotate the upper portion about the midline without support. The youngster has available midline stability reactions to maintain sitting and equilibrium to regain sitting. Protective reactions are available as a part of the self's repertoire to be called up when the demands of the environment exceed the child's independent sitting ability. As automatic balance reactions further mature, the sitting postural set is altered so that the youngster can utilize a narrower base of support and long-sit.

Adaptation of forward and lateral protective support reactions and integrated vertical-rotational righting strategies provides the youngster with the ability to push to sit from prone or side-lying. The baby integrates independent sitting behaviors with the ability to push to sit to assume sitting independently. The process to assume sitting will be explored further in Chapter 6.

The ability to maintain a vertical posture and interact with the environment from that position adds new dimensions to the perceptions of the body in space. The spiraling process of developing sitting will be adapted to the progression for standing, as past acquired behaviors are continually being adapted to higher level purposeful behaviors. In the standing posture, the center of gravity is furthest from the supporting base, therefore a higher level development and modification of the sitting posture will be required to maintain midline stability and equilibrium in the standing position.

Rolling

Rolling is the first purposeful behavior which allows the baby to move his body independently in space — and the baby is usually most surprised the first few times spontaneous rolling occurs. However, he quickly becomes aware of the purpose of rolling. He soon realizes that rolling moves him from one place to another and he rolls for the joy of moving himself. The baby can use the floor for support and move with very little assistance from his extremities. Thus rolling provides the baby with an early behavior to begin to move out into and conquer the world.

Rolling develops rotation patterns of movement. Rotation patterns consist of combinations of flexion and extension which produce diagonal movements. Rolling develops from combinations of behaviors which promote extension in prone and behaviors which develop flexion

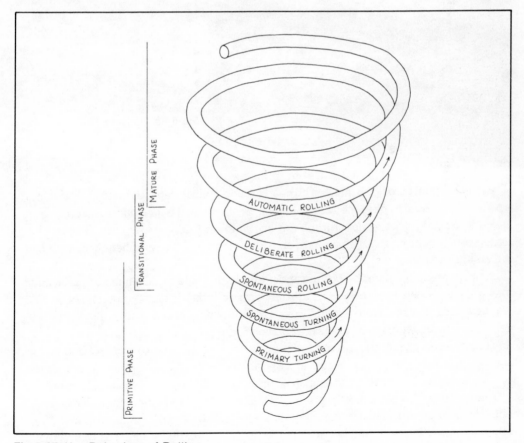

Fig 5-27 Key Behaviors of Rolling.

in supine. However, rolling itself is used to move between supine and prone. The rotation patterns which develop with rolling are adapted as underlying rotary movement strategies for all purposeful behaviors, activities, and skills. The key behaviors of rolling include:

1) **Primitive phase**
   a) primary turning
   b) spontaneous turning
2) **Transitional phase**
   a) spontaneous rolling
   b) deliberate rolling
3) **Mature phase**
   a) automatic rolling

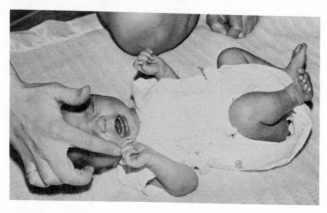

Fig 5-28 Rooting.

Primary Turning

The development of rolling is initiated by head turning. Rolling depends upon and facilitates the ability of head and trunk to move segmentally. Segmentation begins with head turning on shoulders and progresses to upper trunk turning on lower trunk and reverse. The neonate adapts protective and survival behaviors to develop the strategies which differentiate between head and trunk segments.

During the time when primitive posture and movement strategies are influencing protective behaviors, the neonate in prone adapts fetal responses of head dorsiflexion and turns his face from the source of stimulation.[2,6,9] Protective head turning, which accounts for initiation of extension in prone, also serves to initiate rotation in prone.

In supine, head rotation is believed to be adapted from the fetal survival rooting reflex. Rooting is a phasic reflex which occurs in response to tactile stimulation on the side of the face.[7] The accommodation is a snapping of the mouth with head rotation toward the source of stimulation. The reflex is adapted to search and take the nipple into the mouth for nourishment. Head rotation stimulates the labyrinths and activates neck proprioceptors. Neck rotation of rooting becomes a habitual pattern as it is repeated by the infant as spontaneous head turning associated with hunger.

Rooting encourages an interaction with, rather than a protection from, the environment as the infant rotates his head toward the source of tactile stimulation.[6,15,16] Interaction from rooting frequently satisfies hunger, and the infant may associate environmental interaction with pleasure, thus encouraging the infant to seek out sources of satisfaction. This primitive form of association may serve as an underlying motivating force for the baby to move his body through space and interact with the environment. Repeated primary head turning in supine creates opportunity for neck rotation muscle groups to be activated and prepared for strategies which move the body in space.[8,11,13] However, primary head turning is not a sufficient force to facilitate muscle groups which turn both the head and trunk for spontaneous turning leading to rolling.

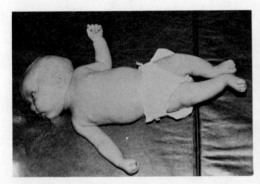

Fig 5-29 Asymmetrical Posture.

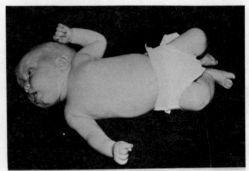

Fig 5-30 Arching.

Spontaneous Turning

Spontaneous turning requires additional influence from reflexes and muscle actions in order to begin to move the body as a unit. Several reflexes interact in the supine posture to activate muscle groups and develop primitive turning strategies. Spontaneous turning combines primary head turning, asymmetrical tonic neck reflex, an occasional Moro reflex, tonic labyrinthine reflex, as well as generalized neonatal movements and tension between muscle groups. As a result, the body may arch and appear to initiate rolling from back to side.[6,10,15] Most significantly, repetition of head turning in supine further facilitates neck proprioceptors and adapts the rooting reflexive behavior to a higher level asymmetrical tonic neck reflex.[5,6,7]

The asymmetrical tonic neck reflex is a tonic response which distributes primitive postural tone asymmetrically along the midline axis of the body. When the baby turns his head to the side, postural tone is distributed in opposite strategies on either side of the midline, ie, extensor tone along the face side of the body and flexor tone along the skull side.[7] Asymmetrical distribution of tone originates from neck proprioceptive assimilations. Trunk and extremity musculature are affected by neck actions, setting a movement strategy by which neck action affects trunk motion. Therefore, this strategy can be adapted to rotate the trunk by initiating neck action.

Hirt[17] proposes that the tonic neck reflexes represent an autonomous component which underlies the rotary body movements of turning or rolling. During the time when the infant assumes the asymmetrical posture, weight-bearing on the supporting surface is still generally distributed on the face side of the body. Pressure from the supporting surface along the face side of the body results in increased tactile and proprioceptive feedback on the side toward which the head is turned. After repeated sensory assimilations from asymmetrical changes in body position, the baby adapts the tendency to turn toward sources of sensory input experienced with rooting behavior and moves from supine to side lying.

The supine position is also influenced by extensor tone from the tonic labyrinthine reflex, which facilitates head dorsiflexion and extension in supine.[6,16] Head dorsiflexion in supine,

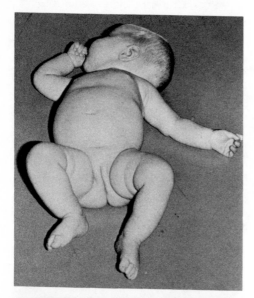

Fig 5-31,32,33 Neck Righting.

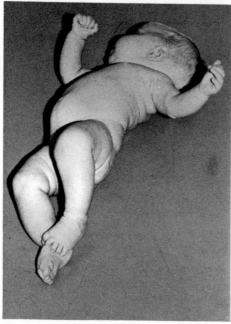

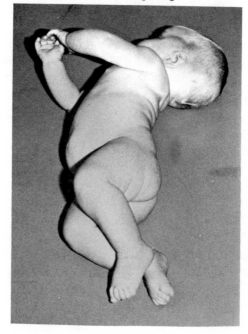

combined with asymmetrical postures, facilitates spinal extension so that the baby lifts the shoulder on the occipital side from the supporting surface and may turn to side lying. As the infant approaches side lying, the tonic labyrinthine reflex influences tonal changes. The body has changed its position in space from a supine to sidelying posture.

The primitive rolling pattern is actually initiated by extensor-flexor movements rather than from rotation between body segments. However, the result is a generalized accommodation of turning toward the source of cutaneous and subcutaneous stimulation following head turning.[16] A primitive strategy develops from integration of sensory feedback from the tactile and pressure stimulation to one side of the body, proprioception from neck musculature together with feedback from the body moving to a new position. The strategy is available to adapt to neck righting so that neck rotation will turn the body.

Primitive preparation for rolling also occurs in prone. As prone behaviors are repeated, extension expands distally and the infant extends his head and lifts the upper portions of the body from the supporting surface. As he turns in the prone supported position, the asymmetrical tonic neck reflex may facilitate extensor tone on one side of the body and flexor tone on the other. Changes in distribution of tone affects a primitive weight shift. As a result, the baby moves laterally, and stability from bilateral support may be lost. Thus, the baby falls to the side and may suddenly turn to supine. He has not truly rolled from prone to supine, but the spontaneous change in position from prone to supine is associated with prone neck extension, head turning and asymmetrical extremity postures. Co-activation of upper body extension against gravity and upper extremity participation in rolling are necessary to fully develop rotation during the transitional phase.[8]

Spontaneous Rolling

As the infant repeats turning patterns in both prone and supine, the influences of transitional vertical and rotational righting reactions and additional contact from the environment results in modifications of the primitive turning processes. As the baby enters the transitional phase, primitive strategies are modified by neck righting reactions and extremity push from prone to develop spontaneous rolling. Spontaneous rolling occurs when the baby turns one body segment; the rotation placed upon the central body axis evokes spontaneous turning by the remaining segments to follow the direction of rotation. Spontaneous rolling facilitates development of underlying rotational chain reactions.

Spontaneous rolling begins in supine when the baby rotates his head, transmits the stimulus for turning to the rest of his body, and rolls to side lying. Sensory assimilations are received from labyrinths as the head moves and from neck proprioceptors as neck muscles are activated and vertebral segments rotated. Underlying rotational neck righting mechanisms facilitate a spontaneous rolling accommodation. Neck righting activates groups of neck flexors and extensors through a full range of rotation.[8,10] By chain reaction, the stimulus from neck righting is transmitted to the trunk. According to the spiraling process, actions from primitive turning are recalled and the baby flexes his trunk in order to automatically follow and align with his head. Rotation between trunk segments has not developed sufficiently to transmit rotational muscle actions, but the righting principle of head and trunk alignment prevails so that lower level flexor reactions (of the trunk) are used to adapt to higher level rotational components of the neck.

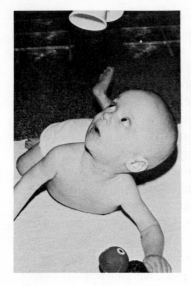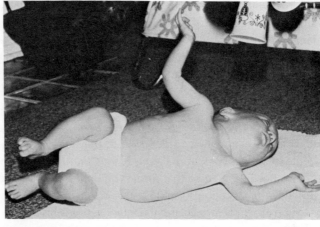

Fig 5-34,35 Push from Prone.

Spontaneous rolling to sidelying occasionally results in log rolling supine to prone. If the baby vigorously elicits rolling to sidelying, the momentum and gravity may carry through, so that the head and trunk move in log fashion to prone. Some babies may also adapt head and upper trunk extension which has been developing in prone so that from sidelying to prone neck and trunk extension are used to complete a spontaneous rolling pattern. In either case, strategies from lower or higher level behaviors are being adapted to modify rolling-to-sidelying to rolling-to-prone. The baby experiences sensory feedback from moving through a complete rolling pattern and achieving a complete change position in space. However, rotational righting chain mechanisms need to be further developed and adapted to smooth strategies for rolling supine-to-prone.

Further development of rotation between body segments comes about with modification of primitive prone turning behaviors. The baby in prone has acquired the ability to raise head and trunk progressively further from the supporting surface and to support on-elbows and on-hands. Increased midline stability in supported prone postures modifies the effect of asymmetrical distribution of tone previously associated with head turning. The baby can combine mobility and stability in supported prone posture to rock from side-to-side on arms and to turn his head without interrupting the symmetry in prone. As he turns his head and rocks side-to-side, neck rotation from head turning is transmitted to rotate the upper trunk, while lower trunk, serving as an anchor to the supporting surface, remains in position. The lower body segments are maintained in extension for stability, which provides a necessary ingredient for segmentation between upper and lower trunk. Rotation can be activated in the upper trunk by chain reaction from the neck because trunk flexors and extensors have been activated and co-activated against gravity in preparation for acting together in rotation.[8,11]

The arms in prone weight-bearing play a major role in transmitting the effect of neck rotation to rotate upper trunk. The lateral movement associated with primitive asymmetrical prone postures is adapted to shifting weight between upper extremities while supported. First attempts at rocking sideways are accompanied by lateral movement to distribute weight from side-to-side. However, these attempts serve to combine mobility with stability around the shoulders so that the arms can move in relation to the trunk as well as support the trunk. The upper extremities can push the upper trunk into rotation while the lower trunk provides stability. The baby plays at combining rotation mobility with midline stability as he rocks. When he integrates prone head turning with upper extremity pushing, the baby rotates head on trunk, pushes with one arm, elicits slight rotation within the trunk and spontaneously rolls prone to supine. Rolling is considered spontaneous when the rolling pattern cannot be interrupted by the baby once turning has initiated the process. When the baby pushes off, he loses control from prone extension-upper extremity support. He quickly aligns head with trunk, using the supporting surface for control, allowing momentum to carry him through the pattern. Expanding rotational righting to include body righting on body reactions is in process at this point, but the reactions are not sufficiently developed to control the complete prone to supine rolling sequence.

In supine, body righting on body reactions develop further as neck righting is modified by the strategies developing with prone rolling. As the child turns his head and approaches sidelying, he begins to prepare for a prone posture. He differentiates the pushing strategy which moved his trunk by abducting the arm with elbow extended and pulling upper trunk toward prone, slightly ahead of the lower trunk. As he reaches sidelying, he extends neck and trunk in anticipation of prone. Pulling with the upper extremity combined with extension of neck and trunk elongates the trunk causing rotation to occur between upper and lower segments. The trunk rights itself and aligns trunk segments with the head in prone.[8] Neck righting reactions are modified to body righting on body reactions combining neck rotation with extremity participation and trunk elongation. As a result neck rotation facilitates upper

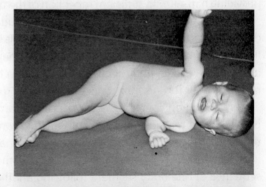

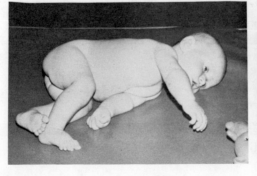

Fig 5-36,37,38 Pulling With Arm.

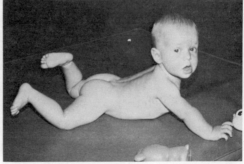

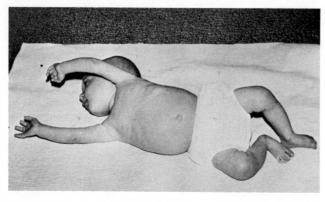

Fig 5-39 Push from Supine.

trunk rotation which facilitates lower trunk rotation instead of turning the body as a whole.

Body righting within the central axis is expanded by lower extremity activity in supine similar to the way in which upper extremity activity in prone modified neck righting. Bridging in supine develops co-activation of pelvic muscle groups against gravity and prepares for combining with rotation. Rotation can be combined when bridging is modified to half bridging. As soon as sides of the body are differentiated and weight can be shifted by combining mobility and stability with support, the baby may flex only one lower extremity and bridge. The effect of the lower extremity push is to rotate the lower trunk on the upper trunk, thereby activating muscle groups for rotation, rotating vertebral segments and promoting segmentation within the trunk.[8] Proprioceptive feedback from changing distribution of lower body muscle tone and pressure adds to the baby's information about rotation within the central axis and movement around the midline. The baby will often play in half-bridging providing himself with sufficient repetition of the pattern to make it useful for deliberate rolling.

In addition, expansion of rotation in a caudal direction means that derotation can be demonstrated. If rotation of one body segment is imposed upon another (example — head on trunk, lower trunk on upper trunk, etc) the other segment automatically rotates in the same direction to re-align body segments. Derotation has been described as an untwisting[12] of the body in order to undo this effect of imposed rotation.

The derotation concept plays a part in imporving the quality of spontaneous rolling once body righting reactions and accompanying segmentation have developed. When the baby rotates one segment, the other segments automatically follow in a smooth sequence, perfecting the chain reaction component. During the time that spontaneous rolling predominates, the sequence of one body segment following another cannot be interrupted by the baby; once initiated the pattern is always completed and position is changed. The sequence of head, upper trunk, lower trunk develops during spontaneous rolling by means of maturation of body righting on body reactions.[7,11,12] The sequence becomes available for use and modification in deliberate rolling.

Deliberate Rolling

Deliberate rolling allows the baby to purposely move himself through space with anticipation of the outcomes of his actions. He combines rotational body righting reactions with

106

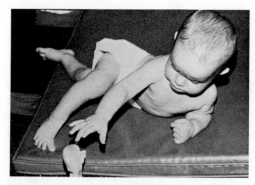

Fig 5-40 Deliberate Rolling.

Fig 5-41 Sidelying with Support.

extremity actions and moves himself between supine and prone, prone and supine at will. His rolling pattern is characterized by rotation between body segments coordinated with extremity movement from one supported posture to another. Rolling can be initiated from any segment of the body.[16] In addition, the change in distribution of pressure to the body surface from the supporting surface elicits a vertical body righting on head reaction.[7] As the baby rolls to his side and localizes pressure from the floor to a more confined area of the body, he automatically rights his head toward vertical facilitating lateral flexion.

In supine, the head is turned, followed by combined upper trunk rotation and pulling of upper trunk with arm, followed by rotating and pushing or pulling of lower trunk with leg. Or, the baby may initiate rolling from supine by means of the lower extremity pulling to rotate the lower trunk followed by rotation of the upper trunk and head. The extremities lead the body in preparation for support to secure the new positions.

In prone, the child initiates rolling with head turning, trunk rotation, and upper extremity push. As the child approaches a side position, he anticipates supine and reaches back with his arm to seek support. He may also push or pull with his lower extremity to roll from prone to supine.

Rotation within the central axis and extremity participation controls posture and movement in free rolling patterns. All rolling does not depend on head movement, as rolling can be initiated from any body segment. The extremities are free to lead or follow as well as be available to protect and support if needed. Generally, the extremity strategies developed with prone-to-supine spontaneous rolling (pushing) are differentiated and adapted to supine-to-prone deliberate rolling (reaching), and spontaneous supine-to-prone strategies are adapted to deliberate prone-to-supine roll. As the baby combines the full range of pushing and reaching with extremities to initiate and control rolling, the extremities are further differentiated from trunk movement.

Along with deliberate rolling, the child develops an ability to stop the rolling pattern at any point within the sequence. The compulsory nature of spontaneous rolling is modified to roll to sidelying by combining vertical-rotational strategies about the midline and by calling up support-protective reactions of the extremities. The child cannot only deliberately initiate rolling but can also stop the process at will. Integration of vertical righting reactions with rotational patterns during deliberate rolling brings the child again into positions which allow extremities to adapt protective reactions and reach out to stop, thus modifying the rolling patterns. The extremity support reactions which accompany protective-reaching patterns are used by the child to support himself in any desired sidelying position between supine and prone.

Acquisition of sidelying provides the child with a new position in which to play. Sidelying also contributes to further development of rotation around the midline. The child can stabilize in sidelying with an upper extremity and rotate the lower body, or he can stabilize with a lower extremity and rotate upper body. The effect of combining rotation and lateral flexion (vertical righting), using extremity support, provides a postural set as background to initiate rotation-counter-rotation patterns about the midline with distal fixation from the extremities.

Playing in sidelying with extremity support also facilitates patterns of movement around proximal joints that eventually contribute to proximal control of distal extremity movement. For example, as the child supports on extremities, the effect of upper trunk rotation back toward supine while the upper extremity is reaching toward prone in support is a higher level differentiation between extremity and trunk. The outcome of the shoulder moving back while the extremity is positioned forward will be adapted to a strategy for control of limb movement forward by a counter movement of the shoulder[8] used with reaching. Differentiation of extremities from trunk as well as trunk segments from each other develops freely moving rolling patterns controlled within the central axis as well as proximal control of extremities, which characterize the automatic rolling of the mature phase.

Fig 5-42 Automatic Rolling.

Automatic Rolling

Automatic rolling is characterized by the ability to move freely, initiating the rolling pattern from any body segment and from any point within the range between supine and prone. Both the movement of automatic rolling itself and any intermediate sidelying postures are controlled by blended strategies resulting from automatic balance reactions. Balance reactions provide an internal means of control around the central axis during rolling or in sidelying positions, thus freeing the extremities from support during position changes. The child develops balance reactions by adapting the transitional rotation-counter-rotation strategies to mature equilibrium reactions which make use of rotation-counter-rotation patterns without support, but with assist from the extremities. In addition, transitional vertical righting reactions combined with rotation are available for adaptation to mature midline stability reactions also providing internal control. The sensory assimilations from the supporting surface to one side of the body as well as movement back and forth through space during deliberate rolling play a major role in adapting combined vertical-rotational righting reactions to midline stability-equilibrium reactions used to control rolling and to function in a sidelying position.

With automatic rolling, the child differentiates rotation-counter-rotation from deliberate rolling to freely rotate one body segment in one direction and balance the rotation by counter-rotating another body segment in the opposite direction; thus, shoulder and hip on the same side are moving in opposite directions. The movement-counter-movement strategy which results provides internal control within the central axis to monitor speed and range of automatic rolling appropriately. In addition, rotation-counter-rotation serves as a postural set to maintain a balance between body segments so that the child can maintain sidelying without relying on extremities for external postural control.

With internal postural control intact, the extremities, especially the hands, are free to play and to lead body segments through a variety of automatic rolling patterns. As the extremities continue to lead, they will begin to cross the midline of the body during rolling further developing integration at the midline. Crossing the midline is dependent upon well developed midline stability reactions and equilibrium in rolling as well as other positions. Automatic rolling provides readily available blended strategies to move through space with control, plus a well developed rotory component to adapt to higher level behaviors and activities.

The development process of rolling is another illustration of the spiraling concept of spatiotemporal adaptation. During the primitive phase, lower level posture and movement behaviors provide opportunities for somatosensory reception of the body in motion. These basic experiences are adapted by the self-system to initiate rotational/vertical righting of the transitional period. As the visual/auditory perceptions from the environment are being integrated with somatosensory receptions from turning and rolling, the baby begins to add new dimensions to his perceptual repertoire. Somatosensory awareness results. With the acquisition of rotational/vertical righting and somatosensory awareness, the more primitive behaviors are differentiated so that essential elements of stability and mobility are maintained and adapted to higher level rolling patterns.

As rolling is repeated, the youngster adapts the process and acquires the ability to respond to visual and auditory stimulation from the environment. The baby automatically sequences his body to roll toward the source of environmental stimulation, thus rolling becomes directed by cues from the environment. Rolling provides the opportunity for the baby to increase his interactions with the environment by promoting a means for him to move out into space and enlarge his world.

Standing/Walking

Standing and walking represent achievement and function at the highest level of vertical antigravity postures. The child's self-motivation toward standing and walking has led him through previous behaviors in pursuit of upright, characteristic of the uniqueness of man. At each stage during development, the child has used his extremities to support the body before entrusting control for movement to the body itself. Extremities play a significant role in upright postures even though ultimately most of the control comes from within.

As soon as the first opportunity appears, after awareness of upright has developed, the baby grasps the opportunity and pulls to stand. The baby pulls up on absolutely everything often without regard for whether the object will support him or not. His interest is in pulling up and walking around objects, not the objects themselves. He is engrossed in selecting appropriate posture and movement strategies from his lower level accomplishments to adapt to his standing/walking goal. The baby soon lets go of objects and delights in pure standing. He will hold on again to move or call up a lower level, more secure posture for movement by creeping. Finally he associates moving with standing and initiates independent steps. The youngster propels forward with delight — falling, getting up, walking, and falling again. Walking is such a joy that once established, the child will initiate the whole process of getting to stand to move rather than roll or creep, even to nearby objects.

The ability to maintain and move the body in the upright standing position is dependent upon delicate alterations in balancing which originate with tactile and proprioceptive stimulation of the soles of the feet of the fetus and neonate.[15,18] Fetal and newborn accommodations possess several reflexes that are characteristic of lower extremity posture and reciprocation. Through the spiraling process, primitive motor accommodations are modified and integrated

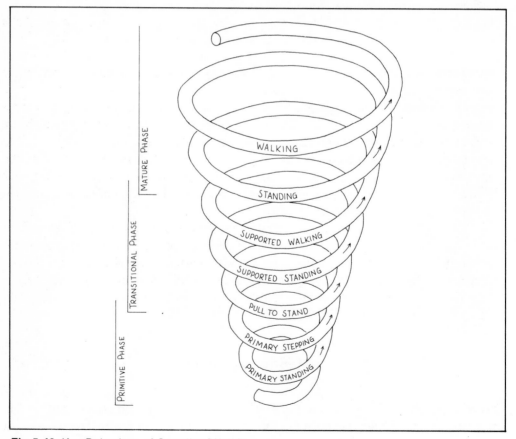

Fig 5-43 Key Behaviors of Standing/Walking.

110

for functional bipedal activities. Somatosensory integration from influences of primitive actions and adaptation of fetal responses serves as the foundation for the developmental progression of standing/walking.

The key behaviors of standing/walking include:

a) **Primitive phase** — primary standing and primary stepping;

b) **Transitional phase** — pull to stand, supported standing, and supported walking;

c) **Mature phase** — standing and walking.

Primary Standing

Primary standing provides the neonate with experiences of supported upright postures. The neonate adapts fetal axial extension of foot contact reflexes to the primitive upright posture. The soles of the feet of the fetus are sensitive to stimulation by 11 weeks gestation.[3] Contact with the wall of the uterus may provide the necessary stimulus for lower limb extension which is adapted to tonic extension reflexes after birth.[6] Two tonic reflexes which activate lower extremity extension patterns are the extensor thrust (magnet) reflex[7,15,16] and primary standing[5,16] The extensor thrust reflex causes extension of the lower extremities from proprioceptive input to the soles of the feet when the infant is in a flexed supine position. Primary standing causes extension when the infant is held upright and the soles contact the supporting surface. Early experiences in orienting to a vertical posture and responding to

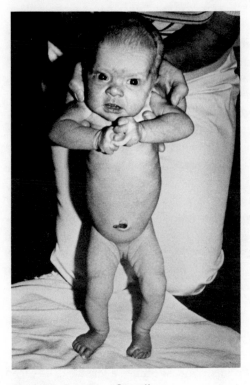

Fig 5-44 Primitive Standing.

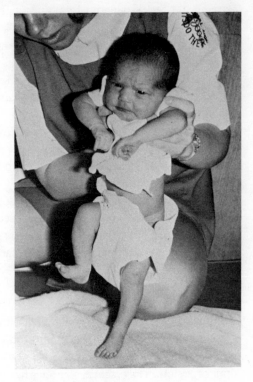

Fig 5-45 Primary Stepping.

pressure with extension from tonic reflexes provides the foundation for holding strategies for the development of weight-bearing. Through the adaptation process, primary standing will be modified and support strategies developed for standing.

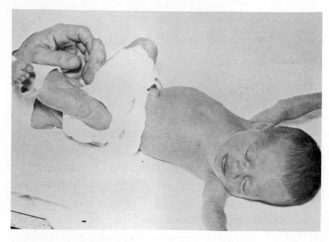

Fig 5-46 Crossed Extension.

Primary Stepping

Fetal foot contact reflexes are also modified by phasic reflexes which mobilize lower extremity reciprocal patterns. Primary stepping activates flexion-extension movements of the lower extremities when the infant is held in vertical, allowing feet to touch the supporting surface, and also when soles of the feet are appropriately stimulated in other positions. In the supported upright posture, the legs first extend and then mobilize into an automatic walking flexion-extension reciprocal pattern as the neonate is tilted forward.[5,16] The neonate will seem to walk and even step over objects; however, the pattern is characterized by total flexion and extension with each step and will need to be modified for true walking. The apparent ability to step over objects is controlled by the placing reflex.[5,16] Placing occurs when the neonate is held in vertical suspension and the dorsum of the foot is stimulated by an object, such as a table edge. The neonate will totally flex the extremity to step onto or over the object, followed by total extension of the extremity.[16]

The reciprocal actions contributing to stepping in vertical occur in a similar manner in other positions. In the supine position an infant accommodates to tactile input on the soles of the feet with total flexion synergies of the flexor withdrawal.[7,16] Crossed extension is elicited by placing one leg into extension and tactually stimulating the sole of the foot on the extended leg. The response is flexion of the opposite leg followed by extension-adduction.[16] Primary crawling (Bauers) provides the reciprocal pattern of flexion on one side and extension on the opposite side following tactile pressure contact to the sole of the foot in prone.[5,6]

Primitive phasic reflexes which mobilize for reciprocation and tonic reflexes which prepare for extremity support reactions are forerunners to standing/walking strategies. However, the primitive phenomena is absorbed while the infant develops strategies necessary to control the upright posture. The essential elements from the primitive phase remain available to be called for higher level transitional and mature behaviors with control.

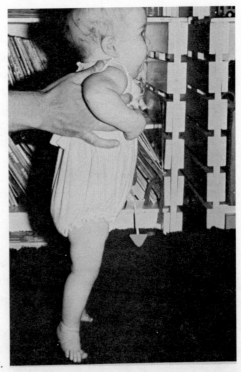

Fig 5-47 Positive Support.

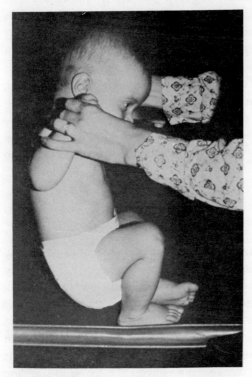

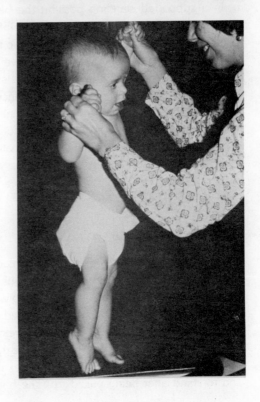

Fig 5-48,49 Pull-to-Stand.

Pull to Stand

With the influence of righting and protective-support reactions of the transitional phase, the baby calls forth the acquired process he experienced being "pulled to sit" and adapts the process to being "pulled to stand." Modification of "pull to sit" to "pull to stand" is influenced by adapting the positive supporting reaction.[7] Positive supporting is elicited when the infant is held in the upright position and moved down toward the environmental surface. The position and movement downward results in protective extension of the legs. Contact of the ball of the foot with the supporting surface places a stretch on the intrinsic musculature of the foot which increases the extensor tone throughout the legs and body for support. The infant will stand on his toes and fully develop extensors in the standing position.[14] The positive supporting reaction calls forth primary standing, but now the reaction encompasses extensors of the neck and trunk as well as the lower extremities. Total extension of positive supporting plays an important role in preparing muscles and joints of the lower extremities for their eventual support functions.[13] In addition, positive support, combined with modifications of the infant's supine posture, are influential in developing pull-to-stand. The infant has differentiated the supine flexed posture with bridging in other postures and movements which allow him to partially flex knees and hips with soles of feet remaining on the supporting surface. Now as the infant is pulled to sit, pressure to soles of feet is increased and positive supporting elicited. The infant pulls to stand. As the infant is pulled to stand and held in that position, the head and shoulders begin to align slightly forward of the pelvis in antigravity postures, further augmenting postural strategies and somatosensory awareness of the body in space.[2]

In a supported standing position the baby may begin to bounce up and down. The movement within the range of standing reinforces stability, since bouncing provides a stretch to the antigravity muscles and resistance to movement against gravity.[14] Bouncing dampens the total extension pattern of the positive supporting reaction so that the feet assume a plantigrade position with the soles and heels contacting the supporting surface. Co-activation of the lower portions of the body is enhanced and the heel-toe contact with the supporting surface prepares the feet for their eventual support role.[2]

Being pulled to stand provides new spatial dimensions. The visual perceptions from the upright position is associated with the somatosensory awareness of the body in space. Visual perceptions and somatosensory awareness are associated for eventual adaptation to pulling self to stand.

Supported Standing

As development progresses in a cephalocaudal direction, the baby integrates previously acquired upper extremity support reactions with newly developed extension of lower body segments. He begins to maintain standing with support from a variety of objects and to seek supported standing. To acquire supported standing, the baby first repeats experiences of being pulled to stand. As he does, he develops a pattern of moving to an upright posture. In addition, as his arms are held he recalls the upper extremity support patterns used to maintain creeping and sitting. He associates upper extremity support to maintain his posture as he holds on to stand after being pulled up. The baby gains security in newly discovered standing

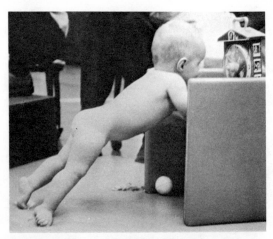

Fig 5-50 Pulling-to-Stand/bilateral linear.

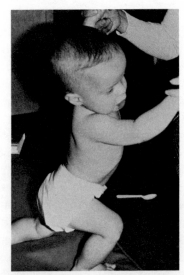

Fig 5-51 Pulling-to-Stand/
Weight-shift.

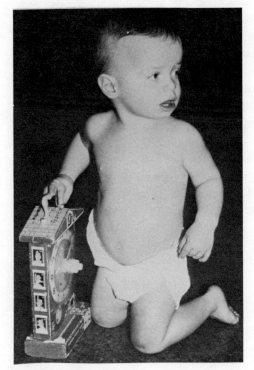

Fig 5-52 Kneel.

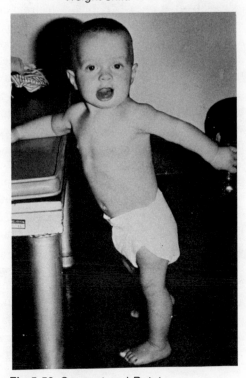

Fig 5-53 Support and Rotate.

postures by holding on to a familiar and trusted person. Now when he is placed in standing, he adapts upper extremity support reactions from previous behaviors with recently developed lower extremity extension-support reactions. The youngster experiences being held and holding on to maintain standing by supporting on objects.

Being pulled to stand, held in stand, and supporting on objects to stand significantly triggers the baby's quest for upright postures. As he moves about his environment on all-fours, he is highly motivated to pull self to stand. The baby creeps toward objects and, with both extremities, pulls himself upward in a bilateral linear fashion. Pulling to stand requires integration of vertical and rotational righting reactions and combined mobility-stability muscle functions. Upper extremities are used to assist with pulling to stand and stabilize while lower extremities move toward standing. The upper extremity stability strategy combined with lower extremity mobility provides a postural set.

Once the baby has attained standing, he will support himself with the upper portions of the body achieving the supported standing behavior by himself.[2] When the youngster has pulled to supported standing he hangs on with both hands and calls up previously acquired bouncing actions. Again, the baby bounces up and down combining mobility and stability in weight bearing with distal segment fixed in support. He begins to differentiate lower extremity segments from each other, further preparing the feet for their support role.

The baby's bilateral linear pattern for pulling to stand is modified by bouncing in standing and by calling forth experiences from bridging in supine. He develops kneeling as an intermediate step between creeping and pulling to standing. The baby differentiates complete extension of the lower extremities which developed from positive supporting influence on pull to stand. He recalls the pattern from bridging which combined his extension with knee flexion and pulls himself to the kneeling position before standing. Kneeling with support provides opportunity to laterally shift weight to one lower extremity and free the extremity to move into half-kneeling. From half-kneeling, the youngster shifts weight back to the foot, extends the lower extremity, and pushes to stand with arms and one leg; the other leg follows into the standing posture. Association and differentiation of bridging, kneeling, and pulling to stand augments posture and movement strategies needed for further development in upright postures.

In the supported standing position, the baby may let go with one hand and rotate the upper portions away from his support, thus combining rotation with vertical righting in standing. In addition, support with only one arm frees the other arm to interact with toys in supported standing. The youngster will throw toys to the floor, motivating himself to lower his body to the floor and providing opportunity to practice pull to standard supported standing. He hangs on with both hands assuming a squat position, thus further enhancing stability of the more proximal joints. Squatting and kneeling enables the youngster to have an opportunity to experience a less demanding upright posture, as the center of gravity is closer to the supporting surface. The more secure squatting/kneeling positions encourage the child to play with toys in these semi-upright positions. The experiences of supported standing, squatting and kneeling, pulling up and letting go, combining rotation with vertical postures, and generally beginning to differentiate sides of the body prepare for moving in vertical postures.

Supported Walking

In the supported standing position, the youngster adapts reciprocal patterns to walk around objects as well as to walk with hands held. The reciprocal walking pattern is an adaptation of earlier stepping movements, but now is accomplished with increased control of the upper

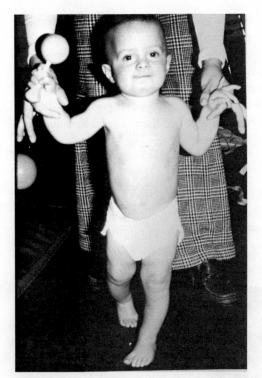 

Fig 5-54 Supported Walking. **Fig 5-55** Cruising.

body and lateral weight shift,[2,13] requiring only a minimal amount of external support. As the youngster repeats experiences of supported standing and walking, midline stability and equilibrium reactions mature until the child can stand and walk independently.

Early supported walking patterns are experienced when the baby is held by both hands. With hands held, needed external stability is provided, and the baby can superimpose mobility upon the supported upright posture. As the baby leans forward into support, the feet follow in reciprocal steps to maintain the upright position, and the baby now walks with support. Early supported walking represents a milestone in the maturation of spatiotemporal adaptation as the child had acquired the ability to maintain and move from the upright posture with support. He has taken his first step out from standing, representing achievement of the beginning of final stages in his quest for upright autonomy.

In addition to walking with hands held, the child also experiences supported walking in the upright by holding onto objects such as tables and chairs. As a child hangs onto an object, he begins to cruise. Cruising can be compared to the earlier experiences of pivoting the body in a circle from the prone trunk-centered position. In pivoting, the baby reached to one side with the upper extremities and "pulled" the body to follow around in a circle. Now, in the supported upright position, the child reaches out to one side, with upper and lower extremities, while stabilizing with his weight on opposite extremities. As the child places the extremities laterally, he shifts support and simultaneously pulls the body sideways. The adapted pattern develops into sidestepping for cruising around objects.

The repertoire of posture and movement strategies experienced during the transitional phase are integrated into the self-system to be used for adaptation to mature unsupported postures. In the process of adapting, the child will repeat previously acquired patterns of mobility/stability in order to differentiate the essential elements for higher level patterns of internal support. Visual perceptions of the body in space are associated with somatosensory awareness and the youngster may begin to make judgments about his abilities to move within his spatiotemporal environment, thus enhancing somatosensory perception. Visual and somatosensory perceptions complement each other for the foundation needed to move out and interact with the environment during the mature phase.

Standing

Experiences in supported standing postures and kneel-standing enhance mature midline stability and equilibrium reactions so that the child may be able to stand unsupported. With independent standing, stimulation from the feet as the sole contact with environmental surfaces gains importance for orientation to space. The importance of foot contact reactions is

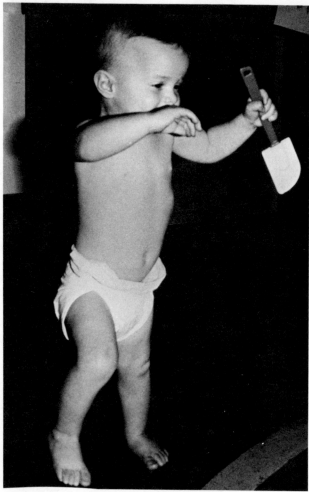

Fig 5-56 Independent Standing.

Fig 5-57 Squat.

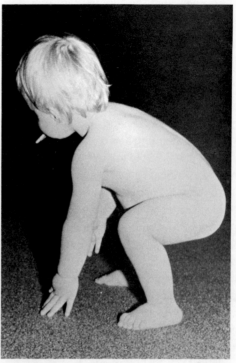

Fig 5-58 Getting to Stand.

emphasized by Twitchell.[3] Twitchell states that the foot contact reactions are more elaborate and dexterous than the crude neonatal reflexes. The primitive reflexes have been integrated and modified so that now the lightest touch on the foot causes an immediate adjustment and placing reactions appropriate to the external stimulus. Adaptation of primitive reflexes to foot contact reactions and acquisition of somatosensory awareness of the feet promotes vertical upright orientation of the body in space. To reinforce upright orientation, a baby will frequently look at his feet while he stands and steps. In addition, delicate instinctive foot grasping reactions enhance orientation for prehending or perceiving the environment in standing. As these experiences are adapted, somatosensory awareness from the feet is integrated with higher-level neural organization of visual perceptions. Adaptation of visual perceptions with somatosensory awareness facilitates the needed somatosensory perceptions for the youngster to achieve independent standing and walking.

During the mature phase, the child frequently assumes an unsupported squat position, maintaining squatting for several minutes while playing with toys. Squatting reinforces necessary stability of the distal portion of the lower extremities and enhances midline stability and equilibrium reactions for upright posture.[14] In addition to squatting without support, the youngster develops independent kneel-standing. He lets go in kneeling to play with toys and kneels unsupported. Both unsupported squat and kneel-stand align midline with the center of gravity while providing an opportunity to experience a less demanding upright posture. The center of gravity is closer to the supporting surface, and the child's base is wider than in the standing position. Although the youngster has acquired the higher level bipedal posture, the

119

lower level squat and kneel-stand postures are called up to reinforce midline stability and equilibrium reactions for adaptation to the higher level standing supported position.

The first experiences of unsupported standing adapt the wide base of support from squat and kneel-stand. As the youngster is engrossed in the purposeful behavior of standing, he may let go of support objects and stand for a few moments, absorbed in the achievement of the behavior. As he repeats his experiences with independent standing, internal stability is enhanced. The child must constantly adjust his posture to align his center with the center of gravity, thus developing midline stability reactions. The child's previous experiences in supported standing and walking, together with newly acquired independent standing, modifies the pattern used to pull to stand. Supported standing and walking brought forth opportunity to combine rotation and lateral flexion with upright postures. Independent standing increases stability to lower body segments. As stability expands in a caudal direction, rotation of lower segments can be imposed and the base of support narrowed in secure vertical postures. Now when the child in kneel-stand holds on to pull-to-stand, instead of laterally flexing the trunk to free his lower extremity, the youngster shifts weight, rotating the pelvis back, and moves his leg forward to stand. [10] Rotation around the midline contributes to a more narrow base and simultaneous weight-shift and movement forward. Besides modifying the pull-to-stand strategy, the youngster blends movement-countermovement into a strategy of pelvis moving back while lower extremity moves forward. [8] This strategy will be adapted to control lower extremity movement in walking and in adaptation of walking to purposeful activities. In addition, integration of pelvic rotation with trunk extension modifies supported walking. The child is not limited to side-step cruising but can begin to walk from object to object by holding on and reaching out or around with increased mobility within the central axis. The association of expanded reciprocal movements with support and newly acquired independent standing results in independent walking.

Walking

Independent standing is combined with the previously acquired reciprocal steps experienced while being held in standing and when walking around objects. The youngster leans forward and the feet follow in reciprocation to maintain the upright posture. [7] At the beginning of independent steps there is poor integration of posture and forward progression, evidenced by the return of wide base of support, lateral weight shift, quick hopping steps, toe gripping, and excessive arm postures. The emergence of more primitive postures and movements are used to compensate for the lack of mature automatic balance reactions and to again differentiate the essential elements from previous behaviors required to develop mature functioning.

Midline stability reactions developing with standing need to be adapted to moving while standing. In addition, equilibrium reactions will have to be developed to regain alignment with gravity with each step. However, the child is motivated now, even before the mature reactions are sufficiently intact. Fortunately, he can call forth previous mechanisms to support his new-found pleasure, and movement in standing will contribute greatly to developing more mature underlying mechanisms. [2] The child may call up certain elements of lower level prone extensor postures to facilitate necessary trunk stability. He begins to walk with arms flexed and

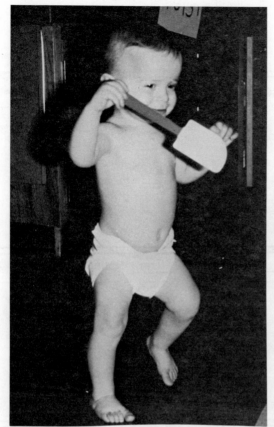

Fig 5-59 Primitive Walking.

Fig 5-60 Mature Walking.

shoulders retracted to increase spinal extension. As the nervous system differentiates trunk extension from shoulder retraction postures, the primitive pattern is modified to a more transitional strategy. The arms begin to extend and abduct in preparation for protection. The arm position is an adaptation of the protective extension reaction.[12] Protective extension posturing of the arms, which was adapted for support in creeping, is now adapted for protection in standing and walking. Adapting previous mechanisms which facilitate development and use of trunk extension and co-activation to enhance midline control against gravity in walking further develops midline stability reactions.

During the time that midline stability reactions are developing by adapting mechanisms which generally increase stability, mobility, particularly rotation, is not easily superimposed on stability in walking. The child's early walking reflects the same strategy as early crawling, creeping, pulling to stand, and walking around objects; the child moves laterally to shift weight to one leg and then moves the opposite leg forward so that he first walks independently with a waddling gait.[12]

The spiraling process continues to be evident with early walking. The youngster may perceive that the environmental demands for walking may sometimes exceed his functional capacities for speed, distance, etc, thus he calls up lower level behaviors of creeping or

Fig 5-61 Developmental Progressions of Purposeful Behaviors*†

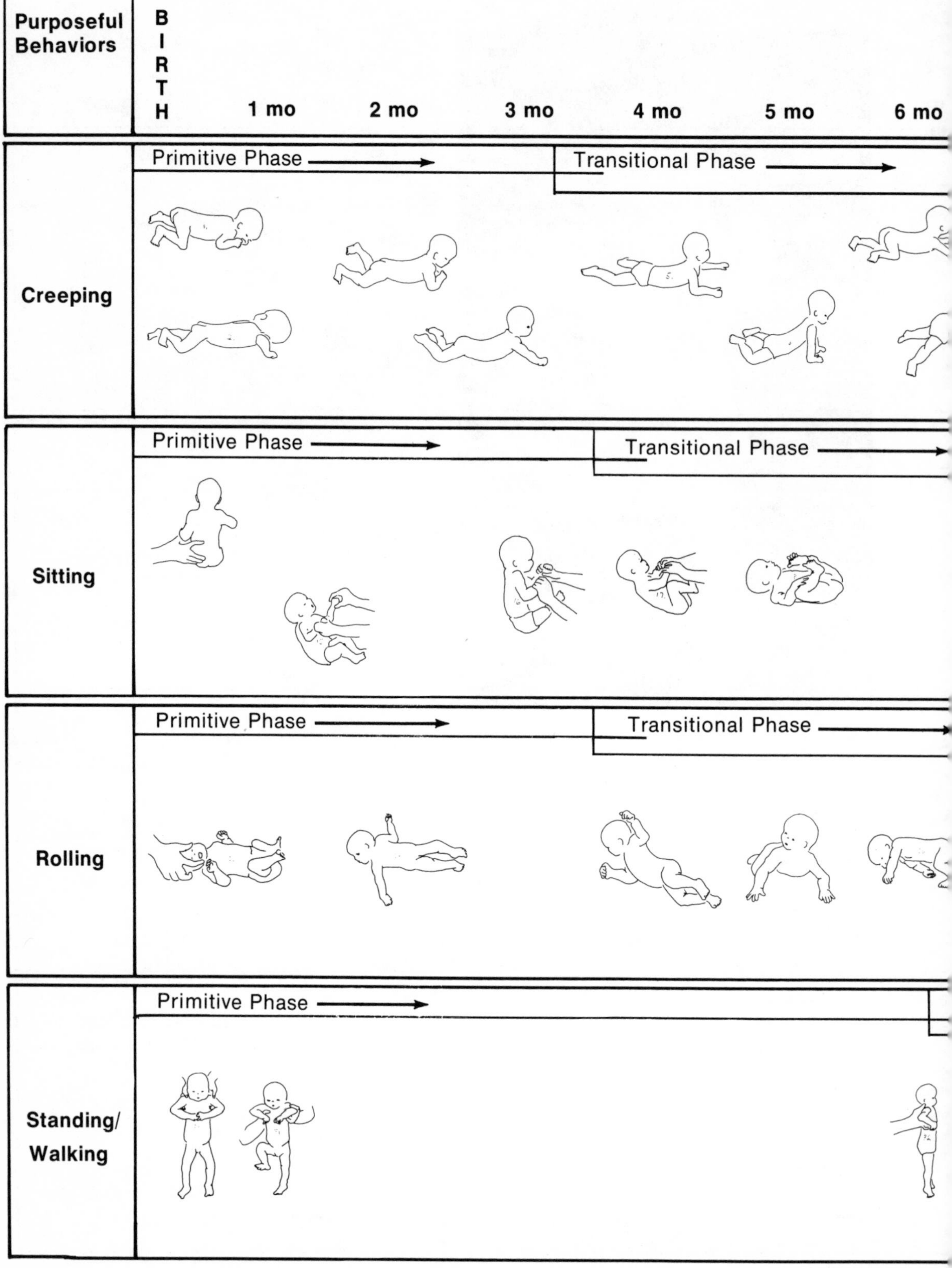

Purposeful Behaviors	BIRTH	1 mo	2 mo	3 mo	4 mo	5 mo	6 mo

Creeping — Primitive Phase ⟶ / Transitional Phase ⟶

Sitting — Primitive Phase ⟶ / Transitional Phase ⟶

Rolling — Primitive Phase ⟶ / Transitional Phase ⟶

Standing/ Walking — Primitive Phase ⟶

* The names of the behaviors illustrated by drawings on this chart can be found accompanying the photographs in Chapter 5.

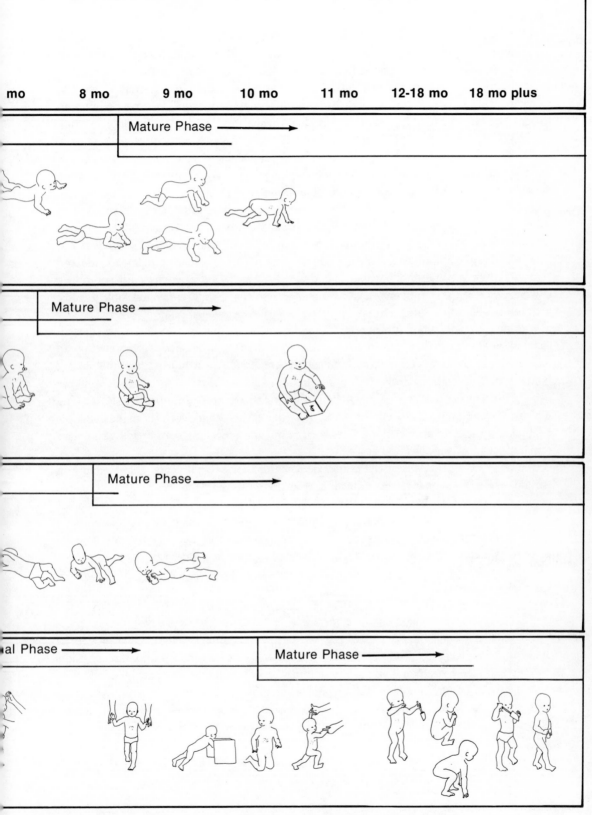

mo 8 mo 9 mo 10 mo 11 mo 12-18 mo 18 mo plus

Mature Phase ⟶

Mature Phase ⟶

Mature Phase ⟶

al Phase ⟶ Mature Phase ⟶

† The primary purpose of this chart is to illustrate the relationships between the key behaviors of each spiral. The specific ages cited for each behavior represent an average age within the normal range for acquiring the behavior.

123

kneel-walking to gain the desired forward progression. As he creeps or kneel-walks quite automatically to get to where he wishes to be, increased midline stability from early walking is combined with expanded rotation about the midline. Creeping and kneel-walking patterns are smoothed out so that the child relies mostly on lower extremities to shift weight and simultaneously move forward to realign the body axis with gravity. The rotation-counter-rotation strategy is needed for equilibrium, both in kneeling and to adapt to standing/walking.

The use of previously acquired behaviors for function under certain circumstances helps the child retain his competence and continue his quest for walking. As he walks and is motivated to stay upright, he associates the higher level strategies which smoothed creeping and kneel-walking with walking. He integrates rotation with midline stability. His arms are lowered and he begins to rotate as he moves forward, decreasing waddling and narrowing his base of support. Equilibrium reactions become available with the advent of rotation-counter-rotation so that he can move more rapidly, change direction, and regain balance whenever it is threatened. Rapid automatic lower extremity movements are controlled proximally. Adapted from patterns to assume standing, the pelvis moves back as the leg moves forward, controlling the speed and range of movement.[8] The upper extremities always remain available to assist with balance and to protect and support whenever balance is lost.

With smooth blending of midline stability and equilibrium reactions as underlying mechanisms for internal postural control, walking is accomplished by simultaneous rotation-counter-rotation and forward movement accompanied by reciprocal arm swing and heel-toe gait.[12,13] Blended midline stability and equilibrium also provide the underlying postural strategies needed to adapt crossing the midline patterns developed with rolling to upright postures. The ability of the extremities to lead body segments in rotation across and away from the midline is controlled by equilibrium reactions. Crossing the midline is necessary for building strategies required for most activities and skills.

The child's walking pattern will continue to mature for several years, culminating in a pattern which is unique to the individual, but encompassing the essential components common to man. Certain elements from standing/walking behavior are available for adaptation to activities and skills such as running, jumping, hopping, skipping, etc. The youngster's ability to assume upright postures also matures over several years. The developmental patterns to assume upright will be discussed and illustrated in Chapter 6.

Summary

The discussion and illustrations of the key behaviors conveys the spiraling process of spatiotempral adaptation. Spiraling represents an unfolding of complex purposeful behaviors by modifying the more primitive posture and movement patterns. Modification of acquired patterns is the primary function of the spiraling process of adaptation. Inherent within the process are the development of neuromusculo-skeletal systems which provide the mechanisms and structures, and sensorimotor-sensory integration which provides the means for functioning.

The child functions as an open-energy system, influencing and being influenced by his own performances and perceptions within the environment. The child's transactions with the environment provide spatiotemporal experiences for maturation and development of a variety of posture and movement strategies. The strategies are integrated and subsequently adapted to purposeful behaviors which become the innate products of spatiotemporal adaptation.

References

1. Jones B: The importance of memory traces of motor efferent discharges for learning skilled movements. Dev Med Child Neurol 16:620, 1974.
2. Hopkins H, Smith H (eds): Willard and Spackman's Occupational Therapy, ed 5. Philadelphia, JB Lippincott Co, 1978, pp 58-80.
3. Twitchell TE: Attitudinal reflexes. The Child with Central Nervous System Deficit. Children's Bureau Pub, US Dept Health, Education, Welfare, Washington, DC, US Government Printing Office, 1965, pp 77-84.
4. Twitchell TE: Normal motor development. The Child with Central Nervous System Deficit. Children's Bureau Pub, US Dept Health, Education & Welfare, Washington DC, US Government Printing Office, 1965, pp 85-89.
5. Andre-Thomas: The neurological examination of the infant. Clinics in Developmental Medicine, no 1. Philadelphia, JB Lippincott Co, 1964.
6. Beintema JD: A neurological study of newborn infants. Clinics in Developmental Medicine, no 28. Philadelphia, JB Lippincott Co, 1968.
7. Fiorentino MR: Reflex Testing Methods for Evaluating C.N.S. Development. Springfield, Illinois, Charles C Thomas Pubs, 1965.
8. Bly L: Lecture Notes, Components of Movement, Neurodevelopmental Treatment Course. Colorado Springs, Colorado, Rocky Mountain Rehabilitation Center, April-May, 1975.
9. Holt K: Movement and child development. Clinics in Developmental Medicine, no 55. Philadelphia, JB Lippincott Co, 1975.
10. Bobath B, Bobath K: Motor Development in Different Types of Cerebral Palsy. London, W Heinemann Med Books, 1975.
11. Bobath K: The motor deficit in patients with cerebral palsy. Clinics in Developmental Medicine, no 23. Philadelphia, JB Lippincott Co, 1966.
12. Milani-Comparetti A, Gidoni E: Routine developmental examination in normal and retarded children. Dev Med Child Neurol 9:631-638, 1967.
13. Bobath B: Abnormal Postural Reflex Activity Caused by Brain Lesion. London, W Heinemann Med Books, 1975.
14. Pearson PH, Williams CE (eds): Physical Therapy Services in the Developmental Disabilities. Springfield, Illinois, Charles C Thomas Pubs, 1972, pp 186-222.
15. Peiper A: Cerebral Function in Infancy and Childhood. New York, Consultants Bureau, 1963.
16. Touwen B: Neurological development in infancy. Clinics in Developmental Medicine, no 58, Philadelphia, JB Lippincott Co, 1976.
17. Hirt S: The tonic neck reflex mechanism in the normal human adult. Am J Phys Med 46:362-368, 1967.
18. Connolly KJ: Mechanisms of Motor Skill Development. New York, Academic Press, 1970.

Chapter Six
Developmental Sequences to Standing

Purposeful behavior has been described according to four goals which children achieve during development: to creep, to sit, to roll, and to stand and walk. Each behavior has its own progression as well as continual influence from other behaviors developing at the same time. Posture and movement strategies developed with each behavior are combined, differentiated, and blended. Selected strategies from each behavior are ultimately integrated into specific patterns used by the child to assume a standing position from supine. The development of sequences to stand takes approximately six years to mature. The effect of the spiraling continuum is evident throughout as transitional strategy combinations are modified for mature blending of strategies. There are no definite norms to determine precisely when a child uses a certain sequence. But rather, the child adapts one pattern to another progressively more demanding pattern. As underlying structures and mechanisms mature, they are adapted to specific behaviors and differentiated for sequences to stand. Observations of children coming to stand affords valuable opportunities to note the way in which a child sequences posture and movement strategies, the synchrony between his use of postural sets and movement flow, and whether or at which point spatiotemporal demands require calling forth lower level strategies to complete the sequence.

The developmental sequences are termed:

1) Pull-up sequence
2) Complete rotation sequence
3) Partial-complete rotation sequence
4) Partial rotation sequence
5) Symmetrical-partial rotation sequence
6) Symmetrical sequence

Pull-up Sequence

Pull-up is the first method used by a baby to get to standing. The pull-up pattern is a modification of creeping adapted to an upright posture.

1) The baby rolls over from supine to prone using rotational righting integrated with vertical righting.

2) Upper extremity support reactions are adapted to support on hands.

3) Weight is shifted laterally to activate the amphibian reaction and the baby adapts vertical righting to get to creeping.

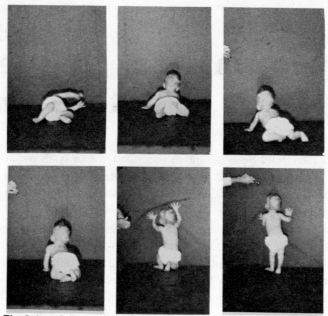

Fig 6-1: a-f Pull-up Sequence.

4) The baby creeps to an object and repeats the sequence used to get to creep.

5) Upper extremity support reactions are adapted to hold onto an object; baby kneels.

6) Weight is shifted either to both upper extremities and baby pulls up with bilateral-linear set until feet are placed flat and weight shifted to stand on feet, or with further maturation.

7) Weight is shifted laterally to one lower extremity, freeing the opposite lower extremity.

8) The free lower extremity moves forward, baby assumes half-kneeling.

9) Weight is shifted to the plantigrade foot, and arms pull body forward and up.

10) Opposite lower extremity follows to join in weight-bearing on feet to stand.

Complete Rotation Sequence

Complete rotation represents the first pattern available to the child to assume standing independently. He adapts the sequence developed with pull-up. As with pull-up, he must first assume the prone position, where development is more advanced for getting to stand.

1) The child rolls over using rotational righting integrated with vertical righting.

2) Upper extremity support reactions are adapted to support on hands.

3) Weight is shifted laterally to activate the amphibian reaction and the baby adapts vertical righting to get to creeping.

4) From creeping, child shifts weight to upper extremities, adapting pull-up pattern from creeping to "hold on" to supporting surface.

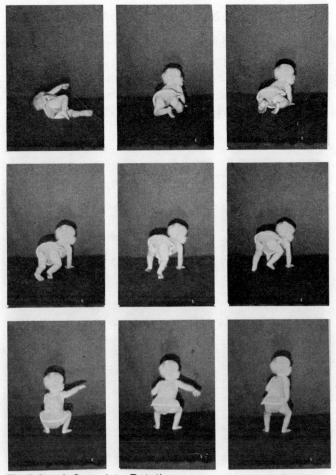

Fig 6-2: a-i Complete Rotation.

5) Weight is either shifted to upper extremities and baby brings both lower extremities to plantigrade position simultaneously in bilateral linear fashion, or with further maturation.

6) Weight is shifted to upper extremities and one lower extremity, freeing the opposite lower extremity from weight-bearing.

7) The free extremity moves to a plantigrade position.

8) Weight is shifted to plantigrade foot and upper extremities as well, freeing other lower extremity.

9) The free extremity moves to plantigrade.

10) Weight is shifted to both lower extremities and the child stands.

11) With maturation, the pattern is modified by movement-countermovement set.

12) The child rolls to prone, supports on arms and brings one leg into standing position, shifts weight and stands up as other leg follows to stand. Maturation of complete rotation leads to modification of the pattern.

Partial-Complete Rotation Sequence

Partial rotation represents a significant change in the child's pattern to get up. Posture and movement strategies have developed sufficiently to get up without using prone to initiate the pattern, although the baby will have to call forth the prone behavior to complete the sequence. Since a child's objective is to get up, initiating the pattern in the direction of getting up represents beginnings of the child's ability to select the most efficient pattern to meet the goal.

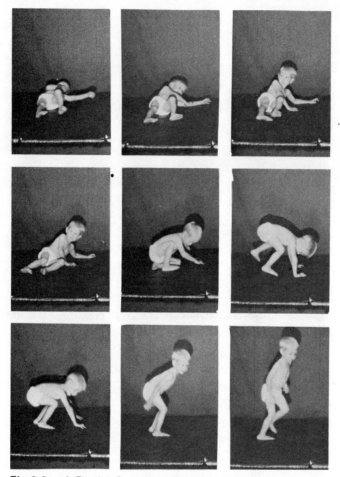

Fig 6-3: a-i Partial-Complete Rotation Sequence.

1) The child rolls toward the prone using rotational-vertiacal righting reactions.

2) As he approaches sidelying, he adapts a protective-support reaction of the upper extremity on that side to stop the complete rotation pattern.

3) From sidelying, he adapts an equilibrium reaction, pushes with supporting arm and pulls with opposite arm up to a sitting position.

4) From sitting, stress becomes a factor. He is unable to complete a forward movement pattern to stand, thus calls forth complete rotation to stand.

5) He rotates toward prone orientation, supports with upper extremities and employs movement-countermovement to bring first one leg, then the other leg into position, shifts weight to feet and stands.

Partial Rotation Sequence

Partial rotation supine to sit becomes more efficient with repetition. The child gains better control over upright posture and is prepared to adapt partial rotation to sit to a process to stand.

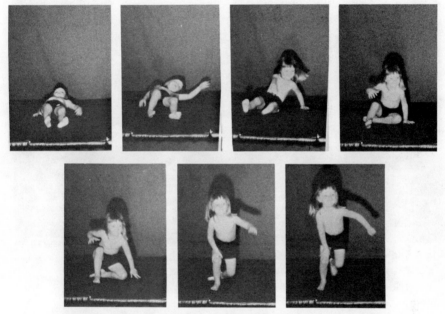

Fig 6-4: a-g Partial Rotation Sequence.

1) The child partially rotates toward sidelying, but rotation is less, due to more influence from vertical righting and direction toward objective of upright.

2) Upper extremity toward supporting surface pushes trunk up toward sitting while opposite extremity pulls.

3) From sitting, child can now continue partial rotation to stand by adapting upper extremity support patterns from complete rotation to partial rotation.

4) He rotates from sitting to one side, supports with arm on supporting surface, and places opposite leg in plantigrade position.

5) With one hand on supporting surface and other hand on knee, he transfers weight to plantigrade foot, pushes on both arms, and stands up.

6) The opposite leg follows to stand and bear weight.

7) With repetition, the child will be able to stand up using partial rotation and push off with one arm, the other arm pulling toward midline with an adaptation of equilibrium. Maturation of equilibrium adapted to partial rotation prepares for the next change.

Symmetrical-Partial Rotation Sequence

The child is striving to develop the most efficient method of getting up. With equilibrium available to pull back toward midline with each partial rotation away from midline, the child rotates less and less away from the center. The ability to maintain midline stability and superimpose movement along the midline develops. A symmetrical process begins to evolve.

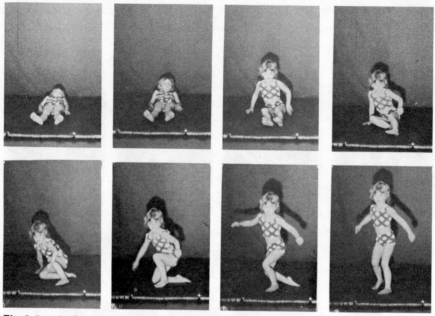

Fig 6-5: a-h Symmetrical-Partial Rotation Sequence.

1) The child raises his head in supine and, by adaptation of chain reaction, comes straight into a sitting posture.

2) The arms may or may not be used to pull forward or push off.

3) From sitting, stress becomes a factor again. The child calls forth the lower level partial rotation process to move from sit to stand.

4) With internal postural control gained from symmetrical sit, the child may only rotate slightly to get up and will probably use his arms to balance rather than push up from partial rotation.

Symmetrical Sequence

Symmetrical sequence to stand is the most mature pattern available. The sequence requires that postures and movements are blended with internal control so that once initiated, a smooth pattern follows.

1) The child raises his head in supine and sits symmetrically.

2) From sitting, he continues on to stand using the symmetrical sequence. He may or may not use arms to pull or push off.

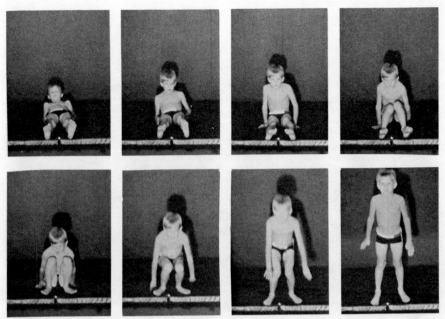

Fig 6-6: a-h Symmetrical Sequence.

All children may not achieve the ability to stand symmetrically. If they do achieve this level, it may not be retained or always available to the child, since stress can easily affect the pattern and cause the child to call forth the next lower pattern. Most normal children achieve and maintain a symmetrical-partial rotation sequence and retain it for normal functioning, although again, stress can cause a lower level pattern to be called forth.

These sequences are presented here for the reader to use for observation of behavior and to consider how the behavioral progressions previously described are linked together by association-differentiation into new sequences for higher level functioning.

Chapter Seven
The Development of Purposeful Activities and Skill

Introduction

Through movement a child is constantly adapting environmental experiences with self. Adaptive behaviors and activities are goal-directed and purposeful as the youngster seeks to expand this world and pursue his quest for autonomy and competence. A child's autonomy and competence depend upon his ability to move about the environment. As the youngster moves out into the environment he becomes involved with the events and activities of his space.

Activity is action and the primary component for modification or change. Joan Erikson states that: "Without change, recovery (rehabilitation, restitution) is illusory. Without activity and change, which is life itself, there is no growth."[1] Activity/action is the vital component of the spatiotemporal adaptation process of development.

Movement can also be equated with change. Movement is basic to action/activity, and through movement the youngster can engage in active participation with activity. The process of modification or change through the child's active participation with activity is dependent upon movement and equals spatiotemporal adaptation.

Through inter-relationships of movement and activity the child develops. Activity requires coordination and regulation of movement in attainment of some particular objective. As the youngster focuses his intent on events/activities, he calls up posture and movement strategies practiced with the development of purposeful behaviors. Essential elements of the behavior are brought forth and adapted to activity performance.

As the child moves out to extend himself into the environment, the acquired behaviors are repeated. Mere repetition of behaviors will not increase a child's ability or facilitate development. There needs to be an increase of demands to the nervous system for maturation to occur and development to proceed. Demands are increased as the child repeats behaviors and begins to combine actions of the behavior with events or activities of the environment. Nervous system maturation occurs with purposeful actions.

As behaviors are adapted to activities there is an arousal of the child's intention. This intention is the initial reaction to the stimulus and promotes the purposefulness of activity performance.[2] Activity becomes purposeful when the nature of and participation with the activity/event facilitates meaningful responses for the nervous system. Responses become meaningful when the feedback associated with actions provide directions and efforts that are more mature or at a higher level than those previously experienced.[3] Thus, purposeful activity augments neural mechanisms and sensorimotor-sensory integration. Through the spiraling process, behaviors are adapted to events and activities, and through the child's intention, newly-acquired goals emerge. As behaviors become goal-directed toward events and activities within the environment, purposeful activities evolve.

Purposeful activities can be differentiated from purposeful behaviors by the child's aim or goal-direction. Purposeful behaviors are those self-starting actions which are body centered and concerned with innate goals, eg, to sit, to stand, and so forth. Purposeful activities are directed toward goals outside the body or to events and activities within the environment and thus become environment centered. The child's intention and participation with both purposeful behaviors and activities results in sensorimotor-sensory integration, thus enhancing maturation. Purposeful activities link together selected actions of posture and movement strategies adapted from purposeful behaviors. Through the linking process the previously acquired postural sets are enhanced.

As a child engages in purposeful activity, association and differentiation of his performance with achievement of the goal of activity affords one aspect of sensory feedback — knowledge of the result of sensorimotor-sensory actions or performance. A child is most concerned with the objective of activity and responds to his intention and end result of his action. The end result provides feedback, for example, a toy is grasped, a shoe is tied, a ball is caught. The youngster measures his success or failure by his view of accomplishment. Determination toward goals, together with feedback about performance, motivates children to repeat successful experiences or experiment with alternate means to resolve problems with unsuccessful experiences.

During development, children seem to utilize certain innate functions that encourage them to seek out those events and activities most related to the specific developmental phase needing reinforcement or development. Thus, the objective of activities or goals provide children with the stimulus to reinforce needed behaviors and activities for higher level performance.

Association and differentiation of the child's intent with the end result augments perception about space and objects in relation to the body and in relation to each other. The end result or goal is an essential attribute to both purposeful activity and the sensorimotor-sensory process to achieve that activity. Achievement of goals challenges children to attempt more complex purposeful activities.

Through the spiraling process of adapting purposeful behaviors and activities, posture and movement strategies are augmented and the self-system acquires visual-motor and auditory-motor perceptual sets. Through repetition of purposeful activities, the child builds up familiarity of the visual/auditory-motor perceptual sets by associating and differentiating his performance with the activity being performed. As children adapt, the perceptual sets become a part of the self-system and are available to be monitored and selected for performance. Hence, the visual/auditory-motor perceptual sets can be likened to internal feedback of the sensorimotor-*sensory* process that is used for directing body accommodations.

As children perform with goal-directed purposeful activities, the self-system integrates posture and perceptual sets of directed movement with feedback of the activity or knowledge of the result. Through the integration process, posture and movement strategies are further enhanced, and skilled performance evolves.

The major functions of skilled performance include the following abilities: to move the body within the spatiotemporal dimensions, eg, dancing, running, skipping; to receive impetus, eg, catch a ball; and to give impetus to external objects, eg, move a pencil or scissors on the paper.[2] These functions are acquired through the child's repetition of and active participation

136

with purposeful behaviors and activities. Through repetition and active participation, actions of behaviors and activities are adapted to postural and perceptual sets used to direct body accommodations during skilled performance.

Skilled performance is characterized by freedom of movement within spatiotemporal dimensions of the environment.[4,5] Skill is appropriate use of posture and movement in relation to the effort (speed, timing, exertion, space, control) for performance of activity. Skilled performance has a quality of natural responsiveness or an unconscious, automatic element to actions. Natural responsiveness of actions results from regulation of flow or blending of postural and perceptual sets in relation to spatiotemporal dimensions. Regulation of the subsets (postural, visual-motor auditory-motor perceptual) for activity performance requires temporal sequencing of posture and movement strategies in relation to spatial confines.[6]

Major outcomes which underlie blending of the subsets include efficiency and accuracy of performance. Efficiency of performance is the relationship between the amount of work that is accomplished and the force or energy expended to accomplish the action. Although the spatiotemporal components affect both efficiency and accuracy, efficiency of movement is more dependent upon the child's ability to perceive and adapt the spatial dimensions. Accuracy is more dependent upon the perception of self in relation to the temporal dimensions of the actions being performed. Accuracy of performance is the perception or judgment of direction, distance, control, and timing of actions.

As purposeful behaviors and activities are being adapted to skill, the self-system builds up familiarity with subsets and the inherent efficiency/accuracy patterns of movement. Perceptual sets from one activity, eg, holding a crayon, can be called forth to adapt to another activity, eg, holding a pencil or pen. Ability to transfer sets from one activity to another is dependent upon the perceptual process inherent within spatiotemporal adaptation.

With skilled performance the sensorimotor-sensory actions are appropriate for a specific performance and therefore there is no need for change or modification of the appropriate actions. Thus, skill can be characterized by consistent patterns of performance and, as such, skill becomes the final degree of spatiotemporal adaptation of postural and perceptual sets.

During the spiraling continuum process, skilled performance of one activity may need to be modified or expanded to achieve a higher level performance of that activity. Thus, consistency of the skilled performance is interrupted and the actions become purposeful again, enhancing neural integration for a higher level meaningful response. The spiraling process repeats itself, certain elements of purposeful behaviors and activities are called up, postural and perceptual sets are expanded, and newly acquired skilled performance emerges.

To illustrate the above concept, consider a child who has acquired skilled performance while skiing on certain intermediate slopes. He becomes motivated to join his peer group on more advanced slopes; hence, the skilled performance he has acquired must be modified to handle the more difficult terrain. In the process of performing, his actions become purposeful again as the nature of, and participation with, skiing on the more advanced areas facilitates a meaningful response for the nervous system. To adapt to the new environment, the child calls forth past behaviors and activities to direct his effort at this higher level. Thus, his performance expands his postural and perceptual sets for future adaptation. As the youngster practices by repeating skiing on more difficult terrain, newly acquired skills emerge.

To further discuss and illustrate the spiraling aspects of developing complex skilled performances, the developmental progression of the visual-motor skills of reaching and grasping will be presented. Throughout the discussion of the spiraling continuum of the development of reaching and grasping it becomes increasingly apparent that inter-relationships of movement and activity provide opportunity for sensorimotor-sensory integration to build postural and perceptual sets for eventual skilled performances.

The text emphasizes visual guidance of directed movement. Although the auditory perceptual system plays a vital role in the development of performance skills, it will not be discussed in this text. In addition, the reader is reminded that the ability to control and direct movements of the upper extremity, as it is projected to explore and manipulate the environment, is dependent upon the body as a unit, as the whole controls and guides the parts.

Primitive Phase

During the primitive phase of development, the baby primarily interacts visually with the environment. Posture and movement strategies have not developed sufficiently to allow the infant to reach out and grasp the environment. Thus, vision precedes action/activity and through the adaptation process, vision culminates in the visual guidance of movement.[5,7] The primitive phase of development of reaching and grasping can best be characterized by somatosensory reception of the body and crude visual auditory perceptions of the environment.

The newborn visually interacts with the environment. The eyes move conjugately and the infant fixates momentarily and monocularly upon objects within his visual field. When the infant sees an object, his roving eyes fixate on it, becoming stationary for a few seconds. Visual attention to the environment is also associated with a suppression of other bodily activities.[5,8] The eye fixation indicates the presence of vision or response to the incoming stimuli, as if the infant is attempting to interact with the environment.[8]

In addition to fixation, the Doll's eye phenomena is prevalent in the neonate.[9] When the head is passively turned, the eyes will remain still as if to turn in a direction opposite to the head. Doll's eye phenomena will eventually be modified to allow the eyes to move with the head.[10] Integration of visual, vestibular/proprioceptive feedback, and pathways enhance modification of the Doll's eye movement. Integration of visual-vestibular stimulation adds new information to previously acquired visual behaviors. Visual-vestibular integration is the intersensory foundation from which the visual process appears to mature.

Not only is vision present at birth, but a primitive form of visual perception has been reported. Peiper[9] reports that infants have color vision identical with adults. Bower's[11] work indicates a preference to solid objects over flat objects, which may indicate a very crude form of depth perception which is not fully developed until approximately nine years of age. Work by Fantz[7,12] indicates that an infant can discriminate patterns differing in complexity and form. Visual discrimination is indicated by a preference to certain patterns over others. During the first two months, visual preferences change and are affected by repeated visual experiences only, not by touching or playing with objects.

What the infant sees and perceives, in all respects, is not what adults see or perceive. The infant has not matured to permit an integration of visual input with other sensory information such as tactile, proprioceptive, and vestibular input from higher level postures and movements. Although visual perceptions are present at birth and do change during the first two months, it is the highly complex SMS integrative process that enhances the perception of objects and space.

As the infant integrates head turning with visual experiences, binocular vision is enhanced. The neonate's monocular vision allows him to fixate on objects by aligning the active eye and relaxing or closing the other eye. Later monocular fixation alternates rapidly between the two eyes with a rhythmic excursion of head turning from side to side.

Eye tracking develops during the primitive phase to allow the eyes to cross the midline.[5,7] During the neonatal period the eyes move to midline. As alternating monocular vision develops, the infant acquires the ability to move the eyes past midline. By three months of age the baby is able to visually track objects through a 180° arc (see Fig 7-1 and Fig 7-2). Although

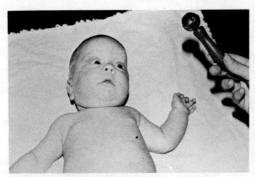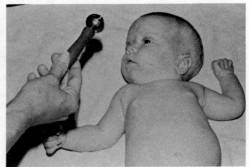

Fig 7-1,2 Eye Tracking.

the baby can visually track, he makes no attempt to grasp an object placed in front of him. Posture and movement strategies and somatosensory perceptions have not progressed sufficiently to allow the infant to move toward the environment and prehend objects.[5,7]

Through adaptation of visual exploration of objects, the self-system acquires higher level visual perceptions which will be integrated with somatosensory information of the body in motion. As the infant tracks, he frequently stops the pursuit and fixates his gaze upon the object. He visually scans or explores the stimulus for prolonged periods, providing the opportunity to associate and differentiate the "distinctive features" being perceived.[7,13]

Adaptation of fetal responses, reflexes/reactions, and primitive muscular functions of mobility and stability prepare the infant for interaction with the environment, providing primary somatosensory information for reaching and grasping. Development of reaching and grasping is influenced by traction, avoiding, grasp responses, and mouth/hand contact.[14,15] In addition, posture and movement strategies of purposeful behaviors as presented in Chapter 5 affect the spiraling progression. Primary hand reactions of the primitive phase are adaptations from fetal responses of sensitivity on the palms to incoming stimuli.[14]

The traction response (Fig 7-3) of the neonate results from deep contact stimulation of the palm which induces finger flexion. Stretch on the finger flexors provides proprioceptive input that results in a flexion synergy of the whole extremity. The proprioceptive holding phase of traction is later modified by finger extension elicited by light touch on the palm or dorsum of hand stimulating extension or the avoiding response[9,14] (Fig 7-4).

The grasp reflex (Fig 7-5) is a modification of the traction response. At this stage of development, contact pressure stimulation induces flexion of the fingers alone, not the total traction response.[14,15] Flexor synergy of traction is believed to be inhibited by postural

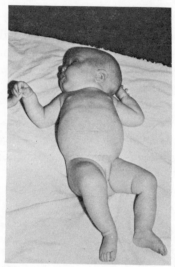

Fig 7-3 Traction.

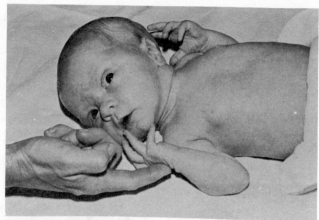

Fig 7-4 Avoiding.

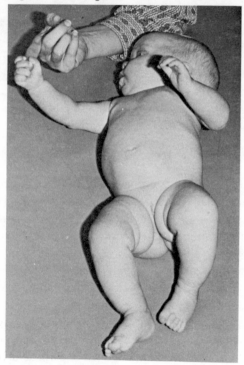

Fig 7-5 Grasp.

influences from tonic neck and labyrinthine reflexes. Postural reflexes affect extensor tone of shoulder, elbow, and wrist to the extent that a proprioceptive stimulation to the hand results only in finger flexion or grasp reflex. [10,14] The remaining extremity position is influenced by the position of head or body rather than specific hand contact. Modification of traction to grasp illustrates the spiraling concept, as adaptation of higher level grasp is dependent upon integration of tonic neck patterns with the lower level traction response. Reactions of traction, avoiding, and grasp are responsible for primitive patterns of mobility in the hand as the reflexive movements facilitate flexion and extension through the physiological range.

Mouth/hand contact (Fig 7-6) expands somatosensory reception of self. The neonate

Fig 7-6 Mouth-Hand Contact.

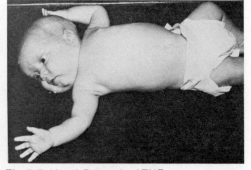

Fig 7-7 Hand Regard—ATNR.

contacts his hand with his mouth by means of primitive head turning. Flexed postures of the upper extremities in both prone and supine combined with survival and protective head turning reflexes brings the mouth and hand in contact with each other.[16]

During the primitive phase, adaptation of hand contact responses is accompanied with visual fixation of hand movement. According to Held and Bauer,[17] viewing of moving hands is necessary for integration of visual-motor direction and later visual guidance of movement. Hand regard is enhanced by the extended position of the upper extremity facilitated by the ATNR.[5] Thus, ATNR places the hand in the infant's visual field, and he fixes his gaze on his hand (Fig 7-7). The visual exploration of hand provides opportunity to visually differentiate the "distinctive features" of the hand.[13] As somatosensory reception of the body and visual perceptions of hands are being integrated by the self-system, somatosensory awareness emerges.

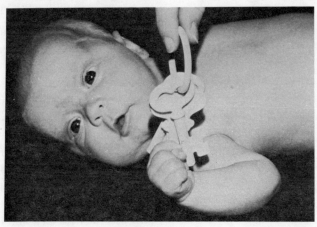

Fig 7-8 Swiping.

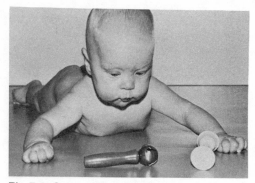
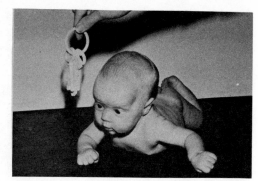

Fig 7-9 Symmetrical Distribution of tone.　　**Fig 7-10** Asymmetrical distribution of tone.

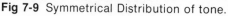

As the infant acquires a somatosensory awareness of the body, he may wave his upper limbs in response to visually perceiving an object. Movement of limbs is suggestive of awareness of the body and its potential for interacting with the environment. With enhancement of body awareness, the infant will visually direct himself to "swipe" at an object[17] (Fig 7-8). Swiping represents a primitive form of unilateral reaching and represents the beginning of purposeful activity with reaching.[5] Due to residual predominance of the grasp reflex, the fingers remain flexed, and the infant cannot grasp the object; however, he has attempted to adapt his actions to events outside the body. Grasp reflex must be modified before the infant will be able to prehend and interact with objects within the environment. During the latter part of the primitive phase, the baby in prone position adapts symmetrical tonic neck distribution of muscle tone. Changing integration of muscle tone results in primitive support reactions. The pronated position of the arms and flexed fingers are similar to the posture of the grasp reflex (Fig 7-9). Pressure on hands from the supporting surface initiates differentiation of the total grasp pattern. In addition, distribution of tone from one side of the hand to the other is facilitated by the ATNR as the baby turns his head and influences tone throughout the extremity (Fig 7-10).

Transitional Phase

During the transitional period of grasp and release development, the baby adapts posture and movement strategies, which are developing with purposeful behaviors, to perform purposeful activities. Adaptation of purposeful behaviors to activities expands spatiotemporal concepts and visual-motor perceptions. The youngster practices grasp-release patterns culminating in appropriate visual-motor interaction.

Transitional behaviors provide necessary components to integrate the grasp reflex and facilitate reaching, crude grasp, and palmar grasp. Supine behaviors influence the development of movement strategies for reaching. Symmetrical postures provide stability to hold the head in midline and bring the arms up to midline.[10,11] Movement strategies are developed so that the baby can reach bilaterally, bring his arms together over his body, and clutch his fists. The baby's visual attention is directed toward his hands as they approach and tactually explore each other.[5] Visual-somatosensory information from this midline activity is a vital component of the development of bilateral arm activity. To further explore the hands, the baby frequently clutches his own fists near his face and brings hands-to-mouth (Fig 7-11).

142

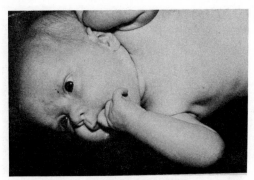

Fig 7-11 Hands-to-Mouth.

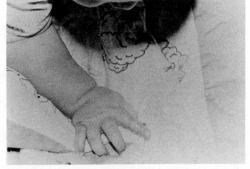

Fig 7-12 Scratching/Raking.

Hands-to-mouth is adapted from the primitive mouth-to-hand behaviors and will ultimately be adapted to mouthing objects.

Postural strategies developing in prone provide background stability to modify the grasp reflex. As the baby gains sufficient upper trunk stability to modify primitive support to support with adduction, weight-bearing is increased on the ulnar side of the hand. Pressure from the supporting surface on the ulnar side promotes finger extension by releasing the fingers from weight-bearing, thus freeing the hands from their total support role. Finger extension is facilitated by the effect of vertical righting spreading distally and combining with the trace affects of the avoiding response. Thus, grasp reflex in prone is modified.

The youngster activates finger flexors with extensors by "scratching" the surface (Fig 7-12). The flexion/extension scratching pattern is a purposeful behavior which is adapted for the purposeful activity of "raking" objects.[11,15] The "scratching" actions ultimately lead to finger differentiation acquired during the mature phase.[9,10]

Modification of grasp reflex also allows the child to hold objects while he supports on-elbows. Interaction with objects in supported prone postures motivates the youngster to reach out for objects in his environment. The pattern for reaching is developed by the purposeful behavior associated with on-elbows weight shift and movement of the upper extremity through space.[18] The baby reaches out with a crude grasp (Fig 7-13). The essential element of crude grasp is the pronated reaching position of the forearm/hand. With crude grasp, the pronated position predominates regardless of object orientation. Therefore, infants adapt objects to the pronated position rather than adapt the forearm/hand position to objects. The

Fig 7-13 Crude Grasp.

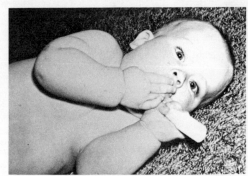

Fig 7-14 Object Mouthing.

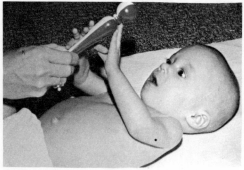

Fig 7-15 Reach and Pat.

Fig 7-16 Palmar Grasp.

crude grasp pattern is not usually the most efficient form of grasping for interacting with activities/events; however, it is meaningful for the self-system as it enhances the baby's awareness of the relationship of the object to the relationship of his limb position.

During this period the baby becomes engrossed in glancing from hand-to-object and object-to-hand in preparation for visual guidance of movement. He visually scans and explores to differentiate the "distinctive features" of hand in relation to object. Differentiation is a vital component for "learning,"[13] and at this time the differentiation of hand and objects provides the self-system with higher level knowledge regarding the body.

Although development of reaching and grasping is more advanced in prone behaviors (the baby can grasp objects by self for visual differentiation), in the supine position the baby will hold objects to midline and visually explore and perceive object/hand relationships (Fig 7-14). Hand mouthing is adapted to object mouthing as the baby bilaterally brings hand and object to his mouth for both grasp and release. The mouth functions to prehend objects, and as a prehender the mouth provides the baby with beginning manipulation of objects by using the mouth for both mobility and stability functions. In addition, mouthing provides sensory exploration of objects for tactile orientation. Mouthing of objects can be viewed as a crude form of external stability as the distal end of the extremities are fixed to the object that is held in the mouth. Holding and mouthing objects further enhances midline stability.

In addition to midline-mouthing behaviors experienced in supine postures, reaching con-

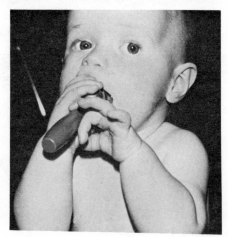

Fig 7-17 Mouthing for External Support.

144

tinues to develop. The baby adapts extension strategies to reach out with extended fingers and "pat" objects (Fig 7-15). Reaching becomes more accurate with visually directed contact with objects. The extended fingers of patting combined with visual direction for reaching modifies primitive "swiping." Now when the baby reaches out and contacts objects, the hand is open and able to grasp. The baby grasps objects between palm and fingers adapting the crude grasp pattern to palmar grasp (Fig 7-16).

The youngster grasps objects and brings them to the mouth for investigation. With the mouth providing external support, the infant can rotate shoulders and forearms through a range of internal-external rotation or supination-pronation while grasping and mouthing toys (Fig 7-17). Mobility and stability are combined in the forearm by using the mouth for fixation. Once mobility and stability are combined to control shoulder movement, the baby expands his investigating abilities. He will transfer an object from mouth-to-hand for kinesthetic exploration. The baby shakes or bangs an object, primarily using shoulder movements for object manipulation. He returns the object to his mouth for more discreet tactile investigation. The baby associates tactile, kinesthetic, visual, and auditory information to expand object judgments for the building of temporal concepts.

During this exploration process, the baby occasionally stops the activity at hand and visually perceives the object. Hand manipulative abilities are not sufficiently developed to support simultaneous extensive visual investigation. After visually perceiving the object, the youngster may look away while he proceeds to manually manipulate the object. He can compare, first, visual investigation with manual investigation, although he cannot simultaneously assimilate visual-somatosensory sensations. However, his limited visual-motor perception of the object is associated with information from the other senses for adaptation and later use.

The baby's manipulative abilities are developing more rapidly in prone. As the baby in prone experiences support on open hands, the weight-bearing function of the ulnar side is further differentiated, freeing the radial side of the hand to develop fractionation of grasp.[10,15] The baby calls up stability by assuming the on-elbows posture to explore the environment with index finger probing (Fig 7-18). Index probing is adapted from "scratching" and "raking" by isolating flexion-extension patterns to the index finger. Index finger probing differentiates the function of the index finger from total grasp in preparation for development of pincer-prehension patterns. Probing of the index finger represents purposeful activity as the participation with and subsequent feedback from the activity of probing facilitates a higher level hand pattern or fractionation of grasp.[9,10,18]

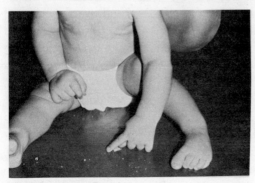

Fig 7-18 Index Probing.

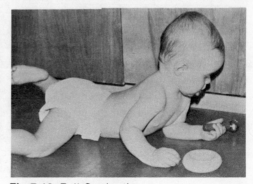

Fig 7-19 Full Supination.

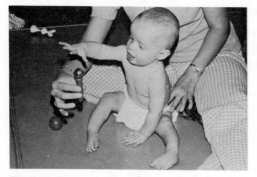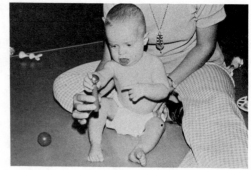

Fig 7-20,21 Instinctive Grasp.

Supination and pronation patterns of the forearm/hand are further developed with the baby in the supported prone posture. As the baby supports himself on-elbows, pressure on the ulnar border of the forearm/hand facilitates supination, and pressure on the radial side facilitates pronation. As support becomes localized around the elbows, newly acquired pronation/supination patterns become useful for grasp and visual investigation of objects. Now when the baby grasps an object he can supinate to manipulate the object, thus viewing it from different perspectives (Fig 7-19).

Development of full range of forearm supination-pronation with support leads to modification of pronated reaching of palmar grasp to instinctive grasp (Fig 7-20, 7-21). With instinctive grasp, tactile stimulation to the radial/ulnar side of the hand is adapted to reach and grasp strategies. Repeated tactile experiences on the radial or skill side of the hand modifies the pronated orientation of palmar grasp to higher level instinctive grasp.[10,15] Therefore, as the child reaches for an object and contacts the object with the radial side, tactile stimulation facilitates forearm supination as the hand grasps.[15] The youngster then grasps the object with an appropriate forearm/hand orientation. The purposeful activity of instinctive grasp enhances maturation resulting in differentiation of forearm/supination-pronation strategies.

Mature Phase

During the mature phase of development of reach and grasp, vision and somatosensory perception are integrated for visual guidance of movement. The tactile orientation of instinctive grasp is integrated with visual experiences of object-hand regard and visual direction of reaching. The youngster guides the hand visually so that he adjusts the forearm/hand position prior to grasping the object. The process is termed visual orientation of hand to objects (Fig 7-22). With the advent of visual orientation, visual-motor integration results in visual guidance of hand movements.

Visual-motor integration is further augmented by the development of purposeful behaviors, such as rolling. As the arms are freed from support, arm and hand movement is also guided by more proximal control from the shoulder, adapting a movement-countermovement strategy so that the shoulder moves back to control movement while vision guides. Repetition of somatosensory control and visual guidance of freely moving extremities culminates in smooth appropriate visual-motor skills and blended strategies for visual-motor

146

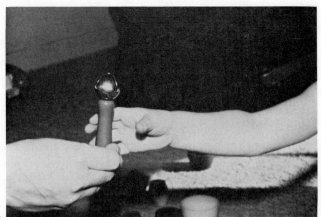

Fig 7-22 Visual Orientation.

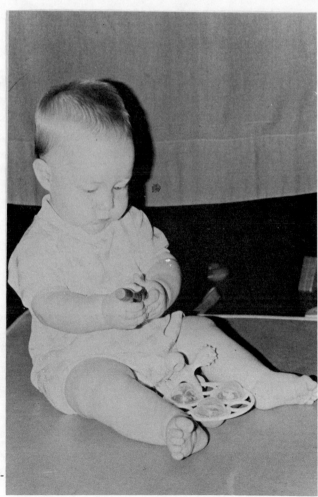

Fig 7-23 Transferring Objects.

perceptual sets.

During the later stages of transitional development of reaching and grasping, the youngster has acquired the mature phase of sitting. The spiraling process of adapting hand patterns from grasp to instinctive grasp to visual orientation in supported prone and supine postures is now adapted to the upright sitting position. The adaptation process repeats itself, and the child engages in purposeful activities in the sitting position.

The youngster can reach out and contact objects within the environment. As he manually explores an object, he frequently shifts his eyes from object-to-hand and calls forth bilateral manipulation of objects experienced with supine and prone behaviors. Transferring objects from hand-to-hand augments the child's control over voluntary release, adding new information for temporal concepts from his tactile-visual explorations (Fig 7-23).

During the advent of the mature phase, somatosensory perception of the hand in relation to objects is further modified. The instinctive grasp response which has contributed to full supination of forearm/hand is eventually adapted to inferior pincer grasp (Fig 7-24). Inferior pincer grasp[10] is adapted from experiences of fractionation or index probing associated and differentiated from instinctive grasp. The youngster not only extends the index finger to point or probe, but he can direct thumb movement to the lateral side of the index finger to grasp the object being probed.[14]

Inferior pincer grasp is adapted to superior pincer grasp (Fig 7-25). Experiences of grasping objects between thumb and index finger, together with the tactile input from index finger probing, encourages the child to rotate his thumb and contact the palmar surface of the finger tips for superior pincer grasp.[9,10]

Experiences with inferior and superior pincer grasp expand differentiated mobility and stability muscle functions to the distal segments of the wrist and proximal joints of the hand. The object being held supplies additional stability for finger-thumb movement strategies. Although the child has developed some visual-motor skills, activities of the environment motivate him to attempt more complex hand behaviors, and he again engages in purposeful activities.

Higher level purposeful activities of reaching and superior pincer are experienced in two major areas: free movement of the upper extremity to grasp and direct the object, such as ball playing, and manipulative activities such as primary coloring or directing the crayon by arm movement. Non-manipulative and manipulative activities are dependent upon the differentiation and blending of mobility and stability.

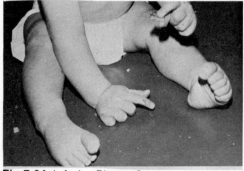

Fig 7-24 Inferior Pincer Grasp.

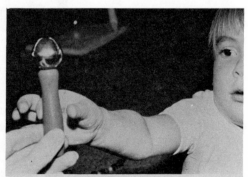

Fig 7-25 Superior Pincer Grasp.

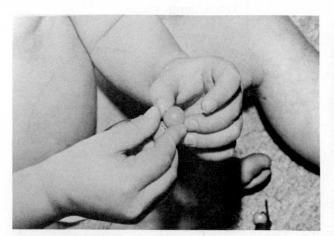

Fig 7-26 Prehension.

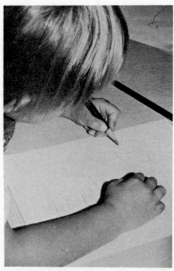

Fig 7-27 Manipulative Prehension.

Moving and directing an object, such as a crayon or scissor, as an extension of moving and directing the hand, requires additional control. The upper extremities develop a higher level of performance skills through manipulation of objects. The demands of fine manipulation which are constantly monitored and sequenced by visual-motor perceptual sets requires that the child call forth trace effects from distal fixation, once used to control movement as it developed. Now the child grasps the object, reinforces more proximal control by holding the object, and blends mobility and stability into strategies which specifically direct the object toward a goal.[16] Muscle functions of co-activation and differentiated mobility and stability have expanded to the distal segments of the wrist and hand. Rotation and counter-rotation patterns of the arm and thumb are blended with the posture and movement strategies for directing the hand as well as the object. Expansion of these strategies are adapted to higher level posture and perceptual sets. Thus, the child acquires the ability to blend thumb abduction and rotation with stability of the joints of the thumb, as well as blend mobility and stability components of finger flexion and extension. The strategy is adapted to the purposeful behavior of prehension (Fig 7-26). Prehension represents the true opposition of thumb and fingers and becomes integrated with visual perceptions of objects being prehended for the visual guidance of purposeful activities.

With the advent of purposeful activities with prehension, the self-system calls forth the manipulative and non-manipulative actions which were initiated with superior pincer grasp and adapts the strategies to prehension. Manipulative prehension evolves (Fig 7-27). The purposeful activities of manipulative prehension are repeated and adapted to skilled performance for smooth sequencing of posture and perceptual sets.

Through the child's active participation with manipulative prehension activities and skills, fingers and thumb musculature and control matures. The self-system adapts fractionation to encompass each finger, and finger differentiation evolves. With finger differentiation the child adds new dimensions to his manipulative prehension activities and skills. Finger differentiation continues to mature over a period of several years, providing a person with fine motor skills needed for activities such as typing or playing the piano.

Fig 7-28 Development of Grasp.*†

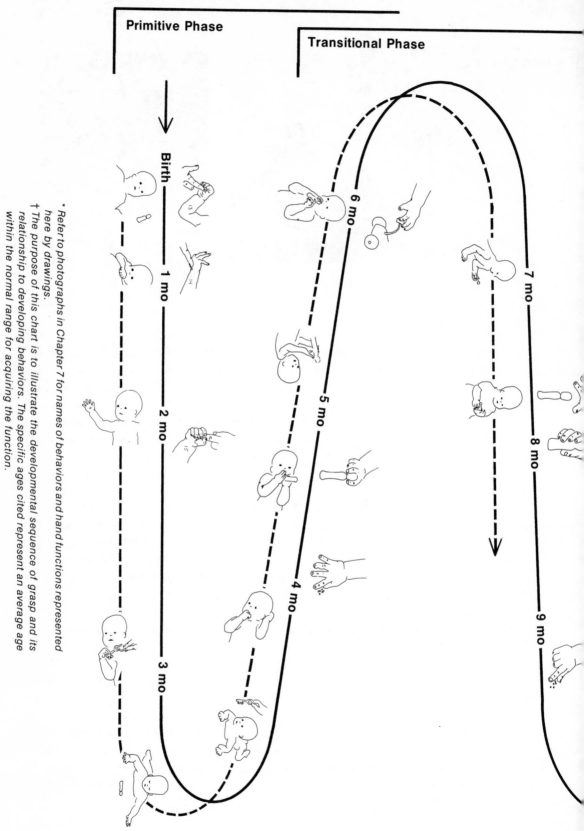

Primitive Phase

Transitional Phase

Birth

1 mo

2 mo

3 mo

4 mo

5 mo

6 mo

7 mo

8 mo

9 mo

* Refer to photographs in Chapter 7 for names of behaviors represented here by drawings.

† The purpose of this chart is to illustrate the developmental sequence of grasp and its relationship to developing behaviors. The specific ages cited represent an average age within the normal range for acquiring the function.

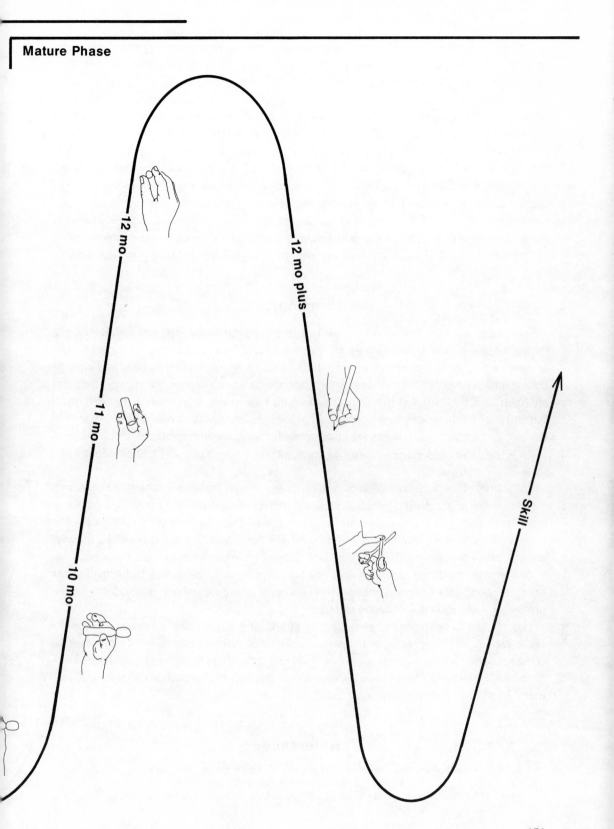

12 mo

11 mo

10 mo

12 mo plus

Skill

With the acquisition of automatic balance reactions and mature pincer and prehension strategies the child expands his abilities to direct upper extremity manipulative and non-manipulative activities while functioning across the midline of the body. The child blends upper extremity crossing-midline patterns developed in rolling, sitting, and standing with upper extremity manipulative activities. As the child adapts crossing midline manipulative activities, he enhances the development of hand dominance.

The child practices manipulative prehension with a variety of purposeful activities, transferring posture and movement strategies learned with one activity to another similar activity. Transferring strategies from performance of one activity to another results from regulation of posture and perceptual sets. Through repetition of purposeful activities, the child's manipulative prehension strategies continues to mature for several years, culminating in prehension patterns which are unique to the person but encompassing the essential components of prehension. The evolution of manipulative prehension contributes to the uniqueness of man.

Summary

The ability to utilize the high level skill of upper extremity manipulative prehension is dependent upon adaptation of posture and movement strategies of the whole body and integration of visual/auditory perceptions. In the mature phase, midline stability and equilibrium reactions have been blended for automatic balance reactions; thus, the upper extremities are freed from their support role. With freedom for movement, upper extremities can reach out and explore the environment. The child moves out into space as one unit, being able to readjust his posture and movement to interact with the changing spatiotemporal dimensions of his world. The child automatically and constantly sequences postural and perceptual sets for skilled performance.

The theory of spatiotemporal adaptation proposes that sensorimotor-sensory integration is inherent within the spiraling process. Through the spiraling process, primitive posture and movement strategies are modified and integrated into complex behaviors that control the body during skilled performance. Through spatiotemporal adaptations, purposeful behaviors are used for environmental interactions. As actions become goal-directed, purposeful activities emerge. With the repetition and practice of purposeful behaviors and activities, the self-system acquires a repertoire of postural and perceptual sets which are available for the regulation and sequential ordering of skill.

The spiraling continuum of spatiotemporal adaptation provides a framework for the understanding of the development of performance skills. Although the theory emphasizes the consistency of the spiraling process, variabilities and differences of each individual is stressed. Each child is unique and expresses his uniqueness through his transactions with the environment. Each child develops a unique "self."

References

1. Erickson J: Activity, Recovery, Growth. New York, WW Norton & Co Inc, 1976, p xi.
2. Wells K: Kinesiology. Philadelphia, WB Saunders Co, 1963, ed 3, pp 327-412.
3. Ayres AJ: Sensory Integration and Learning Disorders. Los Angeles, Western Psychological Services, 1972.

4. Connolly K (ed): Mechanisms of Motor Skill Development. New York, Academic Press Inc, 1970, pp 3-18.
5. White B, Castle P, Held R: Observations on the development of visually directed reaching. Child Dev 35: 349-364, 1964.
6. Bruner J: The growth and structure of skill, in Connolly K (ed): Mechanisms of Motor Skill Development. New York, Academic Press Inc, 1970, pp 63-92.
7. Fantz R, Faga J, Mirand S: Early visual selectivity, in Cohen L, Salapatek P (eds): Infant Perception: From Sensation to Cognition. New York, Academic Press Inc, 1975, pp 249-340.
8. Karmel B, Maidel E: A neuronal activity model for infant visual attention, in Cohen L, Salapatek P (eds): Infant Perception: From Sensation to Cognition. New York, Academic Press Inc, 1975, Vol 1, pp 78-125.
9. Peiper A: Cerebral Function in Infancy and Childhood. New York, Consultants Bureau, 1963.
10. Touwen B: Neurological development in infancy. Clinics in Developmental Medicine. Philadelphia, JB Lippincott Co, 1976, no. 58.
11. Bower TGR: Infant perception of the third dimension and object concept development, in Cohen L, Salapatek P (eds): Infant Perception: From Sensation to Cognition. New York, Academic Press Inc, 1975, vol 2, pp 33-50.
12. Fantz RL: Visual perception from birth as shown by pattern selectivity. Ann NY Acad Sci 118:793-814, 1965.
13. Gibson EJ: Principles of Perceptual Learning and Development. New York, Appleton, Century, Crofts, 1969.
14. Twitchell TE: Normal motor development. The child with central nervous system deficit. Childrens' Bureau Pub, US Dept Health, Education, and Welfare, Washington DC, Government Printing Office, 1965, pp 85-89.
15. Twitchell T E: Reflex mechanisms and the development of prehension, in Connolly K (ed): Mechanisms of Motor Skill Development. New York, Academic Press Inc, 1970, pp 25-47.
16. Stockmeyer S: A sensorimotor approach to treatment, in Pearson B, Williams C: Physical Therapy Services in the Developmental Disabilities. Springfield, C C Thomas Pubs, 1972, pp 186-222.
17. Held R, Bauer J: Visually guided reaching in infant monkeys after restricted rearing. Science 155:362-368, 1967.
18. Gilfoyle E, Grady A: Posture and movement, in Hopkins H, Smith H (eds): Willard and Spackman's Occupational Therapy. Philadelphia, JB Lippincott Co, 1977, pp 58-81.

Chapter Eight
The Development of Personality

This chapter presents a description of the nature of personality development through the spiraling continuum of spatiotemporal adaptation. The purpose is to explore and discuss aspects of the adaptation theory as it relates to the development of the child's personality. Although SMS integration is emphasized in the discussion of the personality, the reader must maintain a holistic view to comprehend human behavior and understand personality development.

Because the groundwork for the theoretical continuum has evolved from the writings of several authors, a brief orientation to the concepts of Allport, Freud, Erikson, Piaget, and Gesell is presented. These persons have addressed themselves to the development of personality, and their theories have influenced the descriptive framework of the spatiotemporal adaptation as related to personality development.

Related Theorists

Gordon Allport

Allport[1,2] discusses the self in terms of the "proprium" (selfhood). He proposes that the development of the proprium has various facets and functions. During the first three years of life there are three aspects to be considered;

1) the sense of bodily self or the bodily me,

2) the sense of continuing self-identity,

3) ego enhancement or self-esteem.

According to Allport, the bodily sense remains as a lifelong anchor for self-awareness, but the bodily me alone never accounts for the entire sense of self. Self-identity and ego enhancement are continuing aspects that are tied to the need for survival, emotions of self-satisfaction, and pride. Self-love or self-esteem are prominent functions for the development of selfhood.

Allport proposes that during the child's years four through six, the development of the "proprium" has two aspects; the ego extension or extension of self, and one's self-image. During the process of ego extension, the child has a high regard for object possessions; the child develops from "me" to "mine." The youngster extends the sense of self to family and neighborhood groups as well as to tangible possessions. In this way, the child is continually expanding his self-image. Allport defines self-image with two facets: the way the individual regards present abilities and what the individual would like to become.[1] According to Allport, self-image helps a person bring present views into line with future.

During the years seven through twelve, the child develops self-awareness. Self-awareness, an extension of self-image, gives a child the ability to cope with problems by means of reason and thought. When a person acquires self-awareness, he or she can begin to synthesize inner needs with outer realities. According to Allport, an important function to self-awareness is the ability to have self-involvement with the environment. In the process of developing self-awareness, the youngster tries out new roles, ie, being a fireman, a cowboy, a nurse, or a mother.

During the adolescent period self-awareness has a new impact, and the adolescent transforms feelings of self-awareness into abstract ideas. The main aspect of the adolescent period is described by Allport[1] as "intentions" or long range purposes and distant goals. To Allport, man is future-oriented and not determined solely by past behaviors.

The nature of man's motivation is in the "propriate" strivings which lead him to seek equilibrium, adjustment, satisfaction, and homeostasis.[1] Propriate strivings are the core of a congruent personality and characterized by conflicts. Conflicts lead to the unification of personality. Thus, personality is a unique entity which functions as a whole. Allport defined "personality" as a dynamic organization within the individual in regard to those psychophysical systems which determine the individual's behavior and thought. The terms "dynamic organization" emphasizes the constantly developing and changing aspects of the personality, and "psychophysical systems" emphasizes personality as a functional integrative process involving both mind and body.[3]

Sigmund Freud

In contrast to Allport, Freud felt that personality was generally formulated by the end of the fifth year. As interpreted by Hall and Lindsey,[3] Freud stresses that growth and development after the fifth year consists of elaborations of the basic structure which developed during the first five years of life. Allport stresses the future as determining man's behavior; Freud stresses the past. Both emphasize *identification* as the method by which the individual learns to resolve conflicts.

The concept of primary and secondary identification originates in Freud's psychoanalytic theory. According to Freud's theories, primary identification is the primitive perception of self in which the external objects of the environment are perceived as a part of the self, while secondary identification begins after the child has differentiated the external world of objects as being separate from self. Secondary identification was believed to be enhanced during the Oedipal period when the child begins to identify with the same sex parent. Identification, according to Freud, is an endeavor to create one's own ego in imitation of a role model.[4]

Freud was one of the first theorists to emphasize the developmental aspects of personality. He defines the role of the early years of infancy and childhood as the time when the basic characteristics of personality are formed. To Freud, personality consists of the id, the ego, and the superego. The ego and the superego slowly become differentiated from the id, which Freud believes to be the original foundation of the personality.

Freud states that the id consists of everything that is inherited and present at birth. The id is the inner self of subjective experience and has no knowledge of reality. The id serves as the reservoir of psychic energy and functions to reduce tension in order to return the organism to a comfortable state of balance. The principle of tension reduction, termed the "pleasure principle," functions to avoid pain and obtain pleasure. Freud believed that two processes enhanced the function of the id: the reflex action and the primary process. Reflex actions are innate, automatic reactions like sneezing and yawning that reduce tension immediately, while the primary process attempts to reduce tension by creating an image of an object that will assist in the removal of the tension. For example, the primary process of the hungry infant will produce an image of the nipple. According to Freud, the primary process or mental image alone will not reduce tension, consequently the ego begins to develop.

Freud believed the ego differentiates between the image and the actual perception of the object. The ego is said to be the executive of the personality because it controls and selects the objects of the environment to which it will respond. The ego will differentiate the image of the nipple of a bottle from a pacifier. If hunger produces tension, the pacifier will not reduce the tension and the ego will direct the child's response accordingly. Freud stresses that the ego is the organized part of the id that eventually develops to enhance the aims of the id.

The third system of personality to develop is the superego. The functions of the superego are to inhibit the basic impulses of the id, to encourage the ego to substitute goals for those that are more realistic for functioning within the person's culture, and to strive for perfection. During childhood the superego develops as a response to rewards and punishments. The superego can be viewed as the "moral arm" of the personality.

These three systems are not separate entities which operate the personality. Rather, they are names given to various developmental processes which have different, but inter-related, functions. The id, ego, and superego function together to guide human behavior. The id can be viewed as the biological component, the ego the psychological component, and the superego the social component.[3]

Erik Erikson

Erikson[5] expands upon the basic theories of Freud. Erikson was greatly influenced by cultural anthropology and therefore put greater emphasis on social interaction. The focus of his theory stresses how the social interaction of a person works together with the biological and psychological influences to affect construction and change of the personality. Erikson also develops a psychosocial conception of drives which had one or more modes of operation which he believed were basic for dealing with reality. His theories are "ego based" as are Freud's; however, like Allport, he views man as continually growing and developing. Erikson, like Freud, presents development in several stages. He accepts Freud's basic premise regarding the basic sequences of development. However, he further elaborates the sequences into eight stages which continue throughout the entire life span of an individual. Erikson considers the eight stages of man as universal because of two underlying assumptions: 1) the personality develops according to predetermined steps, and 2) society is constituted to meet and invite this interaction.[5] Erikson stresses the individual's culture as being an important factor influencing the uniqueness of the person and the mode chosen to solve the polarities or crises at each stage of development. Further, he stresses that the way a person resolves conflicts depends upon one's ego strength which developed during earlier stages. The meaningfulness of environmental reinforcements is the determining factor in resolving the crises of the stages.

The stages are viewed as hierarchical, each depending upon the other. Each stage is described by Erikson's ideas of polarities of function.

In each stage cognitive dissonance exists, one being a positive or healthy response, the other a negative or unhealthy reaction. The first stage of personality development is described by Erikson as a period of "basic trust versus basic mistrust," developing around the nursing experience. Therefore, the first social trust for the infant revolves around his feeding experiences. The baby's first social achievement is to trust mother when she is out of sight without reacting with undue anxiety. Erikson's first sequence is similar to Freud's oral stage.

The second stage is one of "autonomy versus shame and doubt." This can be likened to Freud's anal stage when anal-neuromuscular maturation sets the stage for experimentation with holding on and/or letting go. The newly acquired neuromuscular maturation sets the stage for advanced social modalities, and the child begins to acquire a sense of autonomy. Allport[2] also stresses the importance of autonomy but does not equate autonomy with anal maturation. Allport views the acquisition of a "functional autonomy" as a sign of maturity, stating that the development of functional autonomy is a dynamic, organized process and is not equatable with a specific stage of development.

Erikson's third stage, "initiative versus guilt," is similar to the phallic and the genital stages of Freud. In this period of infant genitality, the superego supposedly functions to bring the child from his pregenital attachment with his parents to the slow continuous process of becoming a parent. During this phase, the child is eager to cooperate and to profit from the teachings of his parents. However, the child remains identified with the parent of the same sex and looks for opportunities where work-identification provides initiative.

The latency period of Freud is described by Erikson as the stage of "industry versus inferiority." According to Erikson the child sublimates his sexual feelings and learns to win recognition by creating things. "To bring a productive situation to completion is an aim which gradually supersedes the whims and wishes of play."[5] To Erikson the fundamentals of technology are developed in this stage, and ego boundaries include the child's tools and skills.

Erikson's fifth stage is "identity or role confusion" when childhood comes to an end and youth begins. The fifth stage is the period of adolescent crises characterized by a "physiological revolution." Erikson believed that earlier stages contribute to the formation of ego identity, but it is the crises and conflicts of adolescence that integrates past experiences into the real sense of ego identity. The adolescent is in a transitional stage between childhood and adulthood, between the "morality learned by the child and the ethics to be developed by the adult."[5] The individual needs this period of upheaval in order to abstractly try out new roles, identify with heroes, and ultimately discover self-identity.

The young adult emerging from this stage of identification begins to seek out identity with others. The person begins to experience intimacy with another person in Erikson's sixth stage, "intimacy versus isolation." This is followed by the seventh stage, described as "generativity versus stagnation." At this time the individual is primarily interested in establishing and guiding the next generation. The last stage described by Erikson is "ego integrity versus despair," which is characterized by the acceptance of self as a part of the order of things in life. Erikson's theory emphasizes that life is an adaptation to one's environment.

Play is an important aspect of purposeful activity, and one can glean insights into the development of a child's personality by examining the child's world of play. Erikson has contributed a theory relating to the developmental sequence of play.[5] Erikson proposes that infant's play is centered on his own body, termed "autocosmic play." During autocosmic play, the baby is learning to master his own body and establish a body sense. The infant is learning to influence the environment with the use of his body. A baby cries to get mother, smiles for pleasure, and constantly explores the body.

The next period proposed by Erikson is termed "microsphere," constituting the small world of manageable objects or toys. With microsphere play, the child learns to master toys and things. As stressed by Allport, ego enhancement is gained by mastering the small world of toys and objects within the environment. During the preschool age period, the social world expands for the child, and play reaches into a world shared with others. Play at this time is termed "macrosphere." The child is extending himself and beginning to acquire self-identity. Erikson states that at this time the youngster's world of social interactions expands to include peers and adults outside the immediate family group, thus enlarging his scope of transaction.

Play, to Erikson is "a function of the ego, an attempt to synchronize the bodily and the social processes with the self."[5] Play, a purposeful activity, becomes the means by which the child develops an identity of self. Self-identity is viewed as the major ingredient for the development of personality.

Jean Piaget

Adaptation of the organism to its environment, together with the concept of stages of development, characterizes the developmental concept of Piaget.[6] Inherent in Piaget's theory is the sequential order of patterns of behavior which are associated with age-related periods and have an organizational process within each stage of development. To Piaget, development is dependent upon the continual formation of new, higher order, intercoordinated systems. Development has its roots in previous experiences and therefore has a direct continuity with the past.

To Piaget, life begins with certain basic neurological and anatomical structures and functions which are inherent in the species man. These structural and functional components of man inhibit or facilitate behavior, but they do not account for an individual's behavior. Piaget argues that function is an organized process of assimilating the new to the old and of accommodating the old to the new. This mode of adaptation is the manner in which an organism develops and is a function of the total system.

Piaget explains the forces that account for development as 1) specific maturational factors, 2) the results of environmental experiences, 3) the results of explicit and implicit teaching of the child, and 4) the process of equilibration. To Piaget, equilibration is a process which eventually harmonizes the child's thoughts and ideas, one with the other. As the child develops, ideas and beliefs are acquired, and these ideas or beliefs are, in essence, unorganized. An unorganized system is not adaptive and this results in conflict. Therefore, the equilibration force is utilized to harmonize the child's ideas, one with another. As a result of equilibration, the child organizes thoughts and beliefs into a coherent, harmonious system.[7] Equilibration, as described by Piaget, appears to be the differentiating, integrating, and organizing process of the nervous system.

Piaget stresses that the perceptions and thoughts of an individual cannot be understood without referring to the individual as a whole. Perceptions and thoughts are organized within the self-system as a oneness. Perceptions and thoughts have been derived from the early SMS schemas of infancy by an internalization process. For example, the visual image of the body is an internalized way of looking at the body. Likewise, the tactile and proprioceptive image of the body is an internalized form of body schema. To Piaget, thinking is an internalized form of talking. [7]

The first stage of development, according to Piaget, is viewed as a period of sensorimotor intelligence and is equated with the age range from birth to two years. When symbolic language becomes available, the child begins a period of preconceptual thought. This stage relates to the ages of two to four years. The period of intuitive thought includes the ages of four to seven years; the period of concrete operations, seven to 11 years; and the period of formal (abstract) operations from 11 to 15 years. According to Piaget, these periods eventually culminate in the identity of self as a member of the group and should result in the formation of a complete personality. [6]

Piaget's theory can be compared with the psychoanalytic theories of Freud and Erikson, as Piaget stresses the egocentrism of the infant, the development of the ego and the superego, and the development from the pleasure principle to the reality principle. Piaget's view, that images are internalized overt responses, has some similarity to the stimulus-response theorists. Likewise, his emphasis upon the developmental sequencing of complex behavior patterns, which begins with simple reflexes, can be likened to the maturational theory of Gesell.

Arnold Gesell

Gesell[8] can best be described as a maturational theorist. His theory is one of "growth process." Gesell describes developmental trends for specific age periods. He considers behavioral trends a dichotomy and emphasizes that, throughout development, the child is trying to pull together or constantly strive for equilibrium. Like Piaget, Gesell emphasizes the need to view development in its entirety.

In Gesell's descriptions of developmental trends, he emphasizes that one developmental period can be evident again at another age or developmental stage. For example, the uniform behavior of the 2-year-old is apparent again at five years and at 10 years. The introverted behavior of the 3½-year-old is seen again at ages seven and 13, whereas the vigorous, expansive behavior of four is also apparent at ages eight and 14.

Gesell veiws developmental trends as universal and maturationally predetermined. He appears to ignore the cultural influences upon developmental trends and has received criticism for this by Mead. [9]

Mead proposes that cultural expectations determined developmental trends and that the characteristics of development as reported by Gesell are not universal, but culturally determined. To Mead, a child's society is constituted with behavioral expectations and invites individual-environmental interaction which encourages the sequence of developmental trends. [9]

Although there are differences among the theorists, each seems to stress the dynamic, organized process of environmental adaptation. We do not attempt to evaluate the theorists nor attempt to integrate their convictions into an eclectic approach for understanding development. Rather, the theories are presented for the reader as the background material used to create a framework for the development of personality. Each theory contributes some insight into a comprehensive percept relevant to the dynamics of personality development. The influence of the theorists upon the presented theory of spatiotemporal adaptation becomes apparent.

Theoretical Framework

The development of personality is enhanced by the organized process of spatiotemporal adaptation. As stated in earlier chapters, adaptation results from the person's transactions with the environment. Adaptation is a process of receiving information from the environment accommodating to the information: associating, differentiating and organizing the information in order to plan and direct one's functioning. Thus, the process of adaptation can be viewed as a three-fold event; that is, past, present, and future are all integrated. With the infant, the process is the immediate tangible future; with the child, the process is a less immediate, more predictable future; and with the adult, the process is a long-term future which helps determine the self's adaptation.

Sensorimotor-sensory (SMS) integration has been described as the major source for adapting to space and time. SMS integration is a function of the nervous system for gathering and processing information for use. SMS integration is reflected in all behaviors, including learning patterns and psychosocial relationships and is an extremely important aspect for the development of personality. Without SMS integration there would be no self-organizing system, and as Piaget points out, without an organized system there can be no adaptation.[7]

To provide a framework for discussion of the development of personality, the following components are termed the spiralis of the continuum: a) survival, b) body sense, c) self awareness, d) self perception, e) self concept, and f) self identification. The components are illustrated in Figure 8-1 and are viewed as the organized continuum of the "self-system."[10] The spiral-effect emphasizes the inter-relationships of the components, with self-identification gradually emerging from the adaptation of lower level components.

Because of the inter-relationships of these components, the reader should keep in mind that one component does not take over where the other one leaves off. The components are both structurally and functionally integrated, one with the other, and adapted as an integral part of the self-system. Aspects of the lower level components are available for use to adapt to the environment whenever stress places a demand upon the system. Because of the variations among individuals concerning developmental growth rates and genetic differences, and due to the cephalocaudal laws of development, the components of the spiraling continuum cannot be equated with specific age ranges. For example, while certain behavioral mechanisms of a child may be developing a body sense, others may be concerned primarily with survival. Therefore, the components should be viewed as names for different aspects of the total process of personality development. The role of SMS integration in the development of personality is stressed. However, each individual must be viewed as a functioning whole, and personality should be understood only in that context.

161

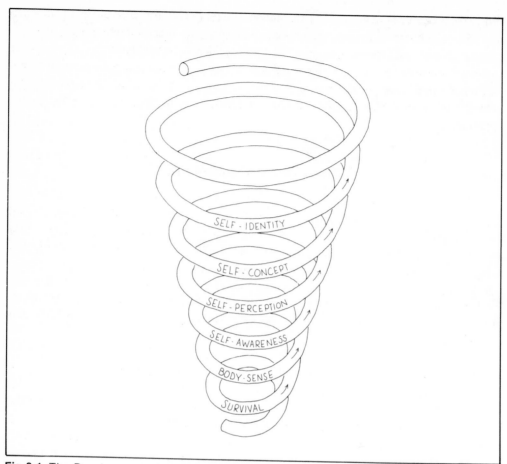

Fig 8-1 The Development of the Personality.

Survival: The First Spiral of the Continuum

Survival is defined as the maturational quest from embryo to birth, encompassing the prenatal, natal, and early neonatal periods. The functions of survival are to preserve, maintain, protect, and defend the organism.[10]

At conception, genetic factors begin to influence the course of development. Also the environment of the mother's womb influences the organism's growth and development. The prenatal experiences of the fetus are considered by Greene[11] as a kind of object perception for the fetus. The mother's activities afford repetitive experiences for the fetus, and this object perception continues for the neonate and "bridges the so-called caesura of birth."[11]

Mussen, Conger, and Kagan[12] stress that the fetus' environment is simple in comparison to the complex world that will be encountered at birth. The environment is a physical one, and the fetus does not need to integrate aspects of a psychosocial environment into its repertoire. Mussen, et al, discuss many variations in the environment of the womb that have a direct influence upon the maturation and development of the fetus, as well as recent research which suggests that the physical, biochemical, and emotional status of the mother exerts an important influence upon the course of development. Factors considered include maternal age, diet, drugs taken by both parents, exposure to radiation, diseases and disorders during pregnancy, hormonal imbalances, blood factors, and the maternal emotional state. The birth process and the time of gestation can affect later patterns of development. [12]

Studies by Twitchell[13] and Jacobs[14] illustrate motor accommodations of reflexive patterns of behavior in the fetus in response to tactile stimulation. Body movements in the fetus provide proprioceptive feedback. The tactile and proprioceptive stimuli are integrated into the developing nervous system and provide the fetus with necessary patterns of adaptation for survival. Fetal experiences of body movements and self-stimulation from these actions help prepare newer posture and movement patterns which the infant will use to adapt to the environment. Therefore, primitive posture and movement strategies, adapted from fetal experiences, provide a means for the neonate to protect the body from incoming sensory stimuli. Through the spiraling process of SMS integration, primitive postural movements become differentiated and organized so that the necessary elements of the strategies can be utilized for higher level adaptations. [15]

In order to survive, the neonate's world must not be exclusively one of protection. Interaction with the environment is a necessity for nutrition, comfort, and survival. Fetal maturation prepares the infant with the necessary components for environmental interaction. Tactile stimulation to the oral region facilitates the rooting reflex in the fetus. The neonate adapts this rooting response and will go toward the source of stimulation. Rooting allows the interaction needed to find the nipple and place it into the mouth.

Although survival forces appear to be primarily biological, an element of psychosocial functioning becomes apparent. The reflex action of the rooting and sucking reflexes ultimately reduces the tension of hunger for the infant. Sucking, which is initially facilitated by the rooting reflex, is an automatic behavioral response to tactile stimuli coupled with the hunger drive. The sucking behavior ultimately becomes a function of the ego to direct that behavior needed to satisfy hunger.

Feeding has a psychological aspect as well as a social communication factor between the infant and the mother or mother-substitute. [10] The nursing experience provides a "biopsychosocial" transaction of the neonate with the environment. The SMS integration of this experience is the foundation upon which the infant begins to develop an awareness of the body. [16] The tactile and pressure stimulation of sucking and swallowing, and of being held and cuddled, the proprioceptive feedback of the postural position, the interoceptive stimulation of satisfying hunger, and the visual stimulation of the mother's face and auditory input from her voice are integrated by the self-system. The SMS integration provides the necessary maturation upon which the nervous system develops a bodily "me."

In summary, the neonate is born into a biopsychosocial world with an already partially organized self-system. [10] The newborn, with help from others, is able to use his self-system for maintaining the survival aspects of protection and interaction in order to preserve, maintain, and protect himself. The spiraling continuum becomes apparent as the neonate utilizes past fetal behaviors for motor accommodations. Through the integration of incoming stimuli the neonate begins to differentiate and organize sensory communication from the environment and from self. This integration leads to an awareness of the bodily "me" or the higher level component of body sense.

Body Sense: The Second Spiral of the Continuum

From Piaget's theories,[6] it becomes apparent that the infant uses innate abilities to direct behavior and assimilate elements of the environment. The stability and mobility components of bodily functions allows for exploration of self and environment. Through the adaptation process the infant begins to associate and differentiate the internal or somatosensory sensations from those that are external to the body. The association and differentiation process leads to body sense. The function of the body sense component is to define the body boundaries for the infant as to what is "me" and "not me."

Through adaptation of experiences, a baby begins to assign some significance or "meaning" to the events in the environment. An important aspect of the development of personality is the significance or meaning assigned to the body. Gordon defined the word "meaning" to imply that the events within the environment signify a cue to action, and that an infant begins to recognize "that some act is symbolic of a coming event that affects him."[10] For example, the act of crying brings mother to him or the act of reaching and grasping for a bottle brings food to his mouth. The significance implied or the meaning attached to the events of the body is the psychosocial aspect of body sense, while the differentiation of internal and external sensations can be more directly related to the biological aspects. The meanings attached to the events of the body and the development of purposeful behaviors have a direct relationship with each other. Body sense can be considered a purposeful behavior as the actions and the significance implied have meaning to the nervous system to enhance maturation. The biopsychosocial aspects of the purposeful behavior of body sense allows the baby to experience himself as a person with some degree of control of the environment. Biopsychosocial interactions lead to higher levels of organization.

Autocosmic play is essential to the acquisition of body sense. Throughout autocosmic play, the infant is adapting to body boundaries. For example, thumb sucking is the body experiencing itself; the mouth "feels" the thumb and the thumb "feels" the mouth. The infant experiences feeling and being felt. Compare this to the sucking of a rattle, nipple, or other objects in the environment. The mouth senses the object and the baby experiences feeling but cannot simultaneously experience being felt. This important differentiation enhances the body sense. Through adaptation of autocosmic play experiences, the infant defines the (first) geography of the body, and this basic map of the child in interplay with persons and objects in the environment remains as a guide for the ego's first orientation to the "world."

When the infant begins to explore the body and objects within the environment, he assigns meanings to the events. Reactions of persons within his environment affect meanings the infant may assign to the body. If body exploration is permitted, meanings attached will probably be healthy. When body exploration is prevented, the infant may develop unhealthy views of the body.[10]

Body sense provides the basic reference point from which environmental interactions take place. A study by Hebb[17] suggests that body sense functions to preserve the orientation of self to the world. Allport[1] stresses that body sense serves as a life-long anchor for man's self-identity.

Body sense contributes to "basic trust" as described by Erikson.[5] The baby's experiences with the purposeful behaviors of body sense augments body control and thus promotes seeking out the environment to satisfy needs, ie, the bottle to satisfy hunger, the toy to satisfy pleasure. The ability to satisfy needs provides a feeling of comfort, thus, the baby can begin to trust his own body. Self-trust provides a sense of stability from which the baby can begin to trust other events within his environment and begin to adapt his purposeful behaviors to purposeful activities.

The spiraling framework demonstrates that the purposeful behavior or body sense of "me" is adapted from the SMS communication of the body during the stage of survival. Primitive patterns of posture and movement become integrated into the self-system. Repetition of the patterns facilitates higher level responses which in turn permit more organization of incoming stimuli. Integration of sensory stimulation from posture and movement strategies of the primitive phase, and the facilitation of higher level purposeful behavior, result in the maturation of the nervous system. Increased maturation is accompanied by an increased repertoire of responses providing the means to establish body sense. By internalizing purposeful behaviors with the meanings attached, the infant begins to develop a schema of the body, leading to an awareness of self.

In summary, body sense provides a schema of what is "me" and "not me." Body sense develops from increased SMS control of purposeful behaviors as the baby adapts to the events of his body. Autocosmic play provides ways by which the infant begins to attach meanings to the body, thus experiencing what the body can provide. The frame of reference of the body is the foundation for the acquisition of self-trust. Body sense is viewed as a fundamental map of the body and remains as a guide for the child's orientation to the world.

Self-Awareness: The Third Spiral of the Continuum

The SMS integrative process of the experiences of the infant during survival and the development of body sense contributes to the awareness of self. These early phases culminate in the sense of the body being "me." However, total differentiation between self and others is not well deliniated at this time. The child must first acquire an awareness of self as a part of the development of "me." Gordon[10] considers the emergence of self-awareness as the line of demarcation between infancy and childhood. The function of self-awareness is the extension of the "me" to seek out the environment and begin to acquire a sense of "mine." The youngster's experiences with purposeful activities augments the development of self-awareness. Through purposeful activities the baby extends the self and the self behaviors to the events of the environment, expanding his goal-directed behaviors to objects outside his own body.

As the child matures and expands his repertoire of purposeful activities, his space increases. The youngster with an ability of locomotion can seek out and explore the environment. With locomotion the child transacts within an enlarged biopsychosocial world, and the body becomes more than "me," that is, the body becomes a social object among other social objects.

Awareness of self develops as the child begins to attach meanings of satisfaction and pride to his body and to his body's accomplishments with purposeful behaviors and activities. As the child interacts with the events of his mileau, he develops high regard for possessions within his biopsychosocial world and extends himself to objects he loves. In this way, the meaning of "mine" develops.

165

The microsphere level of play is important for the development of self-awareness. With microsphere play, the child begins to master objects in the environment, permitting self-satisfaction and pride. The child utilizes the body to accomplish tasks within the biopsychoso-cial world. During microspheric play, a child may experience stress while playing with certain toys, for example, a block will not fit into a hole. The youngster experiences spatiotemporal stress and calls up lower levels of play to adapt to the situation; that is, he may begin to cry, or he may become absorbed with his body, once again experiencing autocosmic play. With increased control of purposeful activities and enhanced sensory awareness through repeated experiences in microspheric play, the need for autocosmic play is reduced. As the child adapts purposeful activities he begins to acquire a sense of autonomy by mastering the events of his environment.

Experiences in this microspheric world of play, including mastery of objects and increased locomotion, encourage the child to further explore the environment and seek out new experience. SMS integrative mechanisms become more complex and the self-system be-comes more highly organized. The child begins to attach new meanings to objects and events in the environment resulting in a "mine" or a new concept of self-awareness.

In summary, self-awareness develops through maturational gains and increased environ-mental experiences. With the foundation of "me," the child acquires awareness of self as a social object in a biopsychosocial world and attaches meanings of satisfaction or pride to the body. With an acquired awareness of self, the child associates experiences and begins to make judgments or evaluations about the body. Thus the spiraling process leads to a perception of self.

Self-Perception: The Fourth Spiral of the Continuum

The major function of self perception is the evaluative or judgmental element. Self-perceptions, like awareness, develop through the child's environmental experiences. How-ever, perception, with a judgmental or evaluative aspect, becomes more of a function of the associate centers of the brain. The child with self-awareness extends himself into the environ-ment; the child with self-perception not only extends himself into the environment but also becomes involved with the self in the biopsychosocial world and begins to evaluate behavior.

The role playing aspects of the newly acquired macrospheric play are characteristic of self-involvement. The child experiences social interactions with peer groups and tries out roles such as fireman, nurse, mother, or father. With role playing, the youngster begins to evaluate the effects of roles upon himself. By evaluating or judging, the child begins to "perceive self as a variety of others: takes on their behaviors as he sees them, tries them out, selects aspects of their roles as meaningful to him, and incorporates them into his own image.[10]

Self-image evolves from self-perceptions. Allport[1] describes two aspects of self-image that are relevant to self-perceptions: 1) the way the child views his present behavior and 2) what he wants to become. Although the young child does not have abstract thoughts of the future, he is beginning to try out adult roles. In a concrete manner, the child is modeling his behavior from the adult's world. He views himself as an adult and attempts to behave in accordance with his perceptions of the adult model.

The child's social interactions with adults and peers provide information about how others feel toward him and his behavior. Gordon[10] believes that the child incorporates the feeling of others into himself. When other persons tell the child how they feel, the child perceives these feelings as his own because self and others are not totally differentiated at this point. For example, the child may go to the garden and pick a rose. He attaches a meaning of pride to the behavior and reinforces this pride by bringing the flower to mother. Her feelings will become incorporated as his. If she smiles, kisses him and is generally pleased, he perceives this as "good" behavior. In contrast, mother may be angry that the child destroyed the flower and the child perceives this as "bad" behavior.

The self experiences behavior as good or bad. This feeling is usually based upon the feelings of others which the child readily perceives. The social component of self (superego) directs the child's behavior according to the perceived feelings which become incorporated into his own self-system. The process of feeling enhances judgmental meanings of behavior, and perception of self develops.

In summary, self-perception is acquired as the child begins to make evaluative judgments and feelings regarding his behavior. The youngster perceives behavior by incorporating the expressed feelings of others into the self-system. The child becomes involved in roles which he models from the adult world. Self-image is developed from the way one views behavior and the way one wants to become. Self-perception, or evaluation of self, is influenced by the feedback the child receives from others concerning his behavior. Self-evaluation becomes a significant influence for future behaviors by promoting differentiation of self from others. Differentiation ultimately leads to a concept of self.

Self-Concept: The Fifth Spiral of the Continuum

The function of self concept is the total differentiation between self and others. The word "concept" conveys a more advanced stage of development and the intellectual quality of learning. Although the aspect of self-concept denotes learning, it also involves a feeling tone. The perceptions of self are ones of evaluation; whereas, the concepts of self are realistic evaluations. Through self-concept the child learns who he is, who others are, how he behaves, and how others behave.

In the process of establishing self-concept, the child differentiates and integrates the various roles of self. The youngster begins to conceive of self as a boy or girl, as a son or daughter, as a brother or sister, as a friend, as a student, and as many other "selves." The concept of self is created by organizing the perceptions of self into one's self-system. As the child learns to cope with the environment he begins to acquire feelings of adequacy or inadequacy. He integrates these feelings with self-perceptions and hopefully establishes a realistic self-concept that serves as the framework upon which many other concepts arise.

In establishing self-concept the child differentiates the fantasy world from fact or "reality from irreality."[18] Previously the youngster perceived self as "father" or "mother" and played the role of being "daddy" or "mommy." As he integrates the schemas of self it becomes apparent that in reality he is not a daddy or mommy but a son or a daughter. The child begins to identify self with daddy or mommy and instead of playing the role, the youngster begins to conceive of himself as a son or daughter working and playing along side of daddy and mommy.

In the SMS process of adapting a concept of self, the child associates and differentiates the components of the purposeful activity of role playing. With repetition of the purposeful activity and the differentiation of fantasy from reality, a higher level behavior or realistic concept evolves. During the spatiotemporal adaptation of self-concept the child frequently experiences stress. The demands of the environment (generally the adult expectations) are too great, and the youngster calls up lower level experiences of fantasy. Repeating purposeful role playing augments association and differentiation components until a realistic concept is established.

Erikson's age of "industry versus inferiority" is fundamental to the achievement of self-concept. During the stage, Erikson stresses that the child becomes ready to apply himself to given skills and tasks.[5] The child adapts to the instruments of the environment and accepts his skill levels as being the realistic mode for coping with the objects of the environment. Learning to cope with the objects of the environment leads to a sense of self-reliance.

In summary, self-concept is the organization of the perceptual schemas of self into a realistic framework. Self-concept is the foundation from which the child creates many concepts. A concept of self is developed from the association and differentiation of purposeful activities experienced with play. With the attainment of self-concept, childhood ends and adolescence begins.

Self-Identification: The Sixth Spiral of the Continuum

Identity, according to Erikson, is "the establishment and re-establishment of sameness with one's previous experiences and a conscious attempt to make the future a part of one's personal life plan."[19] Because future includes vocational identity, the stress of identifying one's self with a specific vocation may be too great, and the adolescent will experience the spatiotemporal stress phenomena. He may over identify with the heroes and leaders, lose his own self-concept, and experience a form of "fantasy" of the role playing period. The identification with heroes and leaders represents a form of identity crises for the adolescent. Erikson feels that if the identity crises of adolescence is not solved with realistic expectations of self, identity is not established satisfactorily, and ego development will be impaired.

In the quest for self-identification, the adolescent utilizes his acquired concept and begins to view himself with a future orientation. Although past development may not overtly determine the adolescent's future, it does influence his perspective or his personal point of view. Piaget suggests that the adolescent begins to reflect beyond the present and seeks a personal place in life.[6] The adolescent models behavior after heroes or leaders as he abstractly views self in preparation for his long range plans and distant goals.[2] The spiraling continuum repeats itself as the adolescent role playing is a modification of the role playing of childhood but has the additional element of abstract thought.

With the spiraling continuum of spatiotemporal adaptation, the adolescent's perspective expands and both the past and the future become important and are eventually differentiated. Mead[20] suggests that the adolescent is in a period of re-examination of the past and re-orientation for the future. A function of adolescence is differentiating past and future or to put aside the *play*/work orientation of childhood and begin to assume the *work*/play orientation of adulthood.

The re-examination of the past is representative of the spiraling continuum and becomes apparent with the descriptions of behavioral traits of the adolescent period. Gesell[21] states that these behavioral patterns can be likened to those of earlier age periods. For example, according to Gesell the behavior of an 11-year-old is similar to the behavior of a 2½ and 5½-year-old; the behavior of 12 years is somewhat characteristic of the behavior of 3 years; the traits of 14 resembles 4 and 8; and the characteristics of 15 are likened to the 4½-year-old. The similarities of the traits represent the influences of earlier periods which become modified through the spiraling process.

With the spiraling continuum of adaptation, earlier lower level behaviors are available for use by the person, particularly in times of stress. During the crises of adolescence, many situations present stress, and the adolescent may call up earlier behaviors in order to cope and adapt to the environment.

Stress has a positive effect upon personality development. When the behavior is influenced by and resembles lower level behaviors, the adolescent has the unique opportunity to re-examine his behavior. However, at this level the adolescent can provide abstract thinking and future orientation to his behavior, ultimately leading to higher level responses and an identification of self as a member of his past, present, and future worlds.

In the spiraling process the adolescent not only re-examines himself through participation with lower level behaviors, but he experiences extremes in behavioral traits which represent conflicts and stress. For example, Gesell states that at age 11 the youth may be negative, argumentative, and impulsive; by 12 he can be reasonable and social; at 13 he may become introverted and reflective; at age 14 he has a tendency toward vigorous expansive behavior; at 15 he may experience increased tensions and hostility; and at 16 his behavior may be smooth and consolidated.[21] By experiencing these oscillating and fluctuating extremes in behavior the adolescent has the opportunity to re-examine himself in respect to his new orientation toward the future. The conflicts are believed to be necessary in order to help establish an identity of self within the biopsychosocial world.

In summary, self-identification is the association differentiation of necessary elements of one's past with the present and in relation to the future of one's personal life goals. Self-identification may be a major hurdle for the adolescent to master because his traits may be extremes in behavior and representative of influences of earlier periods of his life. When establishing self-identification one is in transition from childhood to adulthood. The transition is represented by conflicts and stress. Transitional periods in the developmental process are critical periods of integrating and adapting lower level behaviors to higher level performances. Spatiotemporal stress augments adaptation for the development of self-identification.

The function of self-identification is differentiating past with present reality and the future, as well as making a change from the *play*/work orientation of childhood to the *work*/play orientation of adulthood. The experiences of the adolescent hopefully culminates in self-identification.

Summary

The creation of "self" is a developmental and maturational process, resulting from the transactions of the child with his biological, psychological, and sociological environment. The nature of the development of personality is viewed as a spiraling continuum of spatiotemporal adaptation with increasingly higher level behaviors gradually emerging from the lower level acquired behaviors and continuous stresses of environmental contact. Inherent in the adaptation process is SMS integration. This, in turn, is dependent upon the interaction between nervous system maturation and environmental experiences and the transactions of the child with his biopsychosocial world. Through integration the information from the environment is organized and interpreted by the self-system in order to plan and perform within the person's world.

During the development of personality, the behaviors and activities of the child are goal-directed and purposeful in that they are meaningful for the enhancement of the nervous system. Purposeful behaviors and activities not only enhance the development of skilled performance but are considered as a major attribute in the development of personality. Through the participation with the events of the body and the environment, the child enhances the adaptation of the self-system.

Six components that are characteristic spiraling phases of the development of personality have been presented. The first spiral, survival, functions to preserve, maintain, protect, and defend the organism. The function of the second spiral, body sense, is the definition of the body boundaries. Self-awareness, the third spiral, functions as the extension of the bodily "me" to a sense of "mine." During the fourth spiral, self-perception, the child becomes involved with self in the biopsychosocial world. The function of self-perception is the evaluative or judgmental element of self-behaviors. The function of self-concept, the fifth spiral of the continuum, is the total differentiation between self and others. These phases interrelate and culminate in the final phase of self-identification. Self-identification functions to integrate and differentiate the necessary elements of one's past to the present and future of one's personal life plan. In each of the spiraling phases individuality and uniqueness of the person is the rule. Through interactions with purposeful behaviors and activities, each individual develops his or her own self-system and must be viewed as a functioning whole. Behavior can be thoroughly understood only in this context.

References

1. Allport GW: Becoming: Basic Considerations for a Psychology of Personality. New Haven, Yale Univ Press, 1958.
2. Allport GW: Pattern and Growth in Personality. New York, Holt Rinehart Winston Inc, 1961.
3. Hall C, Lindzey G: Theories of Personality. New York, John Wiley & Sons Inc, 1970.
4. Kagan J: The concept of identification. Psychol Rev 65:296-305, 1958.
5. Erikson EH: Childhood and Society. New York, WW Norton Co Inc, 1963, pp 211, 259, 263.
6. Flavel J: The Developmental Psychology of Jean Piaget. New York, Van Nostrand Co, 1963.
7. Baldwin AL: Theories of Child Development. New York, John Wiley Sons Inc, 1968.
8. Gesell A, Amatruda C: Developmental Diagnosis. New York, PB Hoeber Inc, 1956.
9. Mead M: Coming of Age in Samoa. New York, New American Library, 1950.
10. Gordon IJ: Human Development from Birth Through Adolescence. New York, Harper & Row Pubs Inc, 1969, pp 65, 84.
11. Greene WA: Early object relations, somatic, affective and personal. J Nerv Ment Dis 126:225-253, 1958.
12. Mussen P, Conger J, Kagan J: Child Development and Personality. New York, Harper & Row Pubs Inc, 1969.
13. Twitchell TE: Normal motor development. The Child with Central Nervous System Deficit. Children's Bureau Pub. US Dept Health, Education & Welfare, Washington DC, Government Printing Office, 1965, pp 85-89.

14. Jacobs MJ: Development of normal motor behavior. Am J Phys Med 46:41-50, 1967.
15. Gilfoyle E, Grady A: Cognitive-perceptual-motor behavior, in Willard HS, Spakman CS (eds): Occupational Therapy. Philadelphia, JB Lippincott Co, 1971.
16. Spitz R: The First Year of Life. New York, International Univ Press, 1965.
17. Hebb D: The motivating effects of exteroceptive stimulation. Am Psychol 46:41-50, 1958.
18. Lewin KA: A Dynamic Theory of Personality. New York, McGraw-Hill Book Co, 1935.
19. Muuss R: Theories of Adolescence. New York, Random House Inc, 1968, p 50.
20. Mead M: Male and Female. New York, William Morrow & Co Inc, 1949.
21. Gesell A, Ames LB: Youth: The Years from Ten to Sixteen. New York, Harper & Row Pubs Inc, 1956.

Chapter Nine
Spatiotemporal Stress, Distress, and Dysfunction

Adaptation has been described as the process by which a child organizes developmental experiences to modify and expand his repertoire of behaviors, activities, and skills. Adaptation enhances maturation of one's system and development of a unique "self."

Spatiotemporal Stress

In the process of adapting, a child encounters a variety of experiences that may represent stress. The way a child meets and handles these stress experiences has a direct impact upon results of adaptation. Therefore, stress may be considered as a positive or negative factor of development. Stress, as a positive factor, produces a temporary state that results in higher level functions and maturation. Stress, as a negative factor, is a persistant state that results in dysfunction and interferes with maturation.

Hans Selye[1] describes stress as a relationship between an organism's biological system and changes through which one goes in adjusting to demands of the environment. Selye defines stress as a phenomenon characterized by an alteration of the system's equilibrium. The result of stress is an adjustment made to the environment, with a return to normal functioning or equilibrium following the stress impact.[1] A child will experience stress impact when acquired or learned ways of coping with situations no longer suffice. Therefore, in the process of adapting a child alters learned performances in some manner to resolve the "stress" situation. Alteration of performance results in resolution of the stress situation, modification of learned patterns, and higher level functioning—a positive outcome. Throughout one's development, the self-system must determine ways to regulate accommodations to stress so that experiences do not result in unresolved stressful situations—a negative outcome.

"Stress—the internal drummer, so to speak—truly lies within us," according to Dr. Kenneth Greenspun, Director of the Laboratory for Stress Related Disorders, Columbia-Presbyterian Medical Center. "And so also does the solution to the human predicament. The answer is already there; we just need to learn how to call it forth."[2] Calling forth previously acquired behaviors in order to adapt to stress experiences is inherent within the spiraling continuum of spatiotemporal adaptation.

Spatiotemporal stress is the "internal drummer" phenomenon of the normal developmental process. Spatiotemporal stress is defined as a temporary state, characterized by an inability to adapt one's highest level of posture and movement strategies to purposeful behaviors/activities and/or an inability to adapt one's highest level of behaviors/activities to skills. When the phenomenon occurs the system "calls forth" previously acquired or older strategies, behaviors, or activities to adapt to the demands of the situation. (Fig 9-1, 9-2).

Calling forth acquired patterns to adapt expends only the needed energy to maintain the

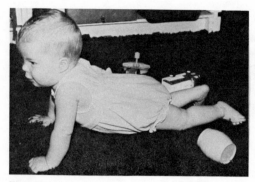

Fig 9-1 This 6-month-old child has achieved postural control to maintain on-hands position in prone.

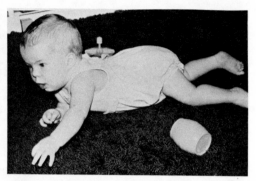

Fig 9-2 However, to move forward in prone (crawl), child "calls forth" postural stability gained from a previously acquired on-elbows position in order to shift weight, maintain balance, and reach out.

system's homeostatsis. Although the system is confronted with change, the amount and degree of change is not past the point for "homeostatic energy expenditure."[3] Therefore, spatiotemporal stress, as a normal developmental phenomenon, is not anxiety provoking to the self-system. Rather, spatiotemporal stress is a motivating force that stimulates us to adapt to the constant changes of our existence.[3]

Spatiotemporal stress is a vital stimulus for normal development according to the spiraling theory. Ability to maintain postural balance within gravitation spatial demands and to gauge movements in accordance with temporal requirements presents a constant challenge to the developmental lifespan. Spiraling sequences adapted by a child to meet the challenges have been described in previous chapters. However, additional attention to the stress component of spiraling is appropriate in order to apply the theory to concepts of distress and dysfunction.

Stress Factors

Gravity was previously identified as a significant force to move against for purposes of developing strategies which support function. In addition to facilitating and strengthening posture and movement strategies, gravity demands that organized strategies be continually available for adaptation to behaviors, activities, and skills. Gravity becomes a significant factor in eliciting selected strategies, organized into postural sets by providing constant, subcortical input for balance. The system monitors changes in body position in relation to gravitational input, and postural adjustments are automatically made. The child is free to attend to activities without expending cortical energy on balance or posture. However, during periods of development and adaptation of strategies, gravity may produce stress rather than promote balance. The child will either seek a more secure posture to perform desired activity, or he may pause to practice balance at a higher level of postural control before attempting activities at that level. In either case, *gravitational stress* is a factor for change in both higher and lower level performance.

A related factor known to produce stress is *complexity of movement* required to complete a behavior/activity or skill. A movement strategy adapted to any situation demands smooth blending of stability and mobility functions to produce coordinated flow. A movement strategy adapted to a complex situation requires even more careful monitoring of movement combinations in order to produce the most efficient and accurate strategy. As long as movement flow and countermovement control are automatically monitored, and blended, the child employs his highest levels of posture and movement for desired behaviors/activities or skills. However, any situation which interrupts monitoring and blending of muscle functions, such as changes in feedback or demands for more intricate movement, may produce spatiotemporal stress. The child will either call forth more secure posture to support more intricate movement, or he will choose a less complex movement strategy to complete the behavior/activity or skill.

A third related factor of spatiotemporal stress is found in the *requirements of the activity or skill* itself. Repeated experiences with a certain activity or group of similar activities combines movement flow and postural sets into perceptual sets. Perceptual sets are automatically activated in the presence of stimuli for a certain activity or skill. If the complexity of an activity or skill increases in terms of spatial, temporal, cognitive, or emotional demands, stress may interrupt automatic use of more recently established perceptual sets. The child may call forth a previously acquired perceptual set to adapt to increased demands from the activity. Or, he may choose a postural set-conscious movement combination to meet the challenge and eventually re-establish the higher level set.

The factors contributing to spatiotemporal stress are inter-related. Several factors are often responsible for change. Gravity usually plays a major role in stress during development of purposeful behaviors when mastery of spatial demands predominates. The gravity factor continues to re-emerge along with the complex movement factor when movement is being matched to temporal demands of activities. Complexity of movement is particularly stressful during the time when perceptual sets are developing. Requirements of activities and skills becomes the intervening variable when perceptual sets are expanding and being adapted to skills.

The following example citing modification of on-hands behavior is presented to illustrate the role of spatiotemporal stress in facilitating normal development:

a) The child can assume an on-hands posture by adapting extension from vertical righting, support reactions of upper extremities and combined mobility, and stability from on-elbows push and pull. On-hands the child can maintain the posture and rock back and forth and side to side. However, the child cannot shift weight to one upper extremity in order to reach out with the other extremity.

b) To reach out for a toy, the child calls forth an on-elbows posture in order to utilize a weight-shift set and free an arm for reaching. Because the child has now had experience in the on-hands posture which expanded stability within the trunk, weight-shift on-elbows is possible, and the child obtains the toy.

c) The child repeats the sequence frequently, moving to on-hands to practice a new behavior and back to on-elbows to play with a toy. Increased control on-hands motivates the child to seek higher postural levels and modify the on-hands posture.

d) From on-hands with back fully extended to pelvis, the child changes position by pushing back on hands and knees and rocking. All-fours posture prepares on-hands posture for change by further expanding trunk stability.

e) Now as the youngster calls forth on-elbows each time he wishes to reach, he associates obtaining a toy by means of the movement for reaching with his now secure higher level on-hands posture. Instead of calling forth the total on-elbows reaching behavior, he differentiates the reaching component and adapts it to on-hands. He has gained necessary stability from all-fours experiences to weight-shift on-hands and is thus prepared to receive differentiated reaching behavior from on-elbows.

f) The last step in this small segment of the adaptation process is the final change which occurs on-elbows. As trunk extension expanded with first on-hands and then all-fours, the stability gained in upper trunk prepared for integration of rotation imposed by rocking side to side. Once rotation is integrated at the midline, on-elbows reaching is modified to include weight-shift with rotation. Movement of the upper extremity forward is controlled by countermovement of the shoulder-scapula developed with rotation around the midline. Accuracy and efficiency of reaching for toys increases with addition of the mature set to on-elbows functioning.

From this illustration, the role of stress as a developmental motivator is apparent. The stress factors which caused the child to alter posture in order to function also provided the opportunity for function to be associated with new behavior, differentiated and adapted so that higher level behaviors change and development proceeds.

During the normal developmental process, spatiotemporal stress primarily occurs in three situations: 1) when adapting to new experiences, 2) when the sensorimotor-sensory integrative process is temporarily altered in some manner, and 3) during transition of one behavior to another. In these three situations, a child may attempt to adapt with his highest level of learned performance. When his method of coping does not suffice, the system will subsequently "call forth" older patterns to resolve the situation and enhance maturation.

Throughout development the self-system learns to manage stress experiences of the environment and ultimately develop methods of coping. Thus development of purposeful behaviors and activities is dependent upon spatiotemporal stress. As a result the system matures. Adapting children thrive on spatiotemporal stress experiences that can be managed and controlled by the self-system.

Spatiotemporal Distress

Stress that is out of control and cannot be managed is termed distress. Distress is a negative factor for development, characterized by an alteration of the system's equilibrium resulting in purposeless performance and maladaptation. With distress there is a lack of return to the system's normal functioning level or equilibrium. When the environment provokes distress, homeostasis is affected, purposeless (meaningless) behaviors and activities prevail, and dysfunction occurs. Repetition of dysfunctional performance during development results in developmental disabilities (Fig 9-3, 9-4, 9-5).

During the spiraling process of adapting spatial and temporal factors of environmental experiences, distress may occur. When the system experiences spatiotemporal distress, lower level behaviors cannot be adapted to new experiences and higher level behaviors do not emerge. Integration of lower level and higher level behaviors/activities does not occur.

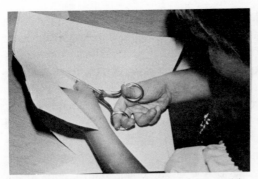

Fig 9-3 Normal Cutting: This 5-year-old with normal adaptation patterns cuts by differentiating mobility and stability within the hand. Stability along the ulnar side provides control for radial mobility to manipulate the scissors.

Fig 9-4 Distress in Cutting: This 5-year-old with learning problems cuts by adapting undifferentiated patterns (full flexion-full extension) to manipulate scissors. Her pattern reflects adaptations used by younger children with scissors.

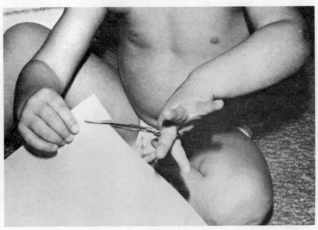

Fig 9-5 Primitive Cutting: The same child in Figure 9-3 at age 2½ used undifferentiated patterns which was a normal adaptation for her age.

Therefore, posture and movement strategies are not adapted to behaviors and activities, and behaviors are not linked with activities for adaptation to skills.

Spatiotemporal distress results from:

a) abnormal assimilations, eg, abnormal sensory reception, sensory deprivation, or sensory overload (jamming);

b) abnormal accommodations, eg, purposeless sensorimotor patterns, abnormal neuromuscular characteristics (tone, range, control, speed, etc);

c) abnormal association/differentiation, eg, faulty sensorimotor-sensory integration.

Origins of spatiotemporal distress resulting in developmental disabilities are numerous. There are hereditary factors, chromosomal abnormalities, unexplained birth defects, fetal distress or lack of expected development in utero, prematurity or dysmaturity, difficulties before, during, or after birth with residual brain lesions, retardation, acquired problems from trauma or disease affecting the central nervous system or peripheral systems, abuse, neglect, or environmental deprivation. There is also a large idiopathic category of developmental disabilities for which diagnosis is not available to explain the origin of the problem, but the problem of spatiotemporal distress still exists for the child, family, educator, health care personnel, etc. Although information about origins of a child's distress/dysfunction is valuable for purposes of evaluation, prognosis, planning, monitoring progress, etc, the most valuable source of information available for analysis of spatiotemporal distress is the child himself.

Spatiotemporal distress affects every aspect of a child's progress toward maturity. The child's relationships within the family and the world outside, his feelings of competence and autonomy, and other persons' responses to him are built upon performance expectations held by the child for himself and others for him. Since so much of measurable performance is built upon spatiotemporal adaptation, especially for the young child, interruptions in the process or failure to develop according to expectations has a reverberating effect upon the SMS process, neurophysiologically and emotionally.

SMS Factors

The quality and quantity of *sensory assimilations* has an obvious effect on the rest of the SMS process.

1) Too little sensory input as experienced by children who are neglected, or in nonstimulating situations, results in absence or poor quality/quantity of motor accommodations. Sensory feedback to self and others from a poor response reduces the possibility of increasing quality or quantity of input. Over a period of time, the cycle may result in sufficient distress to cause dysfunction in adaptation.

2) Too much sensory input which may occur in well-meaning, but overstimulating, situations may overload the system, not allowing adequate accommodation and feedback for association-differentiation. The child may continue to remain responsive to stimulation, but his system cannot make sufficient use of assimilations for adaptation.

3) Sensory assimilations which are threatening or harmful as in child abuse, or input perceived as threatening due to delay in adapting protective responses, may cause the child to withdraw, physically and/or emotionally. Again, the process of accommodation-feedback is altered. Withdrawal from the initial source of modification for the system leaves the child functioning in a primitive state or attempting to function at higher levels with primitive strategies.

4) Sensory assimilations may be received but not recognized by some children. If input is not meaningful, there may be no accommodation or again poor quality accommodation; neither provides the adequate feedback for change within the system. The seemingly purposeless accommodations are often unique or linked into unique sequences characteristic of the child's inability to make adequate use of sensory input and are not always reflective of normal sequences.

It is possible that initial sensory assimilations could be considered adequate for eliciting a response. The difficulty lies with the *motor accommodation* itself. Of course, since accommodations play such a vital role in feedback for change, it is obvious that the whole system is affected rapidly, even though faulty motor accommodation seems to be primarily involved.

1) Sensory assimilation seems adequate and appears to be recognized by the child. Due to difficulty within the system, motor accommodations may be absent, purposeless, or characterized by immature strategies, including aberrations in neural and muscular functions. If accommodations are absent or purposeless, there is lack of feedback for adaptation. If responses are present but abnormal, feedback is abnormal.

2) Sensory assimilations from abnormal feedback become the basis for adaptation with children whose problems are manifested primarily in the motor area. Abnormal muscle tone controlled by primitive neural mechanisms become part of attempts to adapt and develop into a uniquely abnormal process.

Finally, for some children, the SMS process may appear to be intact for achievement of basic behaviors and performance of some activities. However, there may be difficulty making meaningful use of *sensory feedback*.

1) Even if assimilations are received and acted upon by the child, feedback must be associated and differentiated. Failure to adequately associate and differentiate feedback leads to dificits in sensory judgment, thereby interrupting the sensorimotor-sensory integrative process and development of perception.

2. Faulty feedback from poor association-differentiation becomes the basis for adaptation of strategies to progressively higher levels of behavior, activity and skill. As a result, the child's performance may be characterized by attempts to use lower level primitive or transitional strategies to adapt to mature types of behaviors and activities. The process is further complicated because repeated immature adaptations are not meaningful for change. The child does not develop postural and perceptual sets which transfer readily to skill performance.

Since sensorimotor-sensory integration is a spiraling process, any interruption in one aspect of the process has an effect upon the rest of the system. Outcome of distress within the system may be immediately observable or may take years to manifest full impact. Even though specific types of congenital problems may be related to a primary source of distress, effect of distress upon SMS integration is wide-spread and impacts totally upon the child and his environment. Knowledge of primary sources of a problem is important for assessment and intervention as long as cognizance is always given to the effect of interaction between sensory, motor, and feedback components of the system. Generally, children categorized as abused, neglected, over or under stimulated, developmentally delayed, retarded, etc, have problems which originate from difficulty processing or making use of initial assimilations. Their adaptations usually remain primitive or uniquely abnormal. Children grouped as cerebral palsy, motor delay, etc, have initial difficulty manifested in motor accommodation. Their behavior and activity performance may be marked by abnormal movement patterns and development of adaptations not reflective of normal development. Finally, children with sensory integrative dysfunction, learning disabilities, etc, may have integrative problems which begin with a failure to perceive initial sensory assimilations accurately, thus compromising the SMS process as a basis with which to adapt. Other children with sensory integrative dysfunction may have problems which begin with failure to associate/differentiate feedback from sensorimotor experiences. Therefore, aspects of primitive and transitional strategies influence behavior and activity performance.

Children with acquired interruptions in the SMS process present other variables. If trauma or disease, for example, head injury, Reyes syndrome, burns, amputation, juvenile arthritis, etc, interrupts development after the basic foundation for SMS integration has been laid, it is more difficult to determine which aspect of the process is most affected. Just as the SMS system functions as a whole, the system is affected as a whole. Manifestations of acquired spatiotemporal distress include regressions in adaptation, ie, calling forth primitive and transitional strategies and behaviors previously integrated. The child may also acquire some abnormal adaptations with abnormal muscle tone, especially if the central nervous system is involved in the original trauma or disease.

Whether spatiotemporal distress originates with congenital or acquired problems, the factors which tended to cause stress in normal development—gravity, combinations of movement, and complexity of behavior or activity itself—are also factors related to distress/dysfunction. These factors are primary causes of distress resulting in dysfunction, since the child with problems cannot make use of the stress situation to modify his responses. He tends to repeat a limited repertoire of immature or abnormal sequences without change, and dysfunction prevails. In addition, distress factors may cause further progression in dysfunctional performance. The child's attempts to respond to gravity with immature or abnormal muscle functions and patterns of movement, increased demands for more complex adaptations, and the child's own assessment of his competence following unsuccessful, unmodified experiences all comprise some of the secondary factors contributing to dysfunction (Fig 9-6, 9-7, 9-8, 9-9, 9-10, 9-11). The factors related to normal spatiotemporal stress may be unresolved because of nervous system and/or environmental involvement. The stress situation is compounded by secondary factors. Primary and secondary factors impact negatively on development of strategies and adaptation to behaviors, activities, and skills.

As a result of distress, posture and movement strategies are likely to be delayed or develop

Fig 9-6 This 5-year-old boy with cerebral palsy, spastic diplegia, uses a superior pincer grasp for objects requiring minimal manipulation.

Fig 9-7 Adaptation to manipulate a crayon initially calls forth an inferior pincer grasp.

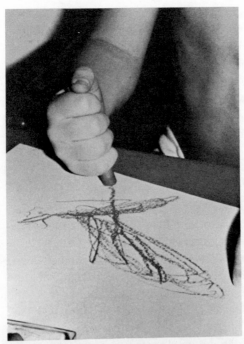

Fig 9-8 However, repetition of complex movements needed to manipulate a crayon calls forth lower level palmar grasp.

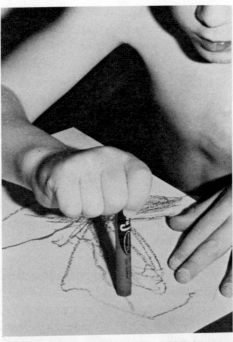

Fig 9-9 Further stress from difficulty controlling movement as well as posture results in lower level pronated palmar grasp.

Fig 9-10 The same boy begins again, trying to maintain pincer grasp, but losing postural control due to stress.

Fig 9-11 Persistant attempts to maintain pincer grasp result in disintegration of postural control over head and trunk.

with deviations in quality and quantity of neural and muscular functions. Strategies may not be adapted or may be maladapted to purposeful behaviors, leaving control to isolated stereotyped strategies rather than a variety of unfolding behaviors. The drive toward purposeful behaviors and activities may or may not be present. If the quest for development is absent or severely delayed, then purposeless, eventually abnormal, strategies prevail. If the drive to purposeful behavior and activities is intact, but if the child cannot modify strategies sufficiently for adaptation, then performance, or attempts to perform, are characterized by either primitive, transitional, or abnormal patterns of movement and postural control.

Distress to Dysfunction

Primitive and transitional strategies are usually identified as dysfunctional whenever the strategies are used to adapt beyond the normal time or at higher than expected levels of behavior/activity.[4] Primitive and transitional strategies reflect early stages of normal development as described previously. The problem is not the strategy itself; the difficulty comes when the strategy is not modified by the association-differentiation process and is only available in the primitive or transitional form for use with mature behaviors or activities. Or, the problem may be evident when primitive or transitional strategies are too readily called forth with the slightest provocation from spatiotemporal stress. Thus, mature functioning is so easily lost that it cannot gain from repetition. Instead, primitive and transitional strategies are repeated more often. As a result, immature neural mechanisms and muscle functions characteristic of these phases continue to be predominate influences on behavior instead of being adapted to mature strategies. Evidence of primitive and transitional strategies used to adapt beyond normal periods for calling forth previous behaviors may indicate pathology in the child's adaptation process. Pathological primitive strategies are usually a cause of dysfunction in younger or less involved children. Pathological transitional strategies usually affect children with sensory integrative dysfunction or children with temporary loss of function due to trauma.

Abnormal patterns of movements and attempts to control posture may resemble some primitive strategies but are characterized by types of muscle tone which is never normal during the usual course of development. Or, patterns may be abnormal because they are comprised of postures or movements not observed at any time in the course of normal development. For example, some particular syndromes or developmental deviations are characterized by posturing or repetitive movement patterns unique to the particular problem. Abnormal movement patterns are considered pathological at any time.

Abnormal patterns of movement and control imply that the brain is not fully developed or that trauma occurred before, during, or after birth. Abnormal patterns may not be apparent in young babies, but can be detected in children after approximately four months of age and any time in severely involved children.

Abnormal patterns make use of abnormal muscle tone, either hypertonic, hypotonic, fluctuating, or combinations of these types of tone. Primitive reflexes assume control over behaviors and activities since abnormal tone interferes with modification of reflexes. Reflexes accompanied by abnormal tone tend to control behavior in an obligatory sense. The child repeats stereotyped, reflex-like patterns building abnormal sequences and reinforcing the effect of the reflex rather than modifying it.

It should be noted that patterns which appear primitive in young babies, or following trauma at any age, can develop into abnormal patterns if abnormal muscle tone, previously undetected, becomes part of a primitive strategy. Effect of gravity and demands for more complex movement at higher levels may bring forth abnormal tone when potential for abnormality is present due to brain lesion. Care should always be taken to recognize developing abnormalities by monitoring change carefully and by avoiding postures and movements known to evoke abnormal responses, even though the posture or movement is usually part of normal sequences for normal children.

Development of purposeful behaviors is interrupted whenever primitive or transitional strategies are retained pathologically, or abnormal patterns are present. The extent and degree of pathology determines lags or arrest in development of behaviors and corresponding spatiotemporal distress/dysfunction. Each time an abnormal response is observed, or a behavioral sequence incomplete, or an immature response used to adapt, the occurrence should be evaluated in terms of its effect on behavior as a whole. Dysfunctional children can be analyzed by *identifying pathology* and by determining *how it interferes* with function. Analysis of behavior yields information about the SMS process, distress factors, strategies retained and adapted or linked together pathologically, strategies and hence behaviors which have failed to develop, and abnormal, as well as normal, patterns present.

Primitive Signs of Dysfunction

During the normal primitive phase of development (0 to 3-4 months) only observations regarding behaviors which have failed to develop or obvious, severe abnormality can be regarded as dysfunctional or potentially dysfunctional. The quality and quantity of behaviors developing during primitive may be suspect, but can only be considered dysfunctional if interfering with higher levels of development after the primitive phase. Some observations which are suspected for pathology* include:

1) **Poverty of movement:**[4] There is a lack of primitive movement. The baby does not make use of phasic activity for reflexive kicking, frequent head turning, or opening and closing hands. Spontaneous movements, cuddling, movement to sight or sound may be diminished or absent. Poverty of movement deprives the child of motor accommodations which lead to development of muscle functions. The baby may appear to be hypotonic.

2) **Stereotyped Movement:**[4] If the baby develops limited movements, the movements may be linked together into stereotyped sequences. Sequences tend to be repeated, reinforcing the stereotype and interfering with development of variability needed for adaptation. If abnormal muscle tone becomes a factor, hypertonicity combined with stereotyped movements produces limited sequences repeated in serial order, ie, the child extends neck, opens mouth, extends upper extremities; or, grasp with hands is followed by flexion of arms, neck and trunk, etc.

Note: Observations of neonates and very young infants will be particularly influenced by the baby's state at the time of observation. Factors like prematurity will also influence posture and movement patterns. Specifically developed evaluation criteria should be used to evaluate neonates or premature babies.

3) **Static postures:**[4] Static postures are related to lack of, or limited, movement. Static postures are mostly indicative of problems when a segment of body usually assumes and remains in the same posture, regardless of changes in position of the rest of the body. Static postures may also include persistant asymmetries in head, trunk, or extremity postures.

4) **Inconsistent patterns:** If there is inconsistency noted between ability in different postures, it may be early evidence of muscle tone problems.[5] A child may appear to be developing appropriate muscle functions in one posture. But, when placed in a different posture requiring the same accommodation, there is an absence of tone noted.[4] Early inconsistencies in primitive muscle functions may indicate that muscle tone developing in one posture is abnormal and therefore not available to transfer to another function.

5) **Suck-swallow problems:** Feeding behavior is one of the bodily functions already established at birth which reflects synchrony of movement. Problems with suck-swallow patterns, not structural in nature, and resulting in feeding difficulty may be a predictor of movement difficulties at higher levels. In addition, the baby is deprived of one of the first intact SMS cycles which he associates with other behaviors. Feeding difficulties also interrupt early infant-parent relationships which are formed around nurturing survival situations. Neither parent nor baby are satisfied by difficult, nonproductive feeding periods.

6) **Lack of visual responsiveness:** Visual interaction and early tracking behaviors may not be apparent during primitive development. A deficit in visual responsiveness deprives the baby of one of his more advanced methods of receiving information about his world. He also eliminates one way by which he can attract others to respond to him. Poor visual tracking also diminishes one of the baby's sources of input for moving and looking.[6]

7) **Lack of transitional preparation:** Failure to develop such behaviors as head lift in prone, head align in supine, and protective or spontaneous head turning in prone or supine deprives the child of necessary neural maturation and muscle development to progress from the primitive to transitional phase.

Throughout primitive development-at-risk for dysfunction, the baby may not be establishing a good basis for development of strategies and behaviors necessary to adapt to higher levels. Specific areas of distress may be emerging, even though definitive dysfunction may not be identified. Primitive behaviors become dysfunctional when not modified by transitional development.

Primitive Pathology

Pathological primitive behavior reflects behavior which is retained to adapt beyond the normal primitive period[4] and corresponding failure to develop some of the higher level strategies/behavior/activities. † Usually gravity is a major distress factor for a child moving from

† *The photographs selected to illustrate primitive pathology (Figures 9-12 to 9-26) were taken over a period of time from approximately four to 20 months of age. The illustrations do not represent this child's complete developmental progression, but are selected to illustrate the points in the text.*

primitive to transitional development. Transitional behaviors require antigravity postures and combinations of posture and movement. Pathological primitive behaviors may prevent transition to higher levels or may significantly influence adaptation of primitive to transitional behaviors. More severely involved children have difficulty progressing to transitional development. There are some general observations of pathological primitive strategies, behaviors, or activities to be noted. These observations are a guide to observing an individual child's performance, at which time this information combined with information about normal development can be used for specific analysis.

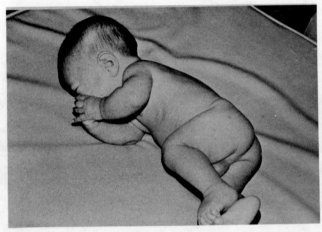

Fig 9-12 Undifferentiated Movements: The child's use of neck flexion to initiate rolling is followed by an undifferentiated use of flexion pattern encompassing trunk and limbs.

1) **Undifferentiated movements:** Use of primitive strategies in a pathological sense may be manifest as continued use of undifferentiated movements, especially those movements affecting neck and limbs. The child continues to initiate movement which is carried through a complete range of motion before an antagonistic movement can be initiated. As a result, the child attempts to function with unmodified activation of muscle groups. A child may be capable of adapting such movements to behaviors and activities if he is so motivated. However, his environment will have to be adapted to undifferentiated movement rather than movement being adapted to environment, negating the possibility that the adaptation process will change primitive movement appropriately. Undifferentiated movements lack variability, and repetition of movements contributes further to stereotyped approaches to tasks (Fig 9-12).

2) **Primitive Phasic Reflexes:** Repeated undifferentiated and stereotyped movements indicate that the neural mechanisms underlying movements have not matured beyond a primitive state.

The child's performance will continue to reflect primitive reflex-like activity, such as stepping or kicking, rooting, total grasp and avoiding, etc, If primitive reflex-like activity persists, the receptors which activate primitive reflex behavior will also remain unmodified. The child may continue to respond to tactile and proprioceptive input with survival and protective accommodations. Instead of adapting primitive tactile responses, the

185

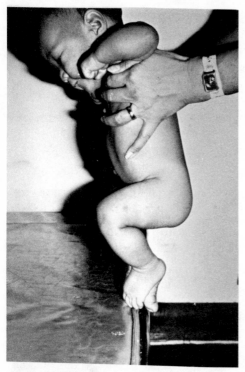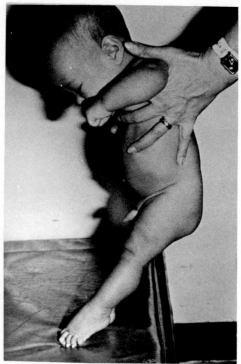

Fig 9-13, 9-14 Primitive Phasic Reflexes: The dorsum of the child's feet contact table edge which stimulates a primitive placing response. In addition to the presence of the primitive reflex, the pattern also reflects undifferentiated movement by the excessive extension in the lower extremities.

child remains hypersensitive to touch, making it difficult for him to reach out and touch, or to be touched (Fig 9-13, 9-14).

3) **Prolonged Retraction and/or Fixation:** Prolonged use of primitive holding strategies is also usually pathological. The child may attempt to maintain higher level postures by means of retraction patterns around the neck, scapula-shoulder, and pelvic-hip regions. The extremities may retain fixation patterns reflecting primitive support functions. Retraction or fixation may be retained to compensate for lack of trunk co-activation. However, prolonged use of these patterns prevents trunk control from developing. Retraction and fixation may eventually be linked together into abnormal holding sets as a basis for postural control. However, primitive holding strategies do not provide adequate background from which to move from one position to another as required at higher levels. Therefore, poverty of movement is again evident, but related more to lack of position changes than diminished extremity movement (Fig 9-15, 9-16).

4) **Primitive tonic reflexes:** Primitive postural reflexes may be retained beyond the primitive phase, even without associated abnormal tone. The child sometimes assumes postures similar to asymmetrical or symmetrical reflexes or uses symmetrical or asymmetrical stabilization patterns in conjunction with retraction or fixation. Both asymmetrical and symmetrical patterns can accompany incomplete development of righting and support reactions. Primitive reflexes along with prolonged holding strategies delay

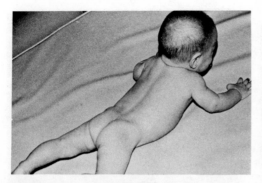 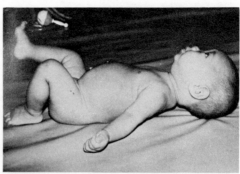

Fig 9-15 Prolonged Retraction and/or Fixation: Neck extension is accompanied by primitive retraction and upper extremity fixation.

Fig 9-16 Prolonged Retraction and/or Fixation: In supine, excessive extension around the neck and upper trunk causes the child to fix head and upper extremities to the supporting surface. Fixation in supine prevents development of hands to midline.

development of stability at higher levels (Fig 9-17).

5) **Incomplete or absent chain reactions:** Chain reactions such as vertical righting and rotational righting, support, and protective reactions do not develop adequately if postures and movements which initiate chains do not develop or are not adapted during the primitive phase. For example, if movement such as neck extension is accompanied by retraction for control, then neck extension is not readily transferred to rest of the body for development of extension. Vertical chains may develop to some extent, but rotational reactions can be incomplete so that rolling patterns are inconsistent, ie, to one direction and not another, or immature, ie, persistence of log roll patterns. Development of rotation will be delayed and unavailable to integrate with flexion-extension for smooth patterns. Since chain reactions facilitate early movement from place to place, lack or delay in chaining reactions causes additional poverty of movement from one position to another. Development of support and protective reactions may also be delayed if chain reactions are not fully activated to bring the child into positions requiring

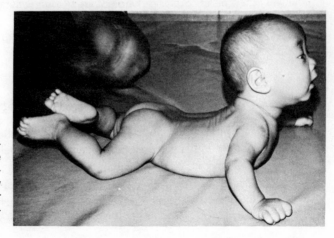

Fig 9-17 Primitive Tonic Reflexes: Influences of the symmetrical tonic neck reflex causes the child to rely on primitive neck and upper extremity extension to maintain prone extension.

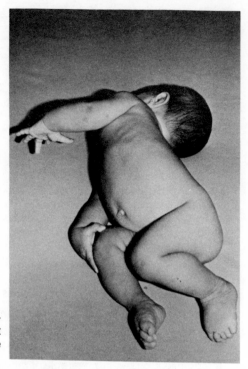

Fig 9-18 Incomplete or Absent Chain Reactions: Neck extension during rolling is not transferred by chain reaction to facilitate trunk extension.

support or protection (Fig 9-18).

6) **Inadequate stability development:** Prolonged fixation/retraction and delay in achieving postures requiring support means that co-activation is not facilitated for development of adequate stability around proximal joints and midline. Fixation/retraction and primitive support reactions continue to influence higher level postural control and provide poor background from which to move (Fig 9-19, 9-20).

7) **Poorly combined mobility and stability:** Delays in differentiating movement and developing co-activation also delays or provides poor components for combining mobility and stability. Some children are motivated to attempt to support and move anyway. Attempts to control movement are by overactivity of primitive support stability causing increased pulling down to move rather than imposing mobility on stable posture. The child will use and may retain poorly integrated bilateral-linear sets to move (Fig 9-21).

Transitional Pathology

Transitional pathological behavior reflects behavior which is retained to adapt beyond the normal transitional period and corresponding failure to develop mature strategies, behaviors, and activities. Transitional behavior may also be considered pathological whenever it is called forth too readily to compensate for loss of mature adaptation. During transition, gravity continues to be a factor in distress since higher level postures and movements are required to move on to mature functioning. However, temporal demands also increase as controlled

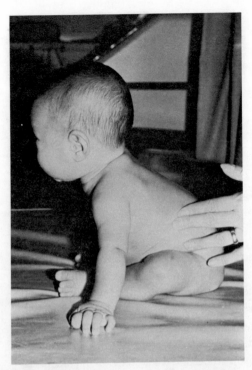

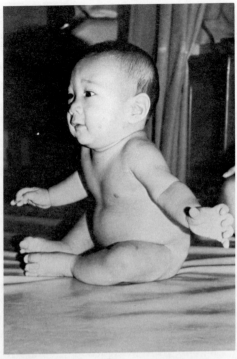

Fig 9-19 Inadequate Stability Development: Supported sitting is accompanied by neck and primitive arm support rather than forward propping.

Fig 9-20 Inadequate Stability Development: Unsupported sitting also reflects retraction and primitive arm posturing in place of midline coactivation.

movement should be developing and adapting to multiple behaviors and activities. More minimally involved children are distressed at the point of developing higher level transitional behaviors/activities and adapting to mature levels.

1) **Undifferentiated movement synergies:** Undifferentiated movement synergies are apparent if either vertical or rotational righting reactions predominate and/or support-protective reactions are easily elicited in lieu of balance reactions. For example, the child

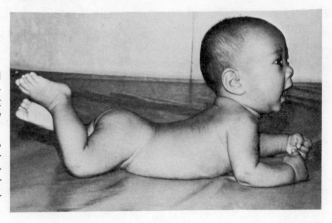

Fig 9-21 Poorly Combined Mobility and Stability: Primitive upper extremity support patterns, characterized by shoulder protraction-abduction with fisted hands, combined with primitive flexion patterns of lower extremities provides poor background as this child attempts to initiate crawling.

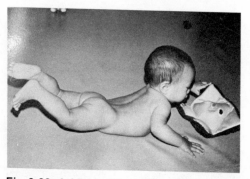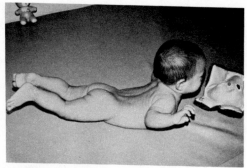

Fig 9-22, 9-23 Undifferentiated Movement Synergies: This child has difficulty modifying prone extension, illustrated by excessive retraction in the upper portions (Figure 9-22), followed by excessive extension in the lowers (Figure 9-23) as upper portions attempt to stabilize during reaching.

may not be able to modify prone extension so that he fully extends the rest of his body whenever he extends his neck; or undifferentiated extension combined with poorly integrated foot support reactions may produce occasional toe walking with the added stress of upright postures. If undifferentiated rotational patterns are active, once rotation is initiated, the child cannot interrupt the pattern and may rotate off of his support base. He lacks counter-rotation to control the pattern and may rely heavily on eliciting support-protective reactions to control rotation. Vertical and rotational righting reactions continue to facilitate full patterns of movement because the reactions are not differentiated and integrated with each other to modify the total pattern. Combined transitional strategies are therefore not available to adapt to mature balance reactions or to add to development of midline stability. The child concentrates on maintaining balance with co-activation of muscle groups associated with vertical righting, decreasing the possibility of integrating rotation component for balance (Fig 9-22, 9-23).

2) **Prolonged stability control:** Stability is developed during transition through co-activation of muscle groups in weight-bearing. Stability needs to be combined with mobility in order to serve as background control. If stability and mobility are not adequately combined and differentiated according to function, stress may prolong the use of unmodified stability for control. Stress from movement in space or control required for extremity movement may call stability to the foreground to control movement. The child increases co-activation patterns for trunk or extremity control. Increased co-activation controls a static pattern but does not provide good background from which to move. A child may also call upon stability too readily to change positions by using arms in weight-bearing to support change at a time when internal postural control should be available for moving about in environment (Fig 9-24).

3) **Use of bilateral-linear sets:** Some children do combine mobility and stability muscle functions but are unable to adequately differentiate functions. These children will continue to use bilateral-linear sets beyond normal expectations, or their activities will reflect the bilateral influence. They may move fairly well in straight patterns, such as jumping, but have difficulty shifting weight and balancing for such activities as standing on one foot or hopping. They depend upon bilaterality for support to balance. How-

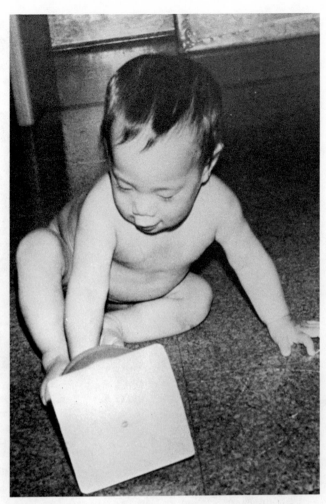

Fig 9-24 Prolonged Stability Control: This child relies upon stability from upper extremity weight bearing in order to reach for a toy.

ever, bilateral integration does not develop since rotation is not integrated into a bilateral-linear pattern, delaying development of midline stability and functioning by crossing the midline. As long as bilateral-linear patterns continue to be used for higher level functions, weight-shift sets are not well developed. Development of weight-shift is a major factor in differentiating stability and mobility functions for adaptation and essential, ultimately, to midline development (Fig 9-25, 9-26).

4) **Use of weight-shift sets:** Weight-shift sets may continue to be used by some children in place of mature movement/countermovement sets. Behaviors and activities based on weight-shift are characterized by lateral side-to-side movement instead of smooth rotation and movement forward. If weight-shift alone is used for balance, balance is easily lost and protective-support reactions called forth since rotation back toward midline for balance is absent. Even children who appear to have developed mature balance reactions may call forth weight-shift when gravity or complex movement or activity requirements produce stress to the system. Subtle problems related to midline integration may result from poor integration of weight-shift sets.

191

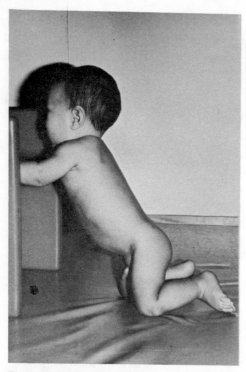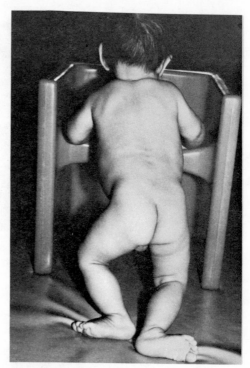

Fig 9-25, 9-26 Use of Bilateral Linear Sets: To move from kneel-standing to standing, the child fixes with upper extremity and pulls to standing using a primitive bilateral linear pattern rather than the more mature weight shift or movement/countermovement sets.

5) **Poor movement control:** The added problem which results from lack of differentiation of muscle functions from poor integration of bilateral linear and weight-shift sets is failure to develop movement-countermovement sets. Without differentiation, smooth blending of muscles cannot occur for coordinated behaviors or adaptation to activities and skills. There is no smooth flow from one position or movement sequence to another from development of mature postural sets. Without movement-countermovement available to adapt movement flow to perceptual sets, the child's motor planning ability is delayed. The child's performance appears clumsy and awkward.

The problems which develop with use of transitional strategies to adapt or failure to develop transitional strategies are reflected in behavior when behaviors are developing. The effects continue to be reflected in activity and skill performance through the child's growing and perhaps adult years without intervention to change the adaptation process.

Delay in maturation of transitional strategies can be observed in the child's pattern to assume standing. Minor deviations from the patterns to get up or perhaps use of a lower level than expected may not be significant. But if a child calls forth a much lower level reflecting immature strategies and sets, it may be significant of dysfunction in the face of other significant findings.

The child's activity and skill performance based on poor perceptual sets is most significant of a lag in the adaptation process. Children functioning with poorly integrated primitive and

192

transitional strategies tend to adapt to activity with patterns which clearly reflect a much younger child's performance.[7] The reason for immature adaptations will depend upon, or change, with the situaiton. A specific mature pattern may even appear to be intact until it is challenged by gravity demands for complex movement or requirements for a new or modified perceptual set.

Abnormal Patterns

There is extensive information in the literature[4,8,9] regarding influences on behavior from abnormal reflexes, stages of abnormal development in cerebral palsy, and abnormal muscle development. Early manifestations of abnormality is often first noted by delayed motor development and retained primitive reflexes. Types of problems depend to some extent on the type of tone developing during the primitive phase and types of behaviors the child is trying to achieve. Abnormal tone is a significant factor which separates primitive and transitional behavior from abnormal behavior.

1) **Hypotonicity/Fluctuating Tone:** Hypotonicity frequently characterizes the young baby's activities. Movement patterns developed from a hypotonic base are frequently accompanied by fluctuating tone leading to athetosis. Patterns appear to resemble undifferentiated primitive strategies since extremity movement is usually through an unmodified range of motion. But control from fluctuating tone does not prepare muscles for co-activation. Control over movement and associated functions remains with athetotic patterns. Lack of control limits variability of movement, reinforcing stereotyped patterns instead. Postural control over hypotonic musculature with or without athetosis is usually accomplished with abnormal asymmetry and retraction around midline and proximal area and distal fixation with extremities.

2) **Hypertonicity:** Hypertonicity, or spasticity, develops with abnormal primitive behavior. The nature of spastic muscles is to pull down in line with gravity rather than to develop antigravity actions. The baby in prone pulls down in flexion rather than develop extension, and in supine spastic extension predominates rather than flexion developing. With strong tonic flexion and extension, integration of rotation will be difficult at higher levels. At this stage, spasticity contributes to inconsistent postural patterns in different positions, reaffirming that it is abnormal tone developing, rather than transferable postural tone. Hypertonicity also accompanies retraction-fixation and asymmetrical patterns. These primitive means to control posture are reinforced by hypertonicity. Spasticity affects the extremities significantly, too. All of the reflexes, asymmetrical and symmetrical tonic neck, grasp, crossed extension, etc, may be combined with spasticity and become obligatory and controlling. The extremities may be involved in prolonged bilateral-linear movement. Spasticity in the arms is increased by pulling down to move. The child will continue to move bilaterally in prone or bunny-hop in all-fours position. Movement in space may also develop with rolling, but hypertonicity reinforces neck righting log roll pattern, so that higher level rotation fails to develop. Repetition of abnormal reflexes creates uniquely abnormal patterns, adding stereotyped components to the pattern not ordinarily present in normal development.

Abnormal patterns and pathological strategies should be viewed for their effect upon behavior, since it is behavior that will need to be evaluated and changed. Each baby will develop unique combinations of normal responses, primitive strategies, and abnormal patterns. Just as there is "competition of normal patterns"[4] in development, there is competition among normal and abnormal factors for control over behavior. An abnormal pattern or reflex may only partially influence a posture, or its influence may change, maybe reverse, depending on the baby's position or movement. Components of abnormality must be carefully analyzed: the type of tone, the presence of reflex or reflex-like behavior, specific influence from too much flexion, or extension in one part of the body or another, in one position or another, lack of rotation, etc. There are usually primary and secondary factors in abnormal behavior. Increased tone, insufficient tone, certain reflexes, may first affect one part of the body. Due to the stress placed on functions related to that body segment, for example, head control, other body segments will compensate with further increase in tone or retraction to hold posture. Over a period of time, the secondary responses may combine into abnormal patterns, and abnormal tone or primitive strategies may begin to influence body segments or behaviors not previously involved.

Summary

Spatiotemporal stress is a phenomenon within the adaptation process that augments association and differentiation of spiraling actions for maturation. Stress that is out of control is distress. Distress affects the child's homeostasis and purposeless experiences occur. The SMS distress factors of abnormal assimilations, abnormal accommodations, and faulty feedback influence the spiraling progressions of development, thus dysfunction prevails. Primitive and transitional strategies used beyond the expected time or at higher than expected levels of behavior characterize the outcome of distress. Abnormal patterns of actions may prevail with the more profoundly involved, presenting behavior/activity performance not characteristic of normal development. This chapter discusses and illustrates pertinent observations of dysfunctional performance relative to spatiotemporal adaptation.

References

1. Selye H: The Stress of Life. New York, McGraw-Hill Book Co, 1956.
2. Fitzgerald S: Stress: the internal drummer. The Denver Post, March 11, 1979, pp 14-15.
3. Moore JC: Concepts from the neurobehavioral sciences. Dubuque, Kendall Hunt Pub Co, 1973, p 38.
4. Bobath B, Bobath K: Motor Development in the Different Types of Cerebral Palsy. London, William Heinemann Books, 1975.
5. Drillien CM: Abnormal neurologic signs in the first year of life in low-birthweight infants: possible prognostic significance. Dev Med Child Neurol 14:575-584, 1972.
6. Fantz R, Fagan J, Miranda S: Early visual selectivity, in Cohen L, Salapatek P (eds): Infant Perception: From Sensation to Cognition. New York, Academic Press, 1975, vol 1, pp 249-343.
7. Kinsbourne M: Minimal brain dysfunction as a neurodevelopmental lag. Ann NY Acad Sci 205:268-273, 1973.
8. Fiorentino M: Normal and Abnormal Development. Springfield, C C Thomas Pubs, 1972.
9. Stockmeyer S: A sensorimotor approach to treatment, in Pearson P, Williams C (eds): Physical Therapy Services in the Developmental Disabilities. Springfield, C C Thomas Pubs, 1972, pp 186-220.

Vignettes

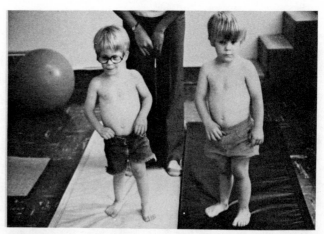

Fig 9-a Twin "K" (on left); Twin "G" (on right). Age 3 years, 2 months.

Twins K and G

Two sets of twins have been chosen to illustrate the effects of distress on performance. The photographs compare the children's performance during one session. Photographs and information do not comprise a complete case study but illustrate selected behaviors and activities.

One set of twins (K and G) are illustrated with the first vignette, Figures 9-a through 9-t. Twin K demonstrates performance affected primarily by primitive-pathological dysfunction. The second vignette illustrates twins M and T with photographs 9-aa through 9-pp. Twin M has been diagnosed as spastic cerebral palsy and demonstrates the effect of abnormal patterns upon performance.

Background Information

K was the second of identical twins born approximately 32 weeks gestation. His birth weight was 890 grams. K was transferred to an intensive care newborn nursery shortly after his birth. He was hospitalized in the nursery for approximately two months. Diagnosis included prematurity, small for gestational age, respiratory distress syndrome, hyperbilirubinemia, and growth retardation. At two years, two months of age K was referred for evaluation because of developmental delay. According to the evaluation he was functioning at approximately 15-16 months in fine motor, gross motor, and social-language development. Following the evaluation K was treated in a coordinated occupational therapy, physical therapy, and speech language program.

The photographs were taken when K was 3 years, 2 months. At that time a re-evaluation indicated that he was functioning at approximately a 3-year-old level in gross motor skills, 2½-year-old level in fine motor skills, and a 3-year-old level in social-language development. However, skill performance was affected by poor joint stability, trunk rotation, difficulty with balance, and incoordinated movements. Participation with behaviors and activities that exceed his ability to perform at his highest level produce distress.

195

ADAPTIVE BEHAVIORS: Supine to Standing

Fig 9-b Twin G on the left and Twin K on right are in the process of assuming standing from supine with an age appropriate partial rotation pattern. Twin G shifts weight to one side, makes use of equilibrium to pull toward midline, and differentiates between upper and lower body segments. Although Twin K can initiate the partial rotation pattern, he is unable to differentiate between body segments for rotation and makes use of generalized tonal increases throughout the trunk, upper, and lower extremities.

Fig 9-c Twin G has already achieved sitting while Twin K is adapting primitive undifferentiated patterns to weight shift, thus affecting temporal sequencing of adaptation.

Fig 9-d Twin G continues the sequence to assume standing by adapting support reactions to stabilize the upper portions of the body and shifts weight to move toward standing. Twin K gains postural reinforcement in sitting before proceeding to stand.

Fig 9-e Twin G transfers weight back to lower extremities, freeing hands from support and stands erect. Twin K is unable to call forth appropriate upper extremity support reactions and thus experiences difficulty shifting weight to one leg. He attempts to adapt to the distress by stabilizing with neck retraction and upper extremity posturing.

Fig 9-f Creeping. Twin G demonstrates good postural stability evidenced by movement-counter-movement creeping pattern. Twin K adapts primitive neck retraction, poor upper extremity support reactions, and utilizes a weight shift set to creep.

Fig 9-g Walking down an incline requires high level adaptations. Twin G maintains his heel-toe reciprocal gait while reinforcing his balance with a readiness to protect. Twin K watches his feet, adapts with shoulder protraction, primitive arm posturing, and a flat-footed gait.

Fig 9-h Standing on one foot requires weight-shift and realignment of the midline with gravity. Although Twin G is not well aligned with gravity, he can shift weight and balance appropriately for his age. Twin K has difficulty shifting weight and maintaining balance. He attempts to adapt arm postures to assist as well as monitor his process visually.

EQUILIBRIUM REACTIONS

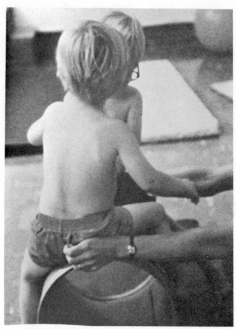

Fig 9-i Twin G experiences a normal rotation-counter-rotation equilibrium reaction in response to movement of the barrel.

Fig 9-j Twin K responds with a variety of abnormal primitive pathological responses. He adapts with neck retraction to reinforce stability.

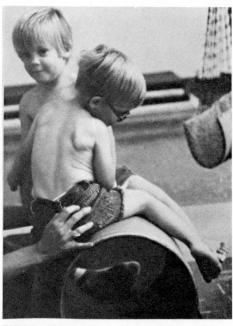

Fig 9-k At times Twin K adapts with lateral trunk flexion instead of rotation.

Fig 9-l Finally, further stress produces asymmetrical upper extremity retraction for stabilization. Twin G can call forth an appropriate upper extremity equilibrium reaction.

ADAPTING ACTIVITIES

Fig 9m Twin G anticipates the approaching ball by adjusting body position in space, preparing arms for catching and visually monitoring the speed (temporal) of the on-coming ball.

Fig 9-n Twin K's primitive response is to concentrate on the spatial adaptation of his hands. He places them in a primitive catching posture. K visually monitors his hands but is unable to simultaneously monitor the temporal component of the on-coming ball.

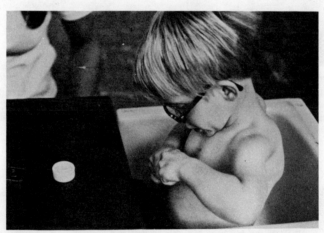

9-o Manipulative Activity: Activities of the upper extremities call forth increased cocontraction from proximal joints in response to distal fixation used to control movement.

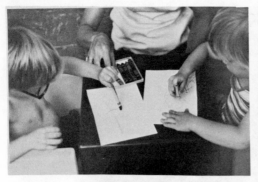

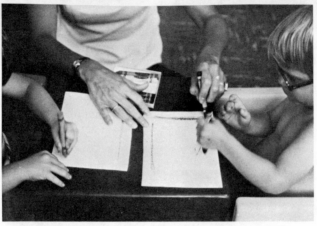

Fig 9-p to 9-r Adaptation to Crayon: In 9-p, K's adaptation to a crayon calls forth a variety of primitive hand functions and a need to switch hands frequently. Development of skill is impeded by his inability to use consistent hand functions and one hand predominately. Note that Twin G consistently uses his right hand and adapts with a superior grasp even though activity seems stressful to him also.

Fig 9-s, 9-t Cutting: Cutting with scissors is stressful to both children. Twin G succeeds in snipping the paper with the scissors by calling forth undifferentiated finger flexion and extension to manipulate the scissors. G's response is an appropriate spatiotemporal stress response for his age and experience with scissors. Twin K calls forth a lower level bilateral attempt to manipulate the scissors. K's response indicates spatiotemporal distress.

Fig 9-aa Twin "M" (on left); Twin "T" (on right). Age 18 months.

Twins M and T

Background Information

M was the second twin born at 28 weeks gestation. His birth weight was 1100 grams. He was transferred to an intensive care newborn nursery shortly after birth and hospitalized approximately two and one half months. Diagnosis included prematurity, hyperbilirubinemia, and respiratory distress syndrome secondary to Hyaline Membrane Disease. M was evaluated by occupational therapy and physical therapy when he was 5 months corrected age. The evaulation was initiated at the request of his parents who noted that M was not using his right upper extremity well. At that time increased flexor tone of the right upper extremity and increased extensor tone of right lower extremity were noted. In addition an asymmetrical tonic neck reflex was present. There were stretch reflexes noted in both right upper and lower extremities. The developmental landmarks achieved by M were at the 2 to 3 month level. Following the evaluation the parents were given a home program and followed periodically by occupational therapy and physical therapy.

SUPINE BEHAVIORS

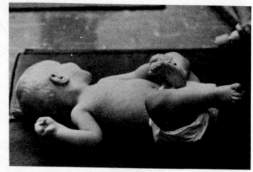

Fig 9-bb to 9-dd Abnormal patterns influence M's supine behavior. The more affected right side is influenced by increased tone, asymmetrical tonic neck reflex, and insufficient sensory awareness from contact with self or toys.

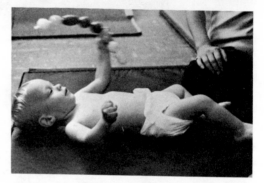

ROLLING

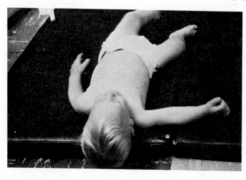

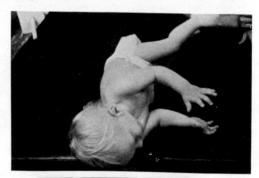

Fig 9-ee to 9-gg M rolls toward his right, more affected side, using his left upper extremity to compensate for poor rotation within the body axis. Lack of rotation between body segments and difficulty with spontaneous adaptive upper extremity movements produces abnormal rolling as well as difficulty adjusting posture in prone.

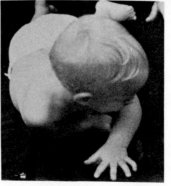

MOVING IN PRONE

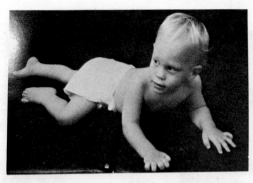 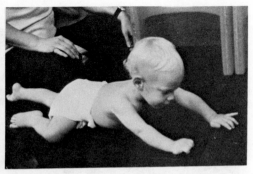

9-hh to 9-ii Use of amphibian crawling and "pushing back" in prone represent significant delay in M's development of locomotion. The patterns are influenced by increased tone in the right side and lack of development around the midline for trunk stability. Compare the effect of upper extremity weight bearing on the development of finger extension and upper extremity support reactions. The right upper extremity remains under the influence of primitive and abnormal patterns.

SITTING

Fig 9-jj Neck retraction, shoulder protraction, kyphotic posture, and lower extremity internal rotation in sitting represent abnormal patterns and inadequate adaptation to perform activities.

PULLING TO STAND

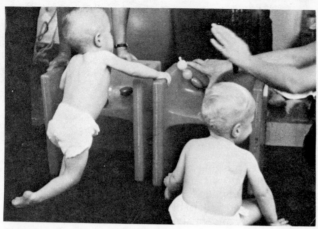

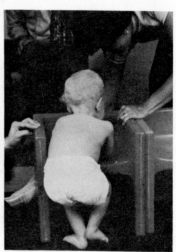

Fig 9-kk to 9-nn PULLING TO STAND: In 9-kk and 9-ll, T pulls to stand with a weight shift set. He holds on with his upper extremities while he shifts weight to one lower extremity, bringing the other extremity into weight bearing. M (illustrated in Figure 9-ll) is under the influence of abnormal patterns. He utilizes neck retraction, pulls down with his upper extremities because of the influence of flexor tone, and adapts an abnormal bilateral-linear pattern to stand.

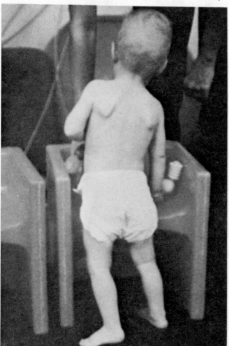

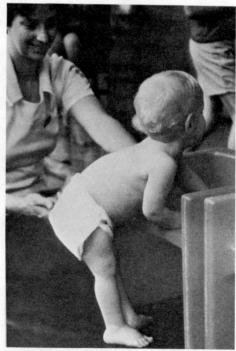

Fig 9-mm T can stand with minimal or no support from his upper extremities while he engages in activity.

Fig 9-nn M cannot attain an upright posture due to influence from flexor tone and dependency on upper extremity support. He attempts to compensate for lack of extension with abnormal neck retraction.

ADAPTATION TO ACTIVITY

Fig 9-oo to 9-pp M's manipulative abilities are severely hampered by increased tone through associated reactions in his upper extremities which prevent bilateral coordination. His highest levels of manipulative activities includes mouthing to manipulate and throwing to watch object movement.

Chapter Ten
A Model for **Therapy**

Introduction

The developmental theory of spatiotemporal adaptation with its spiraling framework provides a model by which occupational therapists can base their therapeutic actions. A model is based on theory, provides a framework for therapeutic reasoning, and implies a mode of action. The spatiotemporal adaptation model has its foundation in the spiraling continuum of development; therefore, the mode of action is based upon the spiraling process of adapting strategies, behaviors, and activities to facilitate development.

Therapeutic reasoning respects the law of "individual differences" that prevails with human behavior; thus, a therapeutic model for intervention must be adaptable for each individual and his assessed needs.[1] The model based upon the spatiotemporal adaptation process does not provide a structured formula or "step-by-step" therapy program. Rather, the model provides a system by which a variety of treatment techniques can be applied to meet individual needs, as each self-system is unique in itself. Not only do individuals possess a unique self-system, but the manner of developing the system has its own individual variations.[1] Due to individual differences and uniqueness of each person, treatment techniques cannot be standardized nor categorized to fit a given population. Rehabilitation must be individualistic in nature, just as each person is.[1] Therefore, the adaptation model presented in this text will provide underlying concepts and principals by which individual treatment programs can emerge.

The spatiotemporal adaptation model has as its core the spiraling process of modifying a child's actions by facilitating higher level functioning. The primary objective of the therapeutic mode of action is linking behaviors and activities to be adapted for skilled performance. Inherent within the evolution of skill is subcortical organization of postural and perceptual sets which become a part of the self-system to be called forth for functional performances.

The spatiotemporal model considers the impact of nervous system attention and transactions of the child with his environment.[1] Maturation is dependent upon the child's attention to and active participation with events of the environment. Thus, learning and memory (including "subcortical learning") are enhanced and performance modified through the child's attention and active participation with goal-directed purposeful behaviors and activities.[1]

A prime responsibility of an occupational therapist is the ongoing process of structuring the environment, including the child, in such a manner to promote an opportunity for the child to attend to and participate with behaviors and activities that facilitate a meaningful response for the nervous system. The child's cortical attention directed toward the end result of the event and the subcortical attention directed to the process to achieve the event are key factors of the occupational therapy adaptation model. Active participation facilitates meaningful or purposeful responses when the environment, including the child, is structured in such a manner to direct higher level functioning adapted from appropriate, acquired lower level performances.

To provide occupational therapy to children with special needs, therapists need to know "why" they are doing what they are doing as well as "what" it is they are attempting to achieve. To understand why, therapists need to think in terms of what is going on biologically, psychologically, and sociologically. The more clearly the biopsychosocial process underlying human behavior is understood, the more effectively a holistic concept can be applied to therapeutic programs. The totality concept in relation to how a child functions is paramount for occupational therapy programs.

To provide the knowledge of what is being attempted through therapy, therapists need to think in terms of adaptation processes, particularly the effect of sensory feedback from the child's therapeutic performance and the impact of association and differentiation of performances. Sensory feedback with association and differentiation are vital for "subcortical learning." The knowledge of why and understanding of what provides needed information for the therapeutic decision of how to implement an individualistic intervention program. The implementation process may include a variety of techniques, eg, behavior modification, activities for sensory integration or neurodevelopmental processes, PNF, etc; however, the techniques must be applied to the individual's needs and uniqueness with the ultimate goal of facilitating a child's adaptation to the spatial and temporal components of his world.

Theoretical Premises

The developmental theory of spatiotemporal adaptation provides guidance for therapeutic reasoning. A theory presents basic premises on which a model can be constructed. The premises implied in the spatiotemporal adaptation theory inlcude:[2]

1) Development is a function of nervous system maturation which occurs through a process of adaptation.

2) Adaptation is dependent upon attention to and active participation with purposeful events of the environment. Without active participation the nervous system is deprived of certain forms of sensation (sensory feedback) which, in turn, affects maturation.

3) Purposeful events (behaviors and activities) provide meaningful experiences for enhancement of maturation by directing a higher level adaptive response.

4) Higher level responses result from integration with and modification of acquired, lower level functions, thus adaptation of higher level function is dependent upon a certain degree of association/differentiation of specific components of lower level performance.

5) Adaptation spirals through primitive, transitional and mature phases of development occurring at the same time within different body segments. The concurrent development of phases considers the adaptation of posture and movement strategies to purposeful behaviors and activities and the linking of behaviors and activities for adaptation to skill.

6) Environmental experiences may present situations of spatiotemporal stress. With stress, the system calls forth past acquired strategies, behaviors, and activities to act upon the demands of the environment and maintain the system's homeostasis.

7) Spatiotemporal distress provokes dysfunction when the adaptation process is inter-

rupted or incomplete resulting in maladaptation. With dysfunction a child repeats purposeless lower level performances. Repetition of purposeless performances results in regression and ultimately leads to developmental disability.

Philosophy of Pediatric Occupational Therapy

The premise statements have been organized into a philosophy or belief system regarding spatiotemporal adaptation as applied to a developmental approach for occupational therapy. Adaptation is the center of the philosophical base. The philosophy presented expands upon the profession's recognized philosophical base that states the belief that "purposeful activity facilitates the adaptive process" (Appendix A).

The philosophical core of pediatric occupational therapy is the use of activities in a manner to facilitate the purposefulness of a child's actions. Activities become purposeful when the process to achieve the activity becomes adapted by the self-system. The nature of, or process to, achieve activity and the child's active participation with activity are necessary components for facilitating purposefulness of actions for adaptation within the system. Adaptation assists organization of neural mechanisms by providing controlled sensory feedback. Sensory feedback includes the interaction of a) the product or event itself, including the child's cortical attention given to the activity stimulus and his perception of the end result, and b) the process to achieve the event which requires subcortical attention and organization. The process or manner in which the child participates provides the desired sensory feedback to enhance maturation. Through active participation with purposeful activities, the self-system organizes the actions of the activity at a subcortical level. Organized actions are integrated into perceptual sets that are subsequently used to direct performance at the subcortical level. In this manner purposeful actions enhances "subcortical learning" and adaptation occurs.

A child who is experiencing dysfunctional performance can benefit from an intervention program designed to facilitate adaptation through active participation with goal-directed purposeful behaviors and activities.

The philosophical framework of a profession should be a major aspect for delineation of that profession's uniqueness, thus distinguishing the profession from other disciplines. Although parts of the philosophy stated can be applied to other health care disciplines, particularly physical therapy, the distinguishing features of uniqueness of occupational therapy is inherent within the philosophy. The uniqueness lies in the manner in which activities are used to facilitate purposefulness of actions for adaptation to enhance development.

Pediatric occupational and physical therapy have similar philosophies and practice techniques. Both professions have the common goal of facilitating a child's highest level of functioning to enhance development and maturation. Both professions use activity as a part of their media. Both professions are necessary for the totality of health care for many children with handicaps. The similarities are multitude and the overlap of philosophy and practice a known factor among the profession's practitioners. However, the distinction between the two professions is paramount and essential for implementing the best possible health care program for many children.

Within the developmental framework of spatiotemporal adaptation, we view the role of the physical therapist as facilitating the adaptation of postural and movement strategies to purposeful behaviors and facilitating the purposefulness of behaviors through the use of body-centered goals (eg, to sit, to stand, to reach, etc). The role of the occupational therapist is facilitating the adaptation of posture and movement strategies to purposeful activities through the active participation toward environmental-centered goals (eg, to feed oneself, to color a picture, to catch a ball).

Since the evolution of behaviors, activities, and skills are on a spiraling continuum, collaborative occupational and physical therapy programs can be most effective for the child. Therapists can work together in planning their separate but inter-related goals. By working together, appropriate behaviors can be facilitated for adaptation to activities, and appropriate activities may be designed to provide the needed motivation to encourage the child's innate goals for purposeful behaviors.

Supporting Literature

The philosophy of occupational therapy based on the adaptation process has support in the scientific literature. The neurophysiological literature portrays the nervous system as a sequence of units that interact to assimilate a variety of information. There is a continual interplay among the units and nuclei at different levels. Therefore, when any unit functions inefficiently, the total integrative process and the efficiency of all units are affected in some manner.[1,3] Damage in one area of the system has a direct effect upon the total integrative ability affecting the delicate facilitatory-inhibitory balance.[1] When the integrative process is upset, an individual's performance becomes disorganized and maladaptation results.[1,4]

In addition, literature stresses that the maturing nervous system is vulnerable to damage with a variety of complex factors affecting maturation.[4] However, the nervous system has plasticity and flexibility which provide the system with the capacity for modification and change.[3,5,6] In addition, the nervous system can regenerate[1] and has a capacity to reorganize and compensate for damage.[1,3,4] The ability to compensate for damage provides a means for the system to direct body accommodations for functioning.[1,4]

The adaptation theory and treatment philosophy gains additional support from the literature in reported concepts of cortical overlay, bias, or scotoma.[1] According to concepts, a nervous system that has never received input from a stimulus or given situation is not capable of comprehending or utilizing the information. The system must direct its accommodations from the repertoire that has been learned or acquired. Man's system has the largest area of cerebral cortex devoted to "association areas." Therefore, integration of the older learned patterns used to assimilate and accommodate to new stimuli can occur. Cortical overlay provides the system with the ability to associate and differentiate old with new for adaptation of higher level performance.[1] The powers of cortical overlay may provide the self-system with the capacity to maintain homeostasis of internal and external environments, therefore bringing some degree of control over the effects of distress.

Cortical overlay may also be the major factor in the development of a unique "self."[1] Individual differences makes it difficult, if not impossible, to categorize or standardize a child's adaptive behaviors and activities. Therefore, each child must be understood in light of his own individuality and uniqueness.[1]

Identification of principals provides insight for identifying methods of treating the child.[7] Underlying principals are the "road map" or essential aspects for guiding therapeutic reasoning. Inherent principles of the adaptation theory have been specified for guidance in developing treatment programs.

Principles

1) The developing nervous system has capacity to compensate for impairments by forming new connections during the early periods of maturation.[1,3,8] Plasticity or flexibility of the formative nervous system enhances its capacity for the sensorimotor-sensory adaptation process to facilitate nervous system modification, eg, changes in degree of myelination, dendritic growth, formation of new synapses.[3,5,6]

2) An intervention program based on the spatiotemporal adaptation process of active participation with purposeful activities prevents sensory deprivation (both initial input and feedback), thus provides appropriate stimulus necessary to help mature synaptic connections.[1,5,6]

3) An intervention program providing appropriate sensory input, motor output and sensory feedback, and employing the spiraling process of linking purposeful behaviors and activities enhances previously unresponsive brain cells, influences neural organization, establishes new engrams, thus facilitates maturation.[3,4,8]

Therapeutic Framework

Purposeful action/activity is the point of departure for occupational therapy intervention programs.[2] The effect of therapy depends upon the change or modification that the child can elicit within himself by adapting the action/activity he is experiencing into his self-system. Adapting purposeful experiences depends upon the competence of the child's internal environment (the mastery level of performance directed by the self-system) together with the expectations of the external environment (the system with which the child interacts) including space, objects, and persons within the child's milieu. Therefore, occupational therapy becomes a multidimensional treatment program; the child, family, therapist, other persons involved with the child, and those physical settings in which a child participates must be a part of the therapeutic plan.[9]

The therapeutic plan has its foundation in the synthesis of an occupational therapy assessment. Assessment includes the collection and review of past data, interviews with the child/family and other persons involved with the child, developmental/occupational performance history of the child, standardized and nonstandardized evaluation procedures, clinical observations analysis and synthesis of findings, recording and reporting. Through assessment procedures, the therapist collaborates with the child/family and significant others to establish short-term and long-term goals and plan the treatment processes.[2]

During the treatment process, the primary role of the therapist is to structure the environment in a manner to promote the "purposefulness" of experiences for the child that the self-system has not been able to do for itself. Therapists guide those appropriate actions/

activities so that the child can explore his environment with "meaningful experiences." Occupational therapy provides an appropriate environment that motivates a child to engage in purposeful experiences for adaptation. Adaptation occurs when the child's level of competence is in harmony with the environment's expectations of the child. When there is a discrepancy between competence and expectations, spatiotemporal distress occurs. [9]

According to Ayres, therapy brings out the child's "inner urge" for action, thus eliciting his potential for self-directing responses that will augment maturation. [3] Self-direction of actions/activities that are purposeful provides success experiences that are pleasing to the child. Self-direction leads to a feeling of "mastery" over the environment augmenting the development of the personality.

Therapy Goals

The ultimate goal of the adaptation model is to facilitate the child's potential to achieve his highest level of performance. [2] Achievement of performance abilities is an individual matter; some children may progress to higher levels or at a faster pace than other children. Paramount within the adaptation model are two primary factors: 1) the child as a unique individual who responds to treatment in his own unique manner and who has his own unique potential, and 2) the acknowledgment and acceptance of realistic expectations for the child's potential. Consideration of uniqueness and realistic expectations provides a climate for healthy intervention, thus "an ideal situation ensues." [9]

Within the therapeutic process toward achieving the ultimate goal of facilitating a child's potential, there are several overall goals. To implement an adaptation program, the overall therapeutic goals include prevention, modification, remediation, compensation, and maintenance. Prevention occurs when the child engages in activity that is designed to keep distress from occurring or to hinder secondary complications from the initial identified problem. Modification occurs when the child facilitates change within the self-system which is brought about by his own participation with actions/activities. Remediation is the process of engaging a child with activity that is designed to correct, remedy, or improve his skill level. Compensation occurs in therapy when the activity promotes another aspect of performance or substituting a different form of actions. Maintenance in therapy is that activity that helps the child keep in condition and retain the acquired, appropriate functions. Repetition of appropriate functions augments perceptual sets.

Within the adaptation framework for therapy, any one or all of the overall goals may be considered. Working toward a goal will be dependent upon the assessed needs and specific treatment plan for each child. The adaptation model permits flexibility for incorporating the overall goals into the program at any given time. For example, during early childhood, it may be realistic to implement a therapy program designed to prevent and modify; whereas, during later periods, such as adolescence, it may be more realistic to emphasize activities and techniques for employing compensation and maintenance. In addition, any one therapy session may include several of the overall goals, depending on the assessed needs and session goals. The decisions for emphasis must consider a variety of variables including age, degree of disability, priorities of immediate health care, expectations and motivations of the child and family, impact upon the family, and available treatment environments.

Therapy Objectives

The objective of occupational therapy is to elicit adaptation through the child's active participation with activities that are purposeful. To achieve the objective, the therapist structures treatment so that the child receives appropriate feedback from his performances; thus, facilitating the linking of behaviors to activities as well as providing the system with successful experiences which enhance skilled performance.

The therapeutic interplay with purposeful behaviors and activities augments perceptual sets. Blending postural sets with movement flow provides the child with internal feedback necessary to select and direct the actions needed to interact with the demands of the environment. Acquisition of perceptual sets leads to competence with performance and a "sense of mastery." Therefore, the objective of an adaptation program is twofold: to facilitate posture and movement competencies and to promote autonomy. Competence and autonomy serve as an internal motivator to encourage the child to extend "self" and seek a variety of experiences within spatiotemporal dimensions.

Therapy Guidelines

Application of spiraling principles (Chapter Three) serves as guidelines for implementing an adaptation program. Spiraling makes its therapeutic impact through a process of "reciprocal interweaving" or reincorporation of several sequential levels of development.[7] Spiraling of actions provides the performances needed by the internal system for engaging in association and differentiation to complete the adaptation process. The interplay of spiraling actions within therapy is based upon the child's homeostasis and the activity being performed by the child. The nature of the activity itself and/or the therapist/child relationship to direct activity performance promotes active participation for appropriate sensory assimilations and motor accommodations. By applying spiraling principles for directing/controlling a child's motor accommodations, accuracy of feedback is more likely to occur.

Therapeutic spiraling occurs when the treatment situation enables the child to participate with an activity that may be designed to call forth certain elements of posture and movement strategies for incorporating with the performance of the immediate behavior/activity being elicited as well as aspects of higher level performances being pulled out and applied to the present functions. Preparing treatment to facilitate spiraling is a most demanding task for the therapist. Care and judgment must be taken in the selection of activity tasks to enhance spiraling and insure some success pleasing to the child.[10]

For the preparation of treatment tasks, therapists may ask themselves several questions to assist with decisions regarding the spiraling process. Using initial and ongoing assessment findings as the foundation for therapeutic reasoning, therapists should ask themselves what it is they wish to change and why, and what the child/family want to change and why. In order to promote meaningful therapy, both internal and external systems may need to be modified. The content of this book has emphasized modification of the self-system; however, therapy must also consider the possible need to modify the external systems with which the child interacts. The child, family, therapist, and other persons involved with the child may need to modify their expectations of the child's performance abilities. Demands and expectations of the environment must compliment the child's potential so that the child can achieve success

213

and be stimulated to engage in a variety of realistic activities. The child, family, and significant others become principal sources for direct involvement with treatment planning.

Another question to be considered is the method of documentation, as ongoing planning and reordering of treatment goals and priorities depends upon the results of therapy. A process for documentation is imperative for success of treatment, therefore, therapists must decide how they will rate or determine a child's progress. Rating progress is an ongoing process and serves as the ultimate guideline for altering therapy programs when necessary, as well as collecting data to document the effectiveness of occupational therapy.

Having specified session goals which have been determined by answering the questions of what it is that therapy will attempt to change and why, a therapist then monitors the session by asking several questions regarding the outcomes of therapy. For example, is the child becoming involved with the activity? The adaptive social-emotional involvement of child with activity is an essential element for modifying actions and facilitating change within the self-system. Adaptive social-emotional responses add meaning to movement. Movement is in close connection with acquisition of general social-emotional attitudes.[10] Should the activity require either too high or too low level accommodations or efforts, the child is not likely to become involved. The therapy process cannot force activity upon the child, rather the child must guide or direct his own actions.[3] The child is the best judge of the appropriateness of an activity; he seems to have an innate sense of his therapeutic needs for adaptation.

A prerequisite to social-emotional involvement may well be the element of success experienced by activity involvement. Therefore, it is imperative to constantly ask if the activity provides a success experience for the child. As stated by Ayres, "there is no reward that has quite the enduring qualities that success holds.[3] Success is the most powerful reinforcer available for therapeutic adaptations.

During treatment, a therapist observes responses and reactions and attempts to assess the child's ability to interpret feedback from his posture and movement stimuli. Appropriate sensorimotor stimulation is therapeutic only when the feedback is appropriate and the child is aware of that feedback. The therapist should constantly be alert to the child's involvement with, interest in, and improvement of his actions. The degree of involvement and self-direction from the child provide valuable clues to the child's awareness of feedback.

The therapeutic use of repetition of actions is another area for monitoring the program and providing guidelines for treatment. Achievement of appropriate purposeful activities provides success experience which motivates the child to repeat performances. Repetition can be likened to the overall goal of maintenance and becomes a vital aspect of therapy, particularly with the planning and implementation of home programs. Once an appropriate activity has been acquired, it is necessary to practice the performance to augment perceptual sets for transfer to performances with similar activities. Providing a variety of activities gives the child an opportunity to not only repeat actions for practice but apply the performances for transference of perceptual sets and expand his repertoire of behaviors, activities, and skills.

The principles and concepts of the spiraling continuum of adaptation provides guidelines for therapeutic reasoning. Therapy programs using the spiraling principles must be based on individual needs and defined session goals. Therapeutic responsibility includes the exploration of effective and efficient methods for enhancing adaptation of purposeful experiences. Consideration of the uniqueness of each child together with the therapist's competence in interpreting the child's performance and implementing a program that promotes purposeful responses approaches the art of therapy.[3]

Considerations of Spiraling

Using spiraling as a framework for eliciting adaptation does not imply that therapy perfects the achievement of one behavior or activity before going to the next. Instead, spiraling stresses the overlap of behavior/activity performances and serves as a major aspect of treatment planning. The child with dysfunction can benefit from a program based upon the spiraling development of behaviors, activities, and skills; however, the program does not recapitulate the normal process. Caution must be taken not to mirror each strategy, behavior, or activity as some aspects of the normal process may only augment the already present dysfunction.[8] For example, facilitating normal posture and movement patterns of the primitive phase may only enhance continued participation in undifferentiated or fixation patterns. Within normal development, a baby frequently calls forth elements of prone extension to reinforce needed trunk stability; to recapitulate this process may only enhance the abnormal pattern by increasing extension tone and repeating the undifferentiated pattern. Facilitation of neck extension or primitive fixation patterns may augment an abnormal retraction pattern. Recapitulating primitive kicking patterns may produce scissoring, increase extension tone, and prevent the development of hip flexion.[8] Caution must be taken regarding the speed and repetition of movement, eg, too fast may increase tone, facilitate an excitatory state, or produce sensory overload. Another factor for consideration includes the temporal aspects of activity performance, eg, activities requiring a quick reaction time, fast movement may elicit a less mature response and present distress. The therapist should not force activity nor present activities at too high or too low a level for the child to adapt. (A good guide is to call forth aspects of performance one level below the child's present functioning level with a specific performance and pull out those appropriate aspects one level above to facilitate association and differentiation for modification.) As sensation is a powerful therapeutic means, the therapist must be aware of the sensory input and feedback the child's system is assimilating. It is important to observe the signs from the autonomic nervous system as a guide for the effect of therapy actions. Throughout the adaptation program, the child is the best indicator of the effect of activity, as the child's performance is a functional expression of the self-system.

Mode of Action

Preparation, facilitation, and adaptation are viewed as the primary processes for occupational therapists engaged in a relationship with a child for the purpose of augmenting development through adaptation. The mode is threefold.

The processes constitute the mode of action inherent within the spiraling framework. The mode has its own threefold spiraling process with each being called forth when needed during a treatment session.

Preparation is both the preliminary and ongoing process of enhancing the neural and muscular functions for their readiness and use as posture and movement strategies. The purpose of preparing strategies for use is to attempt to achieve a state of homeostasis within the self-system. Preparation within a therapy session attempts to do for the child what strategy development accomplishes within the normal adaptation process. Preparation includes normalizing postural tone, eg, increasing, decreasing, or stabilizing tone, increasing range of motion, strength, promoting subcortical attention, securing a balance of the inhibitory-facilitory state as well as controlling sensory input to prevent deprivation and overload. In addition to preparation of the child's internal environment, the process also considers the structures of the external environment to assist in bringing the strategies forth for purposeful use.

Facilitation is the continued successive application of the necessary stimulus to elicit an adaptive response. The facilitory process includes the use of external means applied during therapeutic situations for enhancement of an appropriate reaction. Stimulus may include the position, activity, child and/or what the therapist may provide directly to the child in order to enhance both stability and mobility components. The major purpose of facilitation is to provide the needed and appropriate input for association and differentiation. With distress/dysfunction, the system cannot associate/differentiate the pertinent elements of one action for adaptation to another, thus, therapy stimuli attempts to provide opportunities for the association/differentiation components to occur. The vital components of adaptation are best facilitated through the therapeutic control over the child's accommodations.

Adaptation as a therapeutic mode within occupational therapy gives purpose to performance. Adaptation is the process of promoting a child's abilities to differentiate those aspects of a behavior sequence pertinent for purposeful activity. Adaptation considers the connection or linking of behaviors to events/activities of the environment. Adaptation is the process of "making use" of behavior or applying actions to goals outside the body. Therapeutic linking promotes association and differentiation by structuring and guiding the child's active participation. The therapist must have knowledge of those components, patterns, or sets from a behavior that a child needs to "call forth" for adapting to the demands of the environment. Therapeutic adaptation promotes the positive use of spatiotemporal stress and prevents distress.

Summary

Occupational therapy is a profession whose scientific base is emerging; however, the art of therapy shall remain its most vital characteristic. Although the science of therapy is emerging, individual differences and the uniqueness of each child dictates the necessity of maintaining the art.

Developmental principles and concepts have been organized into a spatiotemporal theory that receives support from literature; a spiraling model of "reciprocal interweaving" of strategies, behaviors, and activities for adaptation to skills; a sensorimotor-*sensory* approach for enhancement of adaptation; and a framework that distinguishes the profession by its use of goal-directed activities that are purposeful for the self-system.

These authors present their theory of the development of spatiotemporal adaptation with its spiraling framework and treatment model as a contribution toward the philosophical base of the profession.

The material is presented for use, analysis, criticism, and application. Hopefully our ideas will stimulate elaboration, refinement, and moderation.

References

1. Moore JC: Concepts from the Neurobehavioral Sciences. Dubuque, Kendall/Hunt Pub Co, 1973.
2. Gilfoyle E, Grady A: Minimal brain dysfunction, in Hopkins H, Smith H (eds): Willard and Spackman's Occupational Therapy. Philadelphia, JB Lippincott Co, 1977, pp 399-414.
3. Ayres A: Sensory Integration and Learning Disorders. Los Angeles, Western Psychological Services, 1972, pp 256, 276.
4. Moore JC: Neuroanatomy Simplified. Dubuque, Kendall/Hunt Pub Co, 1969.
5. Harris FA: The brain is a distributed information processor. Am J Occup Ther 24:264-268, 1970.
6. Norton Y: Neurodevelopment and sensory integration for the profoundly retarded and multiply handicapped child, in Price A, Gilfoyle E, Myers C (eds): Research in Sensory-Integrative Development, Rockville, Am Occup Ther Assoc, 1976.
7. Ames LB, Ilg FC: The developmental point of view with special reference to its principle of reciprocal neuro-motor interweaving. J Genet Psychol 105:195-209, 1964.
8. Bobath K, Bobath B: Cerebral palsy, in Pearson P, Wlliams C (eds): Physical Therapy Services in the Developmental Disabilities. Springfield, C C Thomas Pubs, 1972, pp 31-185.
9. Trupin EW, Townes BD: Neuropsychological evaluation as an adjunct to behavioral interventions with children. Prof Psychol 5:153-160, 1976.
10. Stockmeyer S: A sensorimotor approach to treatment, in Pearson P, Williams C (eds): Physical Therapy Services in the Developmental Disabilities. Springfield, Illinois, C C Thomas Pubs, 1972.

Epilogue
"We Hold These Truths to be Self-Evident...."*

The authors of *Children Adapt* have attempted to integrate into this book a prodigious amount of information concerning growth, development, and behavior, and how these relate to the spiraling continuum of spatiotemporal adaptation. Literature supporting the theory of adaptation and data presented can be found in research papers, books, and scientific reports, including writings of individuals who are specialists in areas of psychology, psychiatry, embryology, ethology, growth and development, the neurosciences, sociology, anthropology, genetics, and so on.

From published reports, our observations, and personal experiences, we believe that everyone who interacts with children (or adults) should "hold these truths to be self-evident" . . . that all men are NOT created equal (except in the eyes of the Creator). Rather, each person is conceived and enters this world as a *unique* individual, "pre-packaged," so to speak, with genetic traits which have never been duplicated before and will never be again. Not only is each human endowed with biochemical and endocrinological individuality but also with such obvious traits as differences in height and weight; variations in hair, eye coloring, skin, and hair texture; 20 entirely different and unique finger and toe prints; an original voice print; and eventually, unique behavioral mannerisms associated with verbal and nonverbal communication. Less obvious differences also exist such as number of cells found in a given individual's nervous system, or in the various parts of that system, or in any given organ of the body.

For example, the variability in distribution and amount of certain nerve endings in a given sense organ or synaptic integrative-relay center could eventually reflect upon one's ability to appreciate such things as 1) temperature differences, 2) degree and kinds of pain, 3) touch and tactile sensations, 4) pressures, 5) gravitational forces, 6) subtle and not so subtle movement patterns, 7) various sounds and intonations, including different forms of vibratory input and visual information (ie, peripheral vision as contrasted or coupled with macular or acute vision), 8) eventually stereognostic capabilities, 9) three-dimensional concepts, and 10) therefore the perception of the environmental surround. Combined with all of these differences are the "degrees of sensitivity" which a given individual possesses in respect to the in-utero and postpartum environment and how each new creation copes with and learns from the innumerable stresses (both positive and negative) which are continually being impressed upon it. These factors are further dependent upon other genetic traits, such as one's intellectual potential, drives, talents, and the various degrees of emotional stability or instability. Likewise, each individual's hormonal make-up will be affected differently by biological or

---

*Reprinted in part with permission of the American Occupational Therapy Association Inc. Copyright 1977, AJOT, vol 31, mo 10.

circadium rhythms which are known to exert an influence upon all living organisms. All of these genetic factors (including many not cited here) are continually being modified, ie, dampened or enhanced (to an unknown and variable degree) by unpredictable and ever-changing environmental transactions and stresses. Each person develops a unique self-system.

From the moment of conception and throughout one's life span the genetico-environmental influences increase, not only in their complexity, but in the way in which they are manifested as the organism matures. For example, environmental stresses, which are constantly impinging upon and modifying the self-system, are in turn being manipulated, interpreted, and re-evaluated by the organism coping with them. Therefore, as a person gains additional experience, he also becomes more cognizant of multiple ways for handling and manipulating the environmental surround. Uniqueness of the original genetic creation eventually incorporates within itself all of the environmental influences which it has experienced or has *allowed itself to experience*. Therefore, each and every human being has blended within it a primordial combination of genetic endowments and environmental overlay. NATURE and NURTURE cannot be considered as separate entities. Together, they constitute a dynamic continuum.

For centuries, man debated the NATURE *vs* NURTURE issue. In the last several decades this argument has been laid to rest. Scientific evidence has demonstrated that both are of equal importance in regard to man's behavioral mechanisms and especially in relation to how man copes with health, disease, deprivation, learning, aging, etc. However, in spite of the fact that the great majority of scientists accept that NATURE *AND* NURTURE are of equal importance, many scientists, doctors, and professionals in the health fields have failed to accept and utilize scientific evidence (accumulated over the last half century) concerning Nature's law of INDIVIDUAL DIFFERENCES. This law is of equal importance to, and is indeed an integral component of, the genetico-environmental law which governs behavioral mechanisms.

Just as the law of NATURE *AND* NURTURE states that man is the combined result of these two determinants, the law of INDIVIDUAL DIFFERENCES reinforces the fact that no two human beings are alike (or any living organism for that matter), nor will they behave or react to a given stimulus, medication, diet, or stress in exactly the same predictable manner. In spite of this knowledge, man continues to rely heavily upon the Gaussian or bell-shaped curve when predicting, prescribing, and/or treating individuals. In so doing, he perpetuates the unscientific practice of forever pushing, shaping, and confining man into the "average bell-shaped human being" and therefore reinforces his "averaged concepts" about himself. This, in turn, seems to give man license to standardize such things as drug dosages, medications, and various treatment techniques and use them up on the masses, forgetting that individuals with unique differences make up these masses. However, man further substantiates his "mass or averaged actions" by continually investigating large numbers of animals or people, litter mates, or groups or societies. Rarely, does man bother to study or treat individuals as unique beings. Because man is able to forget about nature's law of individual differences, he relies upon averages, standardized prescriptions, and/or uniform treatment techniques, all of which can be easily learned, readily repeated, or quickly gleaned from "cookbook" types of publications. However, the more that man relies upon averages or the Gaussian curve for substantiating his actions, the greater is the demand for bigger and better "cookbooks" that will tell him exactly how to treat others. Herein lies a paradox: as the amount of interaction between humans increases so does the demand for bigger and better "cookbooks" which will help man categorize, treat, and understand himself. This floods the market with more and more "recipes" whose sole purpose is to inform man about man and how he fits into or deviates from the "average" individual. Such publications become over-night best sellers. They are momentarily pallative and help comfort the soul. They also help man forget the seemingly intangible, yet all important, law of individual differences including the fact that all living forms and our knowledge of them are forever changing. Nothing is static or permanent. Life and our perceptions thereof constitutes a dynamic continuum. Yet man chooses to forget these laws in his restless search for simple answers. This could remind one of the famous paradox written by a student of Dr. Jess Lair. †

Around and around I run
  in ever-widening circles
    trying to find a center for my life.

For years, therapists, doctors, lay people, and many others have been racing around in "ever-widening circles" seeking the ultimate cookbook that will give them the exact answers for solving the problems of their clients, patients, students, loved ones, or associates. However, when one is in the helping professions, and especially when working with people who are sick or have a handicap, it is of paramount importance to know, understand, and utilize nature's laws. Use of, or attempting to rely upon, the "Gaussian curve philosophy" and/or the law of averages, or trying to mold and treat persons in relation to prescribed "recipes" constitutes a deception, not only upon the individual being treated but also upon the profession doing the treating. Reasons for this are obvious. Each individual is unique and constantly changing, both overtly and covertly, and especially at molecular levels. Each person is affected by and reacts differently to any pathological entity that is capable of altering the direction in which it is progressing. This holds true for all ages and/or stages of growth and development, whether it be prenatal, perinatal, postnatal, youth maturity, or old age. In other words, pathology adds an unquantifiable dimension to a person who is already unique, thus creating even greater individual differences between and among human beings.

It is not surprising then that no two individuals can, or will, react alike to a prescribed medication, treatment technique, or personal interaction. The ART OF THERAPY is in "holding these truths to be self-evident" and treating each human as a unique entity who is attempting to adapt and progress along his or her own primordial pathway. Therefore, the authors of this book make no attempt at supplying the reader with "cookbook" answers. Instead, fundamental concepts have been presented. These should enable one to understand why each individual is a unique and highly flexible creation who is trying to adapt to life by progressing and at times retrogressing along his or her own spiraling continuum.

---

†*Lair J:* I Ain't Much Baby But I'm All I've Got. *Greenwich, Conn. Fawcett Publishers Inc, 1969, p 236.*

Appendix A
The Philosophical Base of Occupational Therapy*

Man is an active being whose development is influenced by the use of purposeful activity. Using their capacity for intrinsic motivation, human beings are able to influence their physical and mental health and their social and physical environment through purposeful activity. Human life includes a process of continuous adaptation. Adaptation is a change in function that promotes survival and self-actualization. Biological, psychological, and environmental factors may interrupt the adaptation process at any time through the life cycle. Dysfunction may occur when adaptation is impaired. Purposeful activity facilitates the adaptive process.

Occupational Therapy is based on the belief that purposeful activity (occupation), including its interpersonal and environmental components, may be used to prevent and mediate dysfunction, and to elicit maximum adaptation. Activity as used by the Occupational Therapist includes both an intrinsic and a therapeutic purpose.

*Adopted by the Representative Assembly, American Occupational Therapy Association Inc, April, 1979.

Appendix B
Suggested Readings

Bower TGR: Repetitive processes in child development. Sci Amer 5:38-47, 1976.

Dement WC: Some Must Watch While Some Must Sleep. WH Freeman & Co, San Francisco, 1972.

Eccles JC: The Understanding of the Brain, ed 2. McGraw-Hill Book Co, New York, 1977.

Held R: Plasticity in Sensory-Motor Systems. Sci Amer 213:84-94, 1965.

Krueger AP, Reed EJ: Biological impact of small air ions. Science 193:1209-1213, 1976.

Luce GG: Body Time: Physiological Rhythms and Social Stress. New York, Bantam Books, 1971.

The Nature and Nurture of Behavior: Developmental Psychobiology. Readings from Scientific American. San Francisco, WH Freeman & Co, 1973.

Melzack R: Effects of early experience on behavior: Experimental and conceptual considerations. Psychopathology of Perception. New York, Grune & Stratton, 1965.

Moore JC: Differences in Electrical Activity of the Biceps Brachii and Brachioradialis Muscles Performing Isometric-like Supination and Pronation Exercises. AJOT 25:391-397, 1971.

Rabkin JC, Struening EL: Life events, stress, and illness. Science 194:1013-1020, 1976.

Sachar EJ (ed): Hormones, Behavior, and Psychopathology. New York, Raven Pub, 1976. (Am Psychopath Association Series).

Smith WL, Kling A (eds): Issues in Brain/Behavior Control. New York, Spectrum, 1976.

Tinbergen N: Ethology and stress diseases. Science 185:41-45, 1974.

Wallace P: Complex environments: Effects on brain development. Science 185:1035-1037, 1974.

Williams RJ: Biochemical Individuality. New York, John Wiley & Sons Inc, 1963.

Index

A

Abnormal
   patterns, 193
   tone, 193
Accommodation
   definition of, 48
   faulty, 178
Activation, 67
   definition of, 61, 65
Activity
   adaptation to, 152
   definition of, 135
   purposeful, 135
   purposeless, 176
   requirements, 175
Adaptation, 159, 210
   components of, 48
   definition of, 2
   model, 207
   of activities, 135-152
   of behaviors, 79-125
   of sequences to stand, 127-133
   spatiotemporal, 47, 49
Adolescence
   development of, 156, 188, 168
   stress of, 168
Allport, G, 155, 166
Amphibian Reaction
   adaptation of, 87
   illustration of, 87
Assimilation
   definition of, 48
   quality-quantity, 178
Association
   areas in brain, 35
   definition of, 48
   failure, 179
Asymmetrical Tonic Neck Reflex (ATNR)
   adaptation of, 27, 84, 101, 102, 141
   definition of, 59

        illustration of, 68, 101, 141, 142
Avoiding Reflex
    definition of, 60, 139
    illustration of, 140
Ayres, A.J., 212, 214

B
Basal Ganglia, 12, 45
Bauer's Reflex
    adaptation of, 81, 112
    definition of, 59
    illustration of, 81
Behaviors
    creeping, 79, 80
    developmental progressions, 122-123
    purposeful, 79, 135, 136
    purposeless, 176
    reaching/grasping, 79, 137
    rolling, 77
    sitting, 90, 91
    standing/walking, 109, 110
    sucking, 163
Biopsychosocial, 163
Body Arching
    adaptation of, 94
Body Righting Acting On Body
    adaptation of, 105
    definition of, 60
Body Righting Acting On Head
    adaptation of, 107
    definition of, 60
Body Sense, 155, 164
Bouncing, 114, 116
Bower, T, 138
Brain Stem, 8
    illustration of, 9
Bridging
    adaptation of, 94, 114

C
Central Nervous System, 7, 8
    developmental stages, 15, 16
    divisions of, 7, 8
    fiber systems, 13

myelination, 18, 19
Cerebellum, 9, 10
  archi, 9, 10
  illustrations of, 9, 10
  neo, 9, 10
  paleo, 9, 10
Cerebral Cortex, 12, 13
Coactivation, 65, 69
  definition of, 61
Corpus Callosum, 12
Cranial Nerves, 21, 22
  illustrations of VII, IX and X, 22
  motor components, 40, 41
  sensory components, 38, 39
Crawling Reflex (Bauer's)
  adaptation of, 81, 112
  definition of, 59
  illustration of, 81
Creeping, 79, 80
  bilateral crawling, 85, 86
  creeping, 88
  developmental progression of, 122-123
  head control—on elbows, 83
  head lift—primitive support, 82
  on hands, 84-85
  primary crawling, 81
  protective head turning, 81
  reciprocal crawling, 86-87
  symmetrical postures, 82
  vertical righting reactions, 82
Crossed Extension Reflex
  adaptation of, 112
  definition of, 59
  illustration of, 112
Cruising, 117
  illustration of, 117

D
Developmental
  environmental factors, 5
  interuterine factors, 3, 4
  motivational factors, 4, 5
  sequences to sit, 127-133
  sequences to stand, 127-133

    trends, 160
Diencephalon
    divisions of, 11
    functions of, 42, 43
Differentiation, 167, 179
    definition of, 48
Distress, 176, 182
Doll's Eyes, 138
Dysfunction, 176, 182

E
Eccles, JC, 36
Embryo, 17, 18
    illustration of, 15, 17
Equilibrium Reactions, 74-75
    adaptation of, 97, 120, 124
    definition of, 61, 74
    illustration of, 75
    in sequences to stand, 130-132
Erikson, E, 157

F
Fantz, R, 138
Feedback, 33
    external, 136
    internal, 136
    sensory, 135-136, 179
Fixation
    object to mouth, 144
    postural, 64, 66, 73
    prolonged, 186
    visual, 138
Flexor Withdrawal Reflex
    adaptation of, 112
    definition of, 59
Freud, S, 156

G
Gesell, A, 160
Goal-Directed, 136
Gordon, I, 2, 164, 165, 167
Grasp
    crude, 143
    development of, 150-151

        fractionation of, 145
        inferior pincer, 148
        instinctive, 146
        palmar, 145
        prehension, 149
        pronated, 143
        superior pincer, 148
Grasp Reflex, 139-140, 142
    definition of, 59
    modification of, 143, 145
Gravity, 63, 65, 174

H
Held, R, 141
Homeostasis, 174, 176

K
Kneeling, 116, 119
    adaptation of, 120
    illustration of, 115

L
Labyrinthine Acting On Head
    definition of, 60
Landau Reaction
    adaptation of, 84
    illustration of, 52

M
Magnet Reflex
    adaptation of, 111
    definition of, 59
Mature
    development of, 65, 74
    eye-hand development, 146
Meaningful, 74, 135, 155, 164
Midline
    and dominance, 152
    and visual tracking, 139
    crossing, 124
    holding, 82, 93
    stability reactions, 61, 74, 75
Midline Stability Reactions, 74
    adaptation of, 97, 118

  definition of, 61
  illustration of, 75, 96-97, 118-119
  in sequences to stand, 132, 133
Mobility
  blended mobility—stability, 62, 76
  combined mobility—stability, 62, 73
  definition of, 61, 62
  poorly combined, 188
Moro Reflex
  adaptation of, 92
  definition of, 59
Mouthing, 140
  illustration of, 140, 143, 144
  prenatal reflexes, 24
Movement, 1, 135
  poverty of, 183
  stereotyped, 183
  undifferentiated, 185, 189
Movement Strategies
  components of, 58
  definition of, 57
  development of, 63-67, 65
  mature, 64, 76
  primitive, 64
  rotation-counter-rotation, 72, 124
  sequencing of, 127
  transitional, 64
Muscle Functions
  activation, 61, 67
  blended mobility—stability, 61, 76
  coactivation, 61, 69
  combined mobility—stability, 61, 73
  definition of, 62, 63
Myelin, 18
  illustration of, 19
  myelination, 27

N
Neck Righting
  adaptation of, 103
  definition of, 59
  illustration of, 102
Neuromusculoskeletal, 57

O

Occupational Therapy, 3
   adaptation model, 207
   framework, 211
   goals, 212
   guidelines, 213
   objectives, 213
   philosophy of, 210, 223
   principles of, 211
   theoretical premises, 208
Optical Righting
   definition of, 59

P

Perception, 136
   definition of, 50
   perceptual sets, 58
   self, 166
   somatosensory, 83, 88
   visual, 138
Perceptual Sets, 58, 76, 136-137
Peripheral Nerves
   illustrated, 19
Personality
   development of, 161, 162
Piaget, J, 159
Placing Reflex
   adaptation, 112
   definition of, 59
   illustration of, 68
Plantar Grasp
   definition of, 60
Play
   definition of, 159
   developmental sequence, 159
Post Natal, 28
   development of, 27, 29, 30
   spiraling concept, 28, 49
Postive Support Reactions
   adaptation of, 114
   definition of, 60, 114
   illustration of, 113
Postures

static, 184
Postural Sets, 136-137
  bilateral linear, 65, 66, 73, 115, 116, 190
  definition of, 58
  fixation support, 64, 66, 73
  movement-countermovement, 64, 66, 76, 120, 146
  weight shift, 64, 66, 73, 115, 116, 191
Postural Strategies
  components of, 58
  definition of, 57
  development of, 63, 65
  mature, 64, 74
  primitive, 64
  sequencing of, 127
  transitional, 64, 69
Postural Tone
  definition of, 58
Pull To Stand
  adaptation of, 114, 127
  illustration of bilateral linear, 115
  illustration of weight shift, 115
Purposeful
  activities, 135-137, 148, 211
  behaviors, 79, 135, 137
Prehension, 149
  manipulative, 149, 152
Prenatal
  development, 14, 26,
  illustration of CNS development, 16
Primitive
  development of, 64, 65
  eye-hand development, 138
  pathology, 184
  signs of dysfunction, 183
Primary Standing
  adaptation of, 112
  definition of, 60
  illustration of, 111
Prone Extension Posture
  adaptation of, 84, 96, 120
Propping
  adaptation of, 95, 98
  illustration of, 95
Protective Reactions

adaptation of, 98, 121
definition of, 60, 73
illustration, 72

R
Reactions, 58, 60, 62
  balance, 74, 75
  chain, 69, 187
  equilibrium, 65, 75
  midline stability, 74, 75
  protective, 72, 73
  righting, 70
  rotational righting, 71
  support, 72
  vertical righting, 70, 71
Reflexes, 25, 58-62
  phasic, 65, 67, 68, 185
  tonic, 65, 68, 186
(Re)habilitation, 2, 207
Retraction, 82, 186
Rolling, 99
  automatic rolling, 108
  deliberate rolling, 106
  developmental progression of, 122-123
  key behaviors of, 99-100
  primary turning, 100
  rotational righting reactions, 71
  spontaneous rolling, 103
  spontaneous turning, 101
Rotational Righting Reactions
  definition of, 60, 71
  illustration of, 71
  in sequences to stand, 127
  rolling, 99
Rooting Reflex, 163
  adaptation of, 100
  definition of, 59
  illustration of, 100
  prenatal, 24

S
Scratching, 143
Self, 169, 210
  awareness, 165

concept, 167

development of personality, 162

evaluation, 167

identification, 168

image, 166

perception, 166

Self-System, 136, 149, 163

definition of, 2, 47

Sensori-Motor-Sensory (SMS), 25, 49, 136, 178

Sequences To Stand

complete rotation, 128

partial-complete rotation, 130

partial rotation, 131

pull up, 127

symmetrical, 132

symmetrical-partial rotation, 132

Seyle, H, 173

Sitting, 90

developmental progression of, 122-123

head align, 92-93

head lag, 92

key behaviors of, 90-91

primitive sit, 91

pull to sit, 93-94

sitting, 96

supported sitting, 94-95

vertical righting reactions, 93

Skill

adaptation of, 137

definition of, 137

regulation of, 137

requirements of, 175

visual/auditory motor, 136

Skills

functions of, 136, 148

performance, 3

Spatial, 48

Spatio-Temporal Adaptation, 47, 135

components of, 48

distress, 176

framework, 49, 50

model, 207

stress, 173

theory of, 47-54

    to play/work, 168
Spinal
  cord, 8, 21, 31
  nerves, 8
  vertebrae, 30, 31
Spiraling Continuum, 49
  considerations of, 215
  effects of, 121, 127
  principles of, 50
  skill, 151
Squat
  adaptation of, 120
  illustration of, 119
Stability
  blended mobility-stability, 61, 65, 76
  combined mobility-stability, 61, 65, 73
  definition of, 61, 62
  poorly combined, 188
  prolonged, 190
Standing/Walking
  developmental progression of, 122-124
  key behaviors of, 110-111
  primary standing, 111
  primary stepping, 111, 112
  pull to stand, 113, 114
  standing, 118
  supported stand, 114, 115
  supported walking, 116, 117
  walking, 120, 121
Stepping
  adaptation of, 112
  definition of, 59
  illustration of, 111
Stress, 169, 173
  factors, 174
  illustrations of, 52, 53
  spatio-temporal, 52
Sucking, 163
  prenatal, 24, 25
  problems, 184
Support Reactions
  definition of, 60, 72
  illustration of, 72, 113
  positive, 114

Survival, 162
Swiping, 141, 142
    adaptation of, 145
Symmetrical Tonic Neck Reflex (STNR)
    adaptation of, 82, 93, 142
    definition of, 59
    illustration of, 82

T
Tactile
    exploration, 145, 148
    orientation, 146
Telencephalon, 7, 12, 46
Temporal, 48
Therapy
    mode, 215
    model, 207
Tonic Labyrinthine Reflex (TLR)
    adaptation of, 81, 82, 92
    definition of, 59
    illustration of, 81
Traction
    definition of, 59, 139
    illustration of, 140
Transitional
    development of, 64, 65, 69
    eye-hand development, 142
    pathological, 188
Twitchell, T, 81, 119, 163

V
Vertical Righting Reactions
    adaptation to prone, 82, 83
    adaptation to roll, 107
    adaptation to sit, 93
    adaptation to stand, 114, 116
    definition of, 60, 70
    effects of, 143
    illustration of, 71, 83
    in sequences to stand, 127, 128, 130, 131
Vision, 138-139
    attention, 142
    exploration, 148
    investigation, 146

    lack of response, 184
    orientation, 146
    prenatal reflex, 24
    tracking, 138-139
Visual Motor Integration, 146